POMPEY THE GREAT

POMPEY THE GREAT

JOHN LEACH

CROOM HELM LONDON

ROWMAN AND LITTLEFIELD

© 1978 John Leach
Croom Helm Ltd, 2-10 St John's Road, London SW11

British Library Cataloguing in Publication Data

Leach, John D
  Pompey the Great
  1. Pompey the Great
  937'.05'0924   DG258

  ISBN 0-85664-659-8

First published in the United States 1978
by Rowman and Littlefield, Totowa, N.J.

ISBN 0-8476-6035-4

Printed in Great Britain by
Biddles Ltd, Guildford, Surrey

CONTENTS

PREFACE

To Romans of later generations the three decades between the dictator-ships of Sulla and Caesar were the age of Pompey the Great. In spite of the fact that the period is central to the most commonly taught Roman History course in schools and universities in Great Britain, there has, curiously, been no full length study in English of its most prominent figure, and for many students he remains enigmatic and shadowy compared with the flesh and blood characters of Cicero and Caesar. Consequently the impact made by Pompey on the history of his own and later times has, I believe, been inadequately understood and emphasised.

In this book I have attempted to re-examine the life and career of Pompey, and to see him, as far as is possible, through the eyes of his contemporaries and of those who wrote about him later using contemporary material which is now lost. If there are few overt references to modern studies of the period, this is because I share the belief of many teachers of Ancient History that it is by an informed study of the original sources that the student can obtain the clearest understanding of the life and people of the Classical world. I have, however, not neglected the works of more modern historians.

Both in the text and the appendix I have made extensive use of quotations (in English) from the sources, and I hope that it will not be difficult for those who wish to read more of these for themselves to obtain copies or translations of them. Except where noted the translations used in this book are my own.

I should like to express my very great thanks to all who have so generously helped me in this enterprise: especially to the President and Fellows of St John's College, Oxford, who welcomed me as a Schoolmaster Commoner in Hilary term 1970 and enabled me to embark on the necessary research under ideal conditions; to many colleagues and pupils at Sherborne and St Edward's; to Mr R.S. Glen, Mr J. Sabben-Clare and Professor J.J. Wilkes, who have read all or part of the text and given me, in our discussions, invaluable advice on very many points; to Mr D.L. Stockton, who in addition to reading the typescript first inspired and fostered my enthusiasm for Ancient History in his tutorials and lectures; and to my wife Rosamund, without whose constant encouragement and support the book could never have been written.

Oxford 1977   John Leach

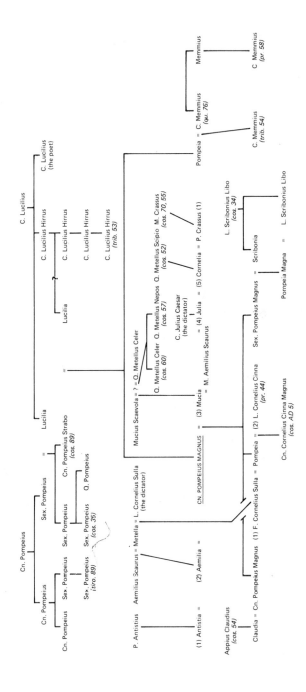

The Family Tree of Pompey the Great

1 THE WAR-LORDS OF PICENUM: SOCIAL and CIVIL WAR 89—79

There is in the Capitoline Museum at Rome a bronze tablet (I)*, which was once nailed to the wall of some public building in the city. It is dated 17 November 89 BC and records the grant on that date of Roman citizenship to a squadron of thirty Spanish cavalrymen by the consul, Gnaeus Pompeius Strabo. The grant was a reward for valour in the Social War, which was then coming slowly to an end. In this war a large number of the communities of central and southern Italy, who had long been allies of the Roman people, were fighting for the right to be not mere allies, but full members of the Roman state.

In November 89 Pompeius Strabo with his army was besieging the town of Asculum in Picenum, the stretch of country between the summit of the Apennines and the sea on the Adriatic coast of Italy north-east of Rome. This town was the focal point of Italian resistance in the northern theatre of the war. In an incident shortly before the outbreak of open hostilities a Roman praetor and all Roman citizens in the town had been massacred, and Asculum itself had been besieged since the early days of the war in 90 by Pompeius Strabo, first in his capacity as lieutenant of the consul of 90, P. Rutilius Lupus, and for the past year as consul himself. This high position he probably owed to his own successes in 90, a year marked otherwise mainly by a series of Roman disasters.

One of the most interesting features of the tablet is the fact that it contains a list of fifty-nine names of the members of the *consilium* or council which Strabo had consulted before making his grant of citizenship, and which added the weight of its authority to his decision. The names seem to be in descending order of rank, starting with five lieutenants (*legati*), who were all members of the Roman Senate. Next comes a quaestor, one of the annual magistrates assigned to the general's staff by the Senate, and sixteen military tribunes or staff officers. There follows a list of thirty-three *tirones*. These were young men who were the sons of senators or knights. When they were slightly older they would expect to serve as officers themselves, and were now

---

* The roman numerals which appear in brackets throughout the book refer to extracts collected in Appendix B, pp. 218-34.

Figure 1: Map of Italy and Sicily.

acquiring valuable military experience. The list is completed by four senior centurions.[1]

For the historian the importance of this inscription lies as much in its value as a political document as in its value for military history. At this period the Roman general was also a politician. As such he was a member of one of the groups of leading senators with their families and clients whose struggles for leadership in the Senate and control over the assemblies of the Roman people are one of the most fascinating and complex aspects of the history of the late Republic.

As consul Pompeius Strabo had reached the position which it was the ambition of every Roman politician to obtain. Not only did it admit him into the company of *consulares*, the men who had held the consulship and who formed the real governing council within the Senate, but it also gave him the opportunity to extend his patronage over less powerful families and communities in Rome, Italy and the provinces. Further, he could cement his alliances (*amicitiae*) with other leading senators. This he could do by appointing as legates men who were his friends and political allies, and by taking on his staff as military tribunes and *tirones* the sons of such men, and also clients whom he wanted to link to his own cause by the bonds of *officium*.[2]

Thus from a document like the Asculum inscription one might expect to discover information about Pompeius Strabo's political affiliations and the families and areas over which he exercised his patronage. Moreover, one might hope to find among the members of the *consilium* men who in the next generation were themselves political allies, and perhaps traced the origins of those friendships to the time when they had served together. Of equal interest will be cases where colleagues on such a *consilium* are later found on opposite sides, in the political arena or even in civil war. It must always be remembered that *amicitiae* could be made and broken with bewildering rapidity as different issues and interests drew men in different directions. A broken marriage or damaged pride could cause political enmity as easily as irreconcilable principles or electoral rivalry.

For the purposes of this study the most important name on the Asculum tablet is the thirtieth, that of Strabo's son, also called Gnaeus Pompeius, who thus makes his first appearance in the records of history. In November 89 he was just over seventeen years of age (he was born on 29 September 106), and had probably been with his father beneath the walls of Asculum since he officially came of age the previous March at the ceremony of the taking of the *toga virilis*.[3]

Like his father he would already be thoroughly familiar with the theatre of war in which he now found himself. His family held a position of very considerable power and influence in Picenum, where they owned large estates in the northern part of the region. The Pompeii were not a family to rank with the long-established aristocratic families such as the Caecilii Metelli, Claudii Pulchri, Cornelii, Calpurnii Pisones or Domitii, and Strabo was the first member of his branch of the family to reach the consulship and thus confer on himself and his descendants the coveted title of *nobilis*.

However, the history of the past fifty years had shown that even a new man, or *novus homo*, could match the noblest families in power and prestige if he could muster enough support in terms of organised manpower at the critical times. The man who had demonstrated this most dramatically was Gaius Marius, Rome's victorious general in two major wars, already six times consul, and in 90 a fellow legate of Strabo in the army of Rutilius Lupus. Strabo will have known him well, even though he seems to have been too much of a 'rogue' in politics to have attached himself closely to the group which looked to Marius as its leader during the nineties. Strabo's position depended not so much on his *amicitiae* as on his *clientela*. This consisted of the men from his estates and from the towns of northern Picenum, and the soldiers in his army, whose pay and prize money depended to a large extent on their loyal service to their general. In fact the bulk of his army probably came from Picenum in any case, and may well have been recruited there at the beginning of the war.

Two incidents in 89 illustrate the ways in which *clientes* could be acquired outside Italy as well. Early in the year Strabo had had a law passed (the *lex Pompeia*) in which the communities of Gaul between the Alps and the river Po had been granted Latin rights. This meant that magistrates of those communities would automatically obtain Roman citizenship for themselves and their families, and could be expected to exercise their right to vote at elections in Rome, especially if required to do so by the patron by whose action they had won the franchise. Secondly the grant of citizenship to the *turma Salluitana* recorded on the Asculum inscription was a way of extending patronage to the communities of Spain.

The inscription also casts light on Strabo's relationship with the Picentines. Twelve of the *tirones* on the list are shown as belonging to the tribe Velina. It was in this tribe that the Roman citizens of Picenum were enrolled, largely for voting purposes, and these young men are clearly sons of the leading families of Picenum who joined the army led by the most important and powerful landowner of the district.

The inhabitants of northern Picenum had long enjoyed Roman citizenship. The region had been conquered by Rome in 268; a Latin colony had been founded at Firmum in 264; allotments of land had been made to Roman citizens by a law of C. Flaminius in 232, and full citizen colonies established at Potentia in 184, and Auximum probably in 157. We know that the Pompeii had not been among those early settlers, as their tribe was the Clustumina, which suggests that they came from one of the settlements in the east Tiber valley north of Rome, the region to which that tribe was originally allocated. The name Pompeius itself is of non-Latin origin, being the Umbro-Oscan form of Quintus (fifth), and exhibiting Etruscan influence in its ending.[4]

On his mother's and grandmother's side young Pompeius was related to another interesting family. His grandmother was the sister and his mother probably the niece of the poet Gaius Lucilius (cf. p. 22 below), who died in 102 and seems to have left considerable property near Tarentum in southern Italy to his niece's new family. Other connections with large landowing families appear later, and it is clear that Picenum was not the only part of Italy which contained clients of the Pompeii (II).[5]

The exact details of the siege of Asculum and the reduction of the neighbouring tribes of the Vestini, Marrucini and Paeligni to the southeast, and the Marsi to the south, are now unrecoverable. A vain attempt by the confederate army to raise the siege resulted in a battle in which 75,000 Romans and 60,000 Italians are said to have taken part, and Strabo's legates were no doubt busy mopping up pockets of resistance in the numerous glens of the Apennines. Of the part played by Gnaeus Pompeius the younger during this year we hear nothing, except the vague statement that he received his early military training in his father's army in a great war and against the fiercest foes. The fall of the town itself followed the dramatic death by suicide of the Picentine leader Vidacilius and a desperate attempt by the inhabitants to break through the besieging forces.[6]

If Strabo was able to distribute rewards for valour on 17 November we may assume that by then Asculum had capitulated. Orosius preserves the story of the whipping and execution of the Picentine leaders, and the sale by auction of all the slaves and booty. The fact that the proceeds of this sale were kept by Strabo and not presented to the treasury, especially at a time of severe financial crisis, probably explains his reputation for greed which later made him so unpopular with the people at Rome.[7]

At all events he was back in the city with his army by 25 December, when he celebrated his triumph over the Picentines of Asculum. Although the Samnites and Lucanians continued sporadic resistance in the south for a considerable time, the serious part of the war was over and Strabo could be acclaimed the hero. Much, however, remained to be done by way of consolidating the victory and restoring the normal pattern of life to what must have been a shattered Italy, and after holding the elections for the magistrates of 88 Strabo returned with his army to Picenum. It is probable that his son accompanied him.

It is now time to consider briefly the main features of the history of the nineties. It is well known that this is a poorly documented period, and there is a serious danger of trying to read too much significance into the references which we have, mainly in the treatises of Cicero, to famous court cases and personal feuds between leading politicians. During the nineties there were few, if any, controversial political issues which might force men to take sides on grounds of principle or even mutual interest, and politicians were mainly concerned with furthering their own ambitions and those of their relatives and friends. Among several such groups, whose composition was probably changing constantly, were one led by the powerful Gaius Marius, and another centred on the noble and prolific family of the Caecilii Metelli. Marius enjoyed considerable support from the class of the *equites*, or knights. This class included such sections of the community as the *publicani* (partners in the tax-collecting companies), bankers, merchants, wealthy traders and the leading families of the citizen communities throughout Italy. The interests of the sections of this class will not always have coincided. The one characteristic which linked them was their wealth, later defined by a minimum qualification of 400,000 sesterces. The sons of senators who had not yet entered the Senate were also counted as *equites* and took part in the ceremonies connected with the order, but as a class they must be considered senatorial and to have shared the interests and prejudices of their fathers.[8]

The struggle for supremacy centred on the *Forum* and the *comitia*. The *Forum* was the scene of the numerous political trials in which, throughout the late Republic, the members of *factiones* attempted to bring disgrace and even exile on their opponents, and to win prestige, position and patronage for themselves. Illustrative of this is the fact that a successful prosecutor could attain the senatorial rank of his defeated opponent, and a successful counsel for defence would expect the political support of his grateful client. The *comitia* were the assemblies of the Roman people for the purposes of passing legislation and electing magistrates. Each year these saw the struggles of the politicians to win the magistracies which would take them step by step towards the charmed circle of the consulars. In normal circumstances these *principes civitatis*, as they were also called, controlled the policies of the Republic. The senior magistracies of praetorship and consulship could also lead to the governorship of one of Rome's provinces, and the opportunity to win a personal fortune, and, if fighting proved necessary or possible, military glory.

The ambitious politician had all the time to be conscious of the need to amass support for himself. During the late Republic the areas from which support could be drawn were rapidly expanding, and new techniques for winning, maintaining and deploying that support were constantly being developed.

In 91 a tribune of the people, M. Livius Drusus, seems to have contemplated the possibility of winning the support of the Italians for the 'Metellan' faction with which he was connected. The Italians had for some time been agitating for Roman citizenship and had already made preparations to demand it by armed force. The failure of his attempt, which would have involved a grant of citizenship to the Italian allies, and his own murder were the sparks which ignited the Social War. His enemies saw an opportunity to attack Drusus' supporters in the courts, and in 90 the tribune Q. Varius had a law passed setting up a court to try people who would be accused of having incited the Italians to revolt. We know of six senators who were prosecuted under this law in 90, all of whom appear to have had connections with the Metelli. The prosecutions met with only moderate success, however, and it appears that by 89 the 'Metellan' faction had reasserted its control. At a time of great crisis this is not surprising, since its members were noted for their traditionalist and aristocratic attitude towards politics and their belief that the dominant group in the Senate should maintain its control over the affairs of the Roman people.

In 90, the first year of the war, some form of compromise seems to have been arrived at in the interests of unity, for it is probably significant that of the two consuls for that year P. Rutulius Lupus was a 'Marian' and L. Julius Caesar a 'Metellan'. Moreover the legates who accompanied the consuls to their military commands seem in all cases to have shared the political sympathies of their respective commanders.

In 89 Pompeius Strabo no doubt owed his consulship largely to his military ability, but his colleague, L. Porcius Cato, who was killed in action during the early part of the year, and the two consuls elected for 88, L. Cornelius Sulla and Q. Pompeius Rufus, were prominent members of the 'Metellans'. Sulla, as one of Rome's most successful generals, was also an obvious choice irrespective of his political leanings. Pompeius Rufus, it may be added, was a distant cousin of Strabo's.

Two main issues faced Rome in 88. One was the reorganisation necessitated by the upheavals of the Social War and the sudden admission under the *lex Julia* of 90 of large numbers of Italians to a share in the privileges of citizenship. The other was the very serious threat of a large-scale war in Asia Minor. For many years King Mithridates VI of Pontus had been extending his control over the surrounding kingdoms, and collecting and training a vast army, which numbered, according to our sources, well over a quarter of a million men. Several times Rome had intervened, attempting to replace Roman sympathisers on the various thrones by means of deputations and commissions, backed by the threat and sometimes the use of force. None of her efforts, however, had brought long-term success. In fact they probably stimulated Mithridates into using his army sooner than he had planned, and in 88 he finally invaded the wealthy Roman province of Asia, which had long been his ultimate goal. Not only did he appear to the Greeks and Asiatics of the province as the liberator from Roman rule and oppression, but on reaching the city of Ephesus he issued a decree that in thirty days' time all Roman and Italian inhabitants of the cities of Asia should be murdered. The eventual death roll is given as 80,000 persons, but this must be a grossly inflated figure.[9]

This survey has been necessary in order to explain the situation which confronted the young Gnaeus Pompeius shortly after his introduction to public life in March 89.

During the early months of 88 he will have listened with interest and, no doubt, some confusion to the reports from Rome which reached his father's camp in Picenum. One of the new tribunes, P. Sulpicius Rufus, whom he had known as a friend of Livius Drusus and a member of a leading aristocratic family, was planning to acquire a square deal for the new Italian citizens by giving them equal voting rights with the old citizens, instead of the inferior rights which had been suggested. The command of the war against Mithridates, of which Pompey's father himself may have entertained hopes, had gone to Sulla, a tried and successful general with experience of negotiating with the king.

Then the news arrived that Rufus, in an attempt to win support for his unpopular legislative programme, had formed an alliance with Gaius Marius. With the aid of violence he had passed his citizenship law and procured for Marius the command against Mithridates. This was followed by the report that Sulla, who had gone to join his army at Nola in Campania prior to embarking for the East, had persuaded his army, but not his officers, to support him and had marched on Rome. There, after a considerable amount of fighting, he had secured the murder of Sulpicius Rufus and the exile of Marius and a number of his supporters. The rivalry between the political factions, which had been kept in check during the Social War, had at last erupted into open war. It was impossible for the Pompeii not to become involved.

Even if Pompeius Strabo had not been an active supporter of Marius during the nineties, there is good evidence that there was little love lost between him and Sulla's faction, and he clearly had a number of powerful friends among the Marians. To Sulla he must have appeared a potent rival. Two passages in Appian and Sallust suggest that Sulla, before leaving Rome again for the East, passed a law recalling Strabo from his command and replacing him with his own colleague and relation by marriage, Pompeius Rufus. Strabo seems to have had a tribune in the city, one C. Herennius, ready to protect his interests, and Herennius interposed his veto. We must presume, however, that the veto was got round somehow, for Pompeius Rufus certainly went out to Picenum to take over Strabo's army. These soldiers were no less loyal to their general than Sulla's had been, and, although Strabo himself made no open move to oppose Pompeius Rufus, they seized control of the situation themselves and took the drastic step of assassinating the consul. Strabo, by popular demand he could claim, remained in control of his army.[10]

It should not be assumed that, because we do not hear of any military activity on Strabo's part during 88, he was merely biding his time and waiting for the opportunity to seize power. There was obviously plenty of work to be done in an area which only recently had been the scene of bloody warfare. Strabo's own clients in Picenum must have suffered during the passage of armies over their land, and many must have died. The job of picking up the pieces and restoring the pattern of normal life will naturally have exercised the organising abilities of the local 'baron', and perhaps given his son valuable experience in manipulating men and materials, which would prove useful to him in later years. It is important to remember that after his father's death young Pompey served no further military apprenticeship. When next he took up arms it was as a commander, not a subordinate officer.

The following year brought still more violence and bloodshed as the new consul, L. Cornelius Cinna, tried to revive the legislation of Sulpicius Rufus and to recall the exiled Marius, only to meet with armed resistance from his colleague, Cn. Octavius. Forced to leave Rome and declared by the Senate to have forfeited his citizenship and consulship, Cinna himself resorted to force. With an army consisting of many of the new citizens and ex-rebels whose cause he had championed and some troops which Sulla had left behind at Nola, he too marched on Rome. He soon heard that Marius himself had returned from exile in Africa, landed in Etruria, and with another force of Numidians and Italians was approaching from the north.

In this desperate situation Octavius and the Senate summoned Pompeius Strabo from Picenum to save the city. From Strabo's point of view the decision must have been a difficult one, for the men he was called upon to fight included several of his friends, and they had in fact taken up arms in a cause which he himself supported — that of the Italian new citizens. On the other hand, those who summoned him, weak and short-sighted though they might be, were the legitimate government, the Senate and People of Rome. There is also a suggestion in Orosius' account that Cinna or Marius had rejected an early approach by Strabo.[11]

His subsequent behaviour appeared then and appears now suspiciously like double-dealing. It is a reasonable conclusion that Strabo's main concern was for his own position. Following the murder of Pompeius Rufus he could, even if successful, expect little support from Octavius and the Senate, who were probably now looking for leadership to an actual Metellus, Q. Metellus Pius, the praetor of 89. His main hope lay in his army, which could help to win him the consulship of 86 and subsequently a further period of military command as proconsul, perhaps against Mithridates.

The records of the fighting which took place outside the gates of Rome are confused, to say the least. Cinna, advancing from the south, seems to have divided his large force into three divisions, and we hear of a fierce battle between Strabo's troops and one of these divisions led by Q. Sertorius. Night intervened before a decision was reached. Marius, approaching from the north, seized the port of Ostia at the mouth of the Tiber, and gained possession of the Janiculan hill, on the north bank of the river opposite the city. In an attempt to dislodge him Octavius led a raid across the Tiber, taking with him a detachment of Strabo's troops, and after fierce fighting both sides fell back to regroup. In the opinion of some a final attack by Octavius might have won the day, but apparently Strabo, whose military experience enabled him to give advice to Octavius (who was technically his superior), prevented any such heroics. Granius Licinianus, probably following Livy's account, connects this action of Strabo's with his desire to win the consular elections for the following year while the military issue was still in doubt. Velleius states that he was thwarted in this desire, and since we hear of no elections it must be assumed that Octavius refused to consider Strabo's candidature. If this is so, it may be at this juncture that Strabo began private negotiations with Cinna, though it appears that he had earlier attempted to keep official channels of communication open. What the terms of these negotiations were can never be known. A pestilence of some sort was by now taking its toll in both armies and Strabo was one of the victims. Not long afterwards Cinna and Marius succeeded in storming the city (IIA).[12]

The effect of his experiences in his father's camp on the eighteen-year-old Pompey is difficult to evaluate. It is tempting, and I think justifiable, to find similarities of temperament and outlook in father and son, and to conclude that the lessons learnt about the power which an army could put into the hands of its commander, and about the uncomfortable fact of life that the hard-core aristocrats were violently unwilling to allow power and prestige to fall into the hands of anyone who threatened to dominate them rather than co-operate with them, must have had their effects upon him in later years. Exactly what sort of position for himself Strabo was aiming at is almost impossible to say, but it is remarkable how similar were the methods used by his son. They were also very much more successful.

The days following the entry of Cinna and Marius into Rome must have been ones of grave danger for Pompey. His house was broken into and plundered by some of the victorious troops. Many of Marius' personal enemies, and many whom his bodyguard of 'toughs', the so-called Bardyaei, thought were his enemies, were murdered. Several of the opposition leaders, including Octavius and four consulars, also lost their lives. But the reprisals were not as bloody or as prolonged as later propaganda suggested; fairly soon the spirit of conciliation prevailed, and in any case Pompey had powerful friends who could protect him.[13]

Two incidents from the record of the next three years serve to illustrate Pompey's situation. In 86 he was prosecuted by some of the many enemies of his father on a charge of illegally possessing part of the booty which had been taken at Asculum, namely some books and hunting nets. Among those who spoke in his defence were the wily L. Marcius Philippus, a rising young barrister named Q. Hortensius, and Cn. Papirius Carbo. Philippus had been consul in 91 and was censor in 86, and his son had probably been at Asculum with Pompey. Carbo had been one of Cinna's lieutenants at the siege of Rome and as his staunchest supporter, was to share the consulship with him the next year. Pompey also had the support of the judge in charge of the trial, P. Antistius, whose daughter, Antistia, he married shortly after his acquittal.

From the account of the episode in Plutarch it appears that there were a number of preliminary hearings in this case, in which Pompey, displaying considerable acumen and rhetorical ability, managed to disprove many of the charges by laying the blame for the disposal or misappropriation of much of the booty on one of his father's freedmen. It was this ability to speak up for himself that brought him to Antistius' notice, and after consulting his friends on the matter Antistius offered Pompey his daughter's hand. The marriage sealed not so much a political alliance, for Pompey was only nineteen at the time, as an agreement by Antistius and his friends to help the obviously gifted Pompey in his career. Gaius Marius and Marcus Tullius Cicero, among others, also owed their start in politics to being patronised by leading political families.[14]

Mention of Pompey's rhetorical skill raises the topic of his earlier education. Two items of evidence may shed some light on this. As has already been said, Pompey's mother was the niece of the poet Lucilius. This man, a supporter and friend of the great Scipio Aemilianus in the mid-second century, was, in addition to being the innovator of the type of poetry known as *satura*, a poet of considerable importance in other ways in the history of Roman literature. An interest and involvement in literature was thus part of the family background, and such a great-uncle must have had his effect on the education of young Pompey; this in its earlier stages was entrusted by Strabo to an Asiatic scholar, Aristodemus of Nysa, and later to a freedman called L. Voltacilius Pilutus. He was a rhetorician, who subsequently won renown as the first freedman to write history. Two of his subjects were the careers of Strabo and his son.

Two years after the trial it was becoming clear that Sulla, who, in spite of having been declared an outlaw, had steadily driven back the forces of Mithridates and come to terms with him at Dardanus in early autumn 85, would soon be returning to Italy with a victorious army and with a large number of old scores to settle. The government would need well-trained and battle-hardened troops to check Sulla's legions. It was possibly in an attempt to provide experience in battle for his soldiers that early in 84 Cinna began to ship an army across the Adriatic from Ancona to Liburnia. A short campaign against the tribesmen of that part of Illyria would give the men battle practice and keep them within easy distance for recall should Sulla make a sudden return. Among Cinna's officers seem to have been M. Terentius Varro, of whom we shall hear later, in charge of the advance party, and Pompey.[15]

While Cinna was trying to embark the rest of his troops during a particularly stormy period, they mutinied and killed him. We need not believe Plutarch's story that they were afraid for the life of Pompey, who had suddenly left the camp following some slanderous accusation; fear of shipwreck and a distaste for a campaign that would bring few rewards and the prospect of a civil war to follow are perfectly satisfactory explanations for the mutiny.

The death of Cinna was followed by a disintegration of government which has been described as being 'as dramatic as anything in history'. This is not the place to discuss the character and the regime of Cinna, but recent research has tried to peer through the cloud of misrepresentation and propaganda which has hung over them ever since Sulla's return. One view suggests that Cinna was able to find considerable support from most political groupings, and that the years which saw Cinna as consul (87–85) were years of stability and legal government. On a perhaps more realistic assessment they were years of inactivity and uncertainty. Many who were not inextricably committed to supporting Cinna or Sulla bided their time until it should become clear who would eventually prove the stronger, meanwhile acquiescing in the military regime of Cinna and his few close supporters. During these years Pompey remained at Rome, gaining valuable political experience, and in the winter of 87-6 he may well have met and become friendly with the great Stoic philosopher Posidonius, who visited Rome then and was to exercise a marked influence on Pompey's outlook in future years.[16]

The disintegration of the government which occurred under the sole consulship of Papirius Carbo during the rest of 84 involved a polarisation of political attitudes which had not been apparent previously. It was due in large part to the threat of Sulla's return and the knowledge that he had with him troops who had already followed him on one successful march on Rome, and had now proved their worth in a number of battles against the numerically far stronger forces of Mithridates.

About a year passed from the murder of Cinna to the arrival of Sulla at Brundisium in spring, 83. During this time many of the *nobiles* and other leading men decided that it was in their interests to join the side that looked like being the winning one. Pompey was in as good a position as anyone to judge the relative military strengths of the two sides, and fairly soon, we may believe, decided that the odds were on Sulla. Instead of returning to Rome after Cinna's death, or co-operating with Carbo, he withdrew to Picenum, where, as we have seen, he could rely for support on the clients and veterans of his father. How active he was during this year is not known, but the speed with which he was able to raise and equip three legions the following spring suggests that secret negotiations and preparations had been going on for some time (IIB).

At any rate opportunity for action came soon in the next year. Carbo, who was now proconsul of Cisalpine Gaul, began levying troops in Picenum, and Pompey, possibly to test the climate of opinion, as Plutarch suggests, opposed the activities of Carbo's recruiting officers. The result was an expression of loyalty to Pompey, who then set up his own recruiting headquarters at Auximum and expelled from the city two of the local leaders who were acting on Carbo's behalf. Soon, from among his clients and the thousands of veterans from Strabo's army who had gone back to their farms in Picenum (or perhaps to a life of virtual unemployment, which was often the lot of the discharged veteran, for Strabo had not lived to see them properly resettled), Pompey had raised and equipped a full legion. Officered no doubt by several of the Picentine *tirones* mentioned on the Asculum inscription, and trained and led by his father's old centurions, it will have been a most useful force.

Sulla landed at Brundisium with his own army of about 40,000 men in the spring of 83, presumably as soon as the weather made the crossing from Greece practicable. As he marched north-west towards Campania, Pompey prepared to lead his own legion south from Picenum to join him, giving orders for the recruitment of two more legions to continue as quickly as possible.

In an attempt to prevent the uniting of the two armies the government at Rome sent out three separate commanders, C. Carrinas, T. Cluilius and L. Junius Brutus Damasippus, possibly with detachments from Carbo's army in Cisalpine Gaul, with orders to intercept and defeat Pompey by attacking him from three directions. Pompey's intelligence service was already working smoothly enough to enable him to take the initiative and break through the encircling net before it could close on him. He attacked the force led by Damasippus, and routed it after a cavalry skirmish in which Pompey was reported to have distinguished himself. The three leaders withdrew, unable to agree on a further course of action, and Pompey was able to add still more recruits to his cause from the local cities. A second battle with some cavalry which had been sent against him by Carbo is recorded by Plutarch as having taken place on the river Arsis (perhaps the Aesis, the northern boundary of Picenum), but this may belong to a slightly later period.

Pompey's engagement with the cavalry of Brutus Damasippus illustrates vividly the split which the arrival of Sulla caused in the ranks of the senatorial families. Damasippus is almost certainly the L. Junius mentioned as the fifth name on the Asculum inscription and, unlike Pompey, he remained a staunch supporter of Cinna and Carbo.

The scene of Pompey's arrival at Sulla's camp caught the imagination of later writers. Plutarch gives us the picture of his soldiers fully armed and marching in good order, with morale obviously high, towards their new commander-in-chief. Sulla dismounted at the sight of them and, on being saluted by Pompey with the official title of *Imperator* (General), did him the unprecedented honour of returning the salute in like terms. In fact the twenty-two-year-old Pompey was the general of a private army, a position as illegal as that of Sulla, who had been declared a public enemy several years earlier. There may well have been a certain amount of irony in Sulla's reply.[17]

Two other aristocrats had also joined Sulla at the head of independently-raised armies, Q. Metellus Pius and M. Licinius Crassus. Pius came from Africa, where he had been since leaving Italy after Cinna's victory in 87, and Crassus from further Spain. Both, like Pompey, had been able to utilise large numbers of clients attached to their families in those provinces. It is difficult to decide whether news of their declaration for Sulla influenced Pompey or not. The sources make it plain that he joined Sulla after the other two, but we have no way of telling how much he was held up by having to fight his way through, nor at what stage he started his recruiting.

Nor is it clear what task Sulla gave to Pompey following his arrival. He may have been with Sulla as he defeated the army of the consul, C. Norbanus, at Casilinum and conducted negotiations with the other consul, Scipio, during which Scipio's army was persuaded to desert *en masse*. During the remainder of 83 both sides were engaged in raising further support, and Pompey probably returned to Picenum to complete his levy there.

When, after a hard winter, fighting broke out once more in 82, the Sullan strategy seems to have involved engaging the government forces on two fronts. While Sulla himself advanced up the Latin Way from Campania towards Rome, Metellus, supported by Pompey, was to try to defeat the forces of Carbo (now consul again) in Cisalpine Gaul, using the friendly Picenum as his base. Plutarch records the story that Pompey insisted on being invited by Metellus to join him in Gaul, saying that it was not right for him to relieve an older and more renowned officer of his command. The implication is that Metellus had been in Gaul for some time without achieving success and that Sulla wanted Pompey to replace him. If this is true we may well believe that Pompey was reluctant to incur the jealousy of the powerful Metellus.[18]

Again, details of the northern campaign are few and not easy to link in a coherent narrative. The first action we hear of was at the river Aesis, where in a six-hour battle Metellus defeated Carbo's lieutenant Carrinas, only to be blockaded by Carbo himself. On receipt of news from the south that the other consul, C. Marius the younger, had been beaten by Sulla at the battle of Sacriportus near Signia, Carbo withdrew to his base at Ariminum, severely harassed by cavalry attacks on his rearguard led by Pompey. Later Metellus defeated C. Marcius Censorinus, another of Carbo's officers, in the same area, and Pompey led the cavalry force which caught Marcius' fleeing troops outside their base at Sena Gallica, defeated them and plundered the town. From his activities as thus reconstructed from Appian's narrative, it would appear that Pompey was acting as Metellus' cavalry commander.

While Metellus remained on the north-east coast, in order to consolidate his control there before advancing north-west into the Po valley, Pompey seems to have been transferred to the southern command under Sulla, and to have moved south-west down the line of the *via Flaminia* towards Spoletium, where he and M. Crassus met and defeated C. Carrinas once again. Carbo had left Norbanus behind in charge of his forces in the north, and was making a two-pronged advance on Rome down the Cassian and Flaminian roads. Carrinas was presumably the commander of the eastern half of this advance. From Rome Carbo's main objective was to relieve C. Marius the younger, who had been blockaded in the town of Praeneste since his defeat at Sacriportus. Pompey laid siege to Carrinas in Spoletium, but carelessly allowed him to escape one night during a heavy rainstorm (IIIA).

Not long afterwards Pompey successfully ambushed another large force under Marcius Censorinus, which was also trying to get through to the relief of Praeneste. It was the failure of these and other attempts to break through the Sullan blockade in Umbria and Etruria, added to Metellus' success in winning complete control in the north, which broke the back of the government's resistance, and Norbanus fled to Rhodes. Carbo set sail for Africa, abandoning the still numerous forces at his base at Clusium to the mercy of Pompey. In the ensuing battle two-thirds of Carbo's demoralised troops are said to have been killed.

Some of the 10,000 survivors with Carrinas, Censorinus and Damasippus moved southwards to join the last hopes of the government's cause. These were the Samnite and Lucanian troops which were continuing their fierce resistance to Sulla, who had held command against them in the Social War (Samnium and Lucania had remained virtually independent during the Cinnan regime). Pursued by Pompey their united forces made for Praeneste. Unable yet again to break through Sulla's blockade, they then marched on undefended Rome, only to be caught just in time and defeated by Sulla at the murderous battle fought outside the Colline Gate of Rome on 1 November 82. It was presumably shortly after this battle, in which he did not take part, that Pompey joined his leader in Rome.

Although only the bare outlines of the events of 82 have been preserved, we can see Pompey as an efficient, if inexperienced, officer, doing what was required of him by his superiors, and giving convincing proof of both his loyalty and his value to Sulla. It is difficult to assess his military ability. Perhaps he had neither the ruthlessness nor the speed to bring some of his encounters to a really decisive conclusion. Carrinas and Censorinus both managed to escape from Pompey's blockades, one by opportune use of weather conditions, the other by a well-worn stratagem (IIIA). A more experienced commander might have foiled both attempts. However, his exploits satisfied that hardened campaigner Sulla, for he now saw fit to link Pompey to himself by a marriage alliance and give him his first independent command.

At the time of, or shortly after, the battle of Sacriportus Pompey's wife had lost her parents. In a vindictive attempt to remove a number of suspected Sullan partisans at Rome young Marius had ordered the praetor Damasippus to murder four leading senators, including P. Antistius. There can be little doubt that Antistius owed his death, and the subsequent suicide of his wife, to his position as Pompey's father-in-law. This was not the only sorrow Antistia had to bear, for Sulla persuaded Pompey to divorce her and marry his own step-daughter, Aemilia, who was already herself married and pregnant by her present husband. As she was the daughter of a Metella, the marriage brought with it a connection with the Metelli, and had the effect of drawing Pompey into the very caucus of noble families with whom his father had by all accounts been so unpopular. In the task of re-establishing the supremacy of this faction Pompey was to be of the utmost value.

Those who continued the opposition to Sulla and his regime after the battle of the Colline Gate will often be referred to by the traditional but anachronistic name of 'Marians'. This should not be taken to imply any close association with the elder Gaius Marius, who had died in January 86, or with his aims, but in the absence of any recognised leader his name seems to have provided an emotive and effective rallying cry for the enemies of Sulla.

Once Rome and Italy were firmly in Sulla's control the laborious task remained of hunting down the enemy leaders who had escaped, and of ensuring that they could not raise the western provinces to arms against the new regime. Moreover, three of these provinces, Sardinia, Sicily and Africa, were of vital importance to Rome as providers of corn. The effects of a severe corn shortage in a city that was already suffering the many hardships attendant on a civil war would have been disastrous.

L. Philippus, who, like Pompey, had joined the Sullan party, had already been sent to Sardinia, and had secured it for Sulla. The consul Carbo, however, had escaped to Africa before Pompey's victory at Clusium, and was reported to be in command of a fleet in Sicilian waters. The corn blockade had obviously started, for that island was under the control of M. Perperna Veiento, another Marian leader.

Although Q. Metellus and M. Crassus might have been considered more suitable by virtue of age and experience, Sulla chose his new stepson-in-law for the important task of recovering Sicily and Africa. Although he had held no previous senatorial office, he was invested with the rank and *imperium* of propraetor, and given an army of six legions and a navy of 120 men-of-war with 800 transport ships. Both men and ships were immediately available: the men from Sulla's own armies, and the ships from the fleet which he had used to transport them from Greece in 83.

For Cicero, speaking in praise of Pompey some sixteen years later, the campaign in Sicily was characterised by the phenomenal speed with which it was planned. No military action is reported. Perperna abandoned the island on hearing the nature of the force sent against him, and Pompey was soon installed in the western capital at Lilybaeum. His task was now to find and capture Carbo. Information as to his whereabouts was procured by a stroke of fortune. One of Pompey's patrols intercepted a fishing boat heading towards Lilybaeum, to find that their suspicions had been justified. The boat was carrying the Marian M. Brutus on a spying mission from Carbo. Brutus himself committed suicide in order to avoid capture and interrogation, but the fishermen must have revealed the purpose of their trip, and a squadron of Pompey's ships was soon on its way to the little island of Cossyra (today Pantellaria) where Carbo was anchored. They had orders to execute the other Marian leaders with Carbo and bring the consul himself to Lilybaeum. Again, no serious resistance is reported.

What is recorded is the manner of Carbo's interrogation and death. Although Pompey was obviously acting under instructions from Sulla, the fact that a young commander of twenty-four who had not even entered the Senate should order the execution of a man who had three times been consul of the Roman People made a deep impression on many of his contemporaries. The episode, with several colourful embellishments, was recalled in anti-Pompeian speeches and propaganda pamphlets for many years, and his enemies were soon calling him by the insulting name of *adulescentulus carnifex*, 'the teenage butcher' (IIIB, IVA).

Favourable counter-propaganda stressed the other side of the picture: Pompey's firm control over his soldiers, his leniency towards Sicilians who had shown support for the Marian cause, his refusal to order a search for the less important Marians trapped on the island, and his restraint and freedom from corruption in his dealings with the Sicilian cities. More recent historians have also noted that his personal *clientela* in Sicily was greatly increased, especially by grants of citizenship to many of his Sicilian friends. Few Roman politicians would have missed such an opportunity of extending their influence.[19]

In view of the absence of organised resistance on the island, it is obvious that a force as large as six legions was not allotted purely for the recovery of Sicily. So, when, before the end of December, Pompey received a decree of the Senate and a letter from Sulla (now elected to the emergency position of Dictator), with instructions to transport his army to Africa immediately, this was no new assignment. It was merely an order to put the second phase of the original plan into operation.

The opposition to Sulla in Africa presented a far more serious threat than did Carbo and Perperna. The influence of the great Gaius Marius himself was still strong there, and the many exiled Marian leaders under the young noble, Gnaeus Domitius Ahenobarbus, had raised a large army of about 27,000 men, supported by a Numidian prince, Hiarbas. They were encamped near the city of Utica.

Pompey handed over control of Sicily to his brother-in-law, C. Memmius, and landed his forces in two divisions at Carthage and Utica. Once more size and speed by themselves produced an immediate effect: 7,000 Marians deserted. This must have decided Domitius to offer battle before the morale of his troops fell further, for Plutarch's narrative suggests that he was the first to draw up his line, which he defended by placing it behind a rugged and difficult ravine, in the hope that the Pompeian soldiers could be lured into attacking across it. A violent storm of wind and rain then broke over the intended battlefield and lasted for the better part of the day, and Domitius finally decided to lead his soaked and shivering troops back to camp. We are not told whether Pompey's army had also been in line all day, but on seeing the start of the withdrawal Pompey ordered an immediate attack across the ravine. At the same time the wind shifted and began to drive the rain into the faces of the Marians as they turned in disorder to meet the charge. Pompey's seizure of the initiative was the decisive move, and in the battle and ensuing rout only 3,000 Marians escaped. The victorious troops saluted their general as *Imperator*.

No doubt remembering his failures the previous year to complete victory by the capture · of the enemy base, Pompey checked the premature celebrations of his soldiers and insisted on an immediate assault on Domitius' camp. This time success was total, and the enemy commander was killed into the bargain.

The war, however, was by no means over. To the west of the small coastal province of Africa the kingdom of Numidia was still in the hands of prince Hiarbas, who now began to rouse his countrymen to war.

A replacement amenable to Rome was ready to hand in the person of ex-king Hiempsal, whom Hiarbas had earlier deposed, and Pompey now embarked on a new campaign aimed at restoring Hiempsal. Success would bring victory over a foreign foe, more glorious than victory over Roman citizens, and the new king would be bound by ties of personal clientship to Pompey himself.

Pompey advanced into Numidia in pursuit of Hiarbas, and at the same time, in response to a request from Pompey, Bogud, son of the king of Mauretania, launched an invasion from the west. The advance in force was calculated to instil terror and respect for Rome into the Numidians, and presumably involved a few skirmishes with Numidian irregulars and the sacking of a few native villages. Hiarbas, withdrawing in front of Pompey up the Bagradas valley, was driven into the arms of Bogud and forced to take refuge in the town of Bulla. On Pompey's arrival Bulla surrendered and Hiarbas was executed.

The restoration of Hiempsal, the arrangement of satisfactory relations between him and other North African princes, and a few days spent hunting lions and elephants in the Numidian hills brought the campaign to an end. Within forty days of his landing at Utica Pompey had returned to join his fleet there.[20]

His sights were now clearly set on a triumph. Just over seven years before, he had been with his father as he drove in procession with the captives and the booty from Asculum through cheering crowds to the impressive ceremony of dedication on the Capitol. Incredibly he now felt that he had the chance to emulate his father and excite the Roman populace with the view of animals and treasure from this strange continent of Africa. The very fact of his presumption in contemplating such an honour marks Pompey as a young man of extraordinary self-confidence and ambition.

What was to come was a test also of his political courage and ability, his determination in the face of powerful opposition from Sulla and the other senior members of his faction. Instructions awaited him at Utica to send home five of his legions and await the arrival of his successor. One of the most critical moments in his career had arrived.

His trump card, as the career of Pompeius Strabo had clearly shown, was the army at his back. He needed to be completely certain of their loyalty and support, and took the most obvious means of testing this by ordering the dismissal and embarkation of five legions. The result was as he had hoped. The soldiers refused to forsake their general, and several times tried to force him to keep his command. Pompey's histrionic attempts to resist by retiring to his tent in tears and threatening to take his own life were consciously reminiscent of similar attempts made by Alexander of Macedon in the face of mutiny by his troops on the limits of the old Persian Empire. This fact, added to an apparent physical resemblance to Alexander, may well have caused the army to salute Pompey at last by the same title which Alexander had enjoyed: *Magnus*, 'the Great'.

In 88 Strabo had been able to claim that his own troops had forced him to retain command in spite of Sulla's instructions. Now his son tried the same move. Exactly what was contained in his reply to Sulla we do not know, but when Pompey landed in Italy with his full army, Sulla was forced to accept the situation. The famous story of the meeting between the two men, and how Pompey extracted from his leader permission to hold his longed-for triumph, is dramatically told by Plutarch. On 12 March 81, possibly no more than five months after he had first set sail for Sicily, Pompey held his triumph. It was officially for his victory over Hiarbas, since his other victories had been over Roman citizens. The story of the chariot drawn by four elephants which was two wide to pass through the triumphal arch and could therefore not be used in the procession has been taken to show that Pompey intended to ride in a chariot of the type traditionally associated with the goddess Venus, bringer of victories and his own patron goddess, and with Dionysus and some of the Hellenistic monarchs. If this is so, the size of the arch may have been no more than a face-saving excuse, following a refusal by Sulla to allow Pompey to exalt himself in this manner. It seems unlikely that a planner of Pompey's calibre would not have foreseen this difficulty.[21]

Another move by Sulla to deflate his ambitious young protégé may be seen in the triumphs later in the year given to L. Murena from Asia and Valerius Flaccus from Spain and Gaul. Neither of these appears to have been particularly well-earned, and Sulla was possibly trying to emphasise to the people of Rome, by a series of impressive triumphs beginning with his own in January, the return of peace and the military achievements abroad which had been brought about by the new regime.[22]

A brief summary of the aims and methods of the Sullan government will be given at the beginning of the next chapter. It is now time to take a closer look at the young man, clad in his brightly embroidered triumphal robe, who mounted the steps of the Capitol to dedicate his spoils to the gods of Rome on that day in March 81. Plutarch, in a well-known passage, describes Pompey's youthful good looks, his air of dignity and majesty, and the glistening look in his eyes, which, with his characteristic way of holding his head, reminded friends of the portrait busts of Alexander. A wayward quiff of hair rose above his forehead, and was to provide later sculptors with an easy means of identifying their subject. The few portraits that we have were copied from originals carved in the mid-fifties at the earliest, but do not in any way contradict the evidence of Plutarch.[23]

More important from the historical point of view is the effect his triumph must have had on the other political leaders of the time. Centuries of tradition decreed that the aspiring politician should, by the use of his own talents and the influence of his family and friends, slowly work his way up the ladder of promotion in the Senate to reach the consulship at the age of forty-two (at the earliest), and then as consul, propraetor or proconsul command the armies of Rome overseas. At home he could guide the deliberations of the Senate and the policies of the magistrates as one of the powerful group of consulars, the experienced elder statesmen. Thus he would win *gloria* and *dignitas*.

Within the Senate different factions would be for ever struggling to win temporary predominance for themselves, but at the same time would be determined to prevent any single member of their own or any other faction from reaching a position of personal domination. The leaders of the factions themselves had to be no more than *primi inter pares*, firsts among equals.

And yet here was a young soldier who had not even entered the Senate; his family was not long established in Roman politics; his father had had few friends, if any, among the nobility, and had won many enemies by his greed and unscrupulous ambition; like his father he scorned traditional methods of advancement, and was using Italian and foreign clients and his own army to bring him positions which should be the fruits of long apprenticeship and victory at elections. He had taken advantage of a time of upheaval and civil war, when irregularities were justified on grounds of expedience, and he had the foresight to make himself indispensible to the victor of that war and the most powerful man in the Roman world. Already he was behaving like a senior senator and winning a dangerous amount of personal popularity with the people. The natural reaction of most *nobiles* would be *invidia*, jealousy and a determination to clip the young man's wings.

2 THE SENATE'S GENERAL: ITALY and SPAIN 78–71

Julius Frontinus includes in his collection of military stratagems an interesting incident which occurred shortly before Pompey's triumph. When his troops threatened to plunder the money which was to be carried in the procession and it looked as if mutiny might break out, Pompey rapidly took command of the situation and, with one of his now familiar dramatic gestures, restored discipline in the ranks (VA). According to Plutarch, who also records the story, one outcome of the episode was that Pompey won the admiration and support of the powerful senator Publius Servilius Vatia, grandson of the famous Metellus Macedonicus, and a leading figure of the Metellan faction, who had previously been strongly opposed to the whole idea of a triumph for Pompey.[1]

This anecdote is certainly illustrative of the fact that, in spite of his defiance of the new dictator Sulla, Pompey succeeded in forming an alliance with the faction which was to benefit most from Sulla's constitutional reforms. As a successful and popular general and a masterful commander of men he was an important ally to win, especially in the early days of the regime. Jealousy was, temporarily at least, laid aside and Pompey was welcomed into the faction. During his absence in Sicily and Africa his wife Aemilia had died while bearing the child with which she had been pregnant at the time of their marriage. At some date between his triumph and the summer of the following year (80) Pompey married Mucia, a girl of impeccable family. Her father had been Q. Mucius Scaevola, consul in 95 and Pontifex Maximus from about 89 to 82, when he had been one of the four consulars murdered at the command of the younger Marius. Her mother had also been married to Q. Caecilius Metellus Celer, the tribune of 90, and Mucia was thus half-sister to two of the rising generation of Metelli, Q. Metellus Celer the younger and Q. Metellus Nepos.[2]

The death of Aemilia and his own independent attitude before his triumph seems to have caused a cooling of relations between Pompey and Sulla. This is reflected in the fact that no more commands were found for Pompey, and he was apparently the only one of Sulla's friends who did not benefit by his will. Nevertheless Sulla's faction, looking towards the rising rather than the setting sun, realised that

Pompey's ambition would be better harnessed to their own cause than to that of their opponents, the surviving Marians, who could still muster support, especially in the western provinces.

Among other aristocratic friends of Pompey can be counted his old patron L. Philippus, now one of the senior surviving consulars, his own brother-in-law C. Memmius, and possibly M. Pupius Piso. Piso like Pompey had been ordered by Sulla to divorce his wife, Cinna's widow, and thus to demonstrate his loyalty to the new regime. He was a member of a distinguished family, the Calpurnii Pisones, and was to be a firm supporter of Pompey in later years in spite of the spirited resistance offered by several of his relatives.

Equally significant are the friendships which Pompey was developing with talented men from non-aristocratic families, especially with men from his own country of Picenum. The Picentines T. Labienus, L. Afranius and A. Gabinius had probably been officers in Pompey's army in 82 and were to prove his loyal aides and legates as they climbed their way up the ladder of political advancement under his patronage. Not yet powerful enough to form a *factio*, they and others such as M. Petreius and M. Terentius Varro were the men on whose friendship Pompey would rely heavily in the years to come. All were sound officers, Varro indeed one of Rome's few outstanding naval commanders, and since they were not of noble birth would not be jealous of their leader's success.

Pompey also enjoyed great popularity among the equestrian class, of which he was now the most distinguished member. The people too, were dazzled by his military successes and triumph, and according to Plutarch were delighted by the fact that he did not yet show any intention of entering the Senate.

It is noteworthy that, with the exception of his sister's marriage to C. Memmius, the other members of his family were of no help to Pompey at all. His uncle Sextus Pompeius was a philosopher and jurist who steered clear of politics, and his mother's brother Lucilius seems to have been solely concerned with running his country estates. The Pompeii as a family were neither a coherent nor an effective political unit, and of necessity Pompey would have to win his support by means other than those traditionally employed by the sons of noble families. If he was not content to remain an adherent of the Metellan faction or some other aristocratic clique, he would have to gather round him *clientes* who owed loyalty to him personally. As we have seen, he had inherited a large number of these from his father, mainly in Picenum and Cisalpine Gaul. But to be effective support had to be utilised in Rome, where the elections were held and government carried out. This was to prove one of Pompey's hardest problems.

Under the Sullan regime, however, Pompey was still a subordinate, even if a very important one, and we should now look briefly at the policies and actions to which he was being called on to subscribe. After his victory at the Colline Gate Sulla's purposes were two-fold: (i) to restore some semblance of law and order to a city which had been racked by war and the threat of war for the past decade, and (ii) to ensure once and for all the dominance of the Senate in Roman politics and of the Optimates in the Senate. Much of his legislation as Dictator, an office to which he was elected late in the year 82 for the express purpose of 'writing the laws and reconstituting the state', was aimed at putting an end to the methods by which the authority of the Senate had been successfully challenged in the past. The powers of the tribunes were drastically curtailed; they could no longer propose legislation, at any rate not without senatorial approval, their power of veto was limited, and they were prohibited from holding any further office. The activities of provincial governors and other army commanders were also strictly controlled by laws redefining the crime of treason (*maiestas*). Marius and Pompeius Strabo had shown how effectively an army could be used as a political weapon if it was brought into Italy, and although Sulla had himself used his own army in such a way, he tried to ensure that at least the movement of armies would in future be more effectively controlled by the Senate. Any sign of independence in a general would be checked by the threat of prosecution for treason, and the courts were once more to be in the hands of juries drawn exclusively from the ranks of the Senate.[3]

Other measures further strengthened the position of the Senate and especially its senior members, in particular the law which prescribed the order, interval and age-limits of the main magistracies and forbade the holding of a second consulship within ten years of the first. The way to the top was to be even more difficult than before for the non-noble politician.

It is not necessary here to discuss at length the legalised murder of opponents and the blatant profiteering by his supporters which accompanied Sulla's reforms. It is significant, however, that Pompey does not seem to have been accused in later years of having enriched himself by his support for the regime or of having used the proscriptions as a means of taking vengeance on his enemies. Quite apart from the fact that Pompey must have been a very rich man already, both from his family inheritance and from the proceeds of his military victories, there is no need to doubt the insistence on his personal honesty and moderation which we find in many of the sources. If his support for Sulla was a matter of expediency, we should not necessarily suppose that he approved of his leader's methods, or that he was whole-heartedly in sympathy with his aims. It is obvious that Pompey's own rise to a position of power was an example of the kind of thing which Sulla was trying to check.[4]

It is therefore not surprising that we hear of no political activity on his part between his triumph and the campaign for the consular elections in 79. In all probability he withdrew into private life with Mucia and started raising the family that had not proved possible in his first two marriages. In the space of four-and-a-half years Mucia bore him three children, two sons, Gnaeus and Sextus, and a daughter, Pompeia. For a while Rome had no immediate need of his generalship, and Pompey had little taste for domestic politics. To enter the Senate he would, under the Sullan law, have had to win election as a quaestor, and this was no post for a triumphant general who had probably had several quaestors under his own command in the past. He may also have genuinely disliked the political climate of the years 81 and 80.

By the end of 80, however, Sulla had abdicated his dictatorship, leaving the guidance of the Republic in the hands of two consuls from famous noble families, P. Servilius Vatia and Appius Claudius Pulcher. It remained to be seen whether the Optimates could continue to produce from their own ranks the leaders which Rome would need; whether they could justify the responsibilities which Sulla had placed upon them. Already there were a number of serious problems facing the government.

Abroad the main focus of attention was the provinces of Spain. Here one of the few surviving Marian leaders, the tough Sabine Q. Sertorius, was successfully holding out against a succession of Sullan commanders, helped not only by the remnants of the Marian forces but also by considerable numbers of Spanish tribesmen. Praetor in 83 he had left for his allotted province of Nearer Spain in 82, and although expelled in the following year by the proconsul C. Arrius, he had managed to find support in North Africa and returned to Spain in 80 at the invitation of the Lusitanians. An inspiring, some would say brilliant, commander, he was quick to adapt his Roman military training to the requirements of the Spanish country-side and the flexible tactics of guerrilla warfare. In 79 the Sullan proconsuls in Spain were Q. Caecilius Metellus Pius, Sulla's consular

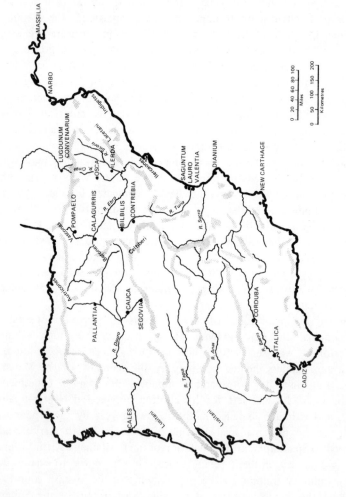

Figure 2: Map of Spain to illustrate Pompey's campaigns against Sertorius.

colleague of the previous year and one of the foremost Optimate leaders, and a praetor of 80, M. Domitius Calvinus. Of these the latter was defeated and killed by one of Sertorius' lieutenants in a battle on the river Anas, and Metellus suffered a number of reverses at the hands of Sertorius himself.

At home Sulla's legislation had failed even to touch, let alone solve, many of the pressing problems of Italy. In particular the difficulties of the small farmers and farm labourers, which had been increased by over ten years of civil war, still cried out for attention. It was hard enough in settled times for the small farmers to make a living from their holdings or their rented farms, but in time of war they formed the bulk of the legionary troops and many farms must inevitably have fallen into disuse with the menfolk away fighting and whole armies foraging and pillaging in the most fertile regions of the peninsula. What is more Sulla had had to resettle most of his own troops on new farms after his victory, and in order to do so had confiscated large areas of land both from private individuals and from cities and towns which had failed to give him support.

Thus although 120,000 veteran soldiers are said to have been settled on land in colonies situated near enough to Rome for their inhabitants to be called to the support of the Optimates if necessary, there were also thousands of dispossessed farmers and labourers who now had no visible means of support.

Added to these discontented citizens were the sons of those who had died in the proscriptions, who had lost all their property and the right to stand for any public office. The equestrian class, more than 1,600 of whose members had died in the same purge, and who had lost their control of the law courts, were also embittered against the new regime. The *plebs* had lost the right to the distributions of cheap corn, which had done something in the past to alleviate hardship even if they had been used as a vote-catching bait by *popularis* politicians. Finally, those Italians who had supported the Cinnan cause in the civil war, especially the Etruscans, Samnites and Lucanians, felt nothing but bitter resentment against a government which had punished them ferociously for loyalty to the losing side.

During the year 79 Pompey reappeared on the political scene to support M. Aemilius Lepidus, one of the candidates for the consulship of the following year. Since Lepidus had probably been a fellow officer of Pompey's in Strabo's army at Asculum, it was not surprising that Pompey should see fit to put his resources at his friend's disposal. However, the anecdote concerning the election which Plutarch records has given rise to considerable speculation about Pompey's motives and the soundness of his judgement.

> When in spite of Sulla and against his wishes Pompey helped Lepidus to the consulship, canvassing for him and turning the people in his favour through their goodwill towards himself, seeing him go off with a crowd of supporters through the forum, Sulla said to him, 'Young man, I see that you are revelling in your victory. To be sure, it was a splendid and noble result for Lepidus, the worst rogue in the world, to be elected consul ahead of Catulus, the finest of all men, thanks to your influence over the people. It is high time you woke up and paid attention to what is going on, for you have made your rival stronger than yourself.'[5]

It has often been thought that this was evidence that Pompey had supported Lepidus against a (third) Sullan candidate and was thus already challenging the settlement which he was later called upon to defend. Recently, however, Syme has pointed out that there is no evidence that there were any other candidates beside the two *nobiles*, Lepidus and Q. Lutatius Catulus, and that both must have had the ex-dictator's blessing on their candidature. Stories about Sulla's prophetic utterances are in any case of doubtful authenticity, and one should also avoid the danger of assuming that Lepidus' hostility to Sulla came into the open before the latter's death.[6]

In fact, although Lepidus appears to have been married to Apuleia, the daughter of Saturninus, the violent *popularis* tribune of 103 and 100, he had obviously thrown in his lot with Sulla at some time during the eighties and owed his consulship primarily to the fact that he belonged to a noble family of long standing. In Sulla's eyes Pompey's mistake had not been to help him to election but to secure for him the senior position and privileges which went to the candidate who topped the poll. Catulus had always been, and remained, one of the staunchest of Sulla's followers and will have been considered to have deserved that honour.

In Roman politics personal friendship and obligation frequently meant more than policies or principles. Even if Lepidus' support for Sulla was superficial and did not survive the latter's death, Pompey probably had no desire in 79 to encourage the dissident elements in the state which were to rally under Lepidus' leadership in the following year. On the contrary, it appears from Plutarch that when, on Sulla's death in 78, Lepidus tried to prevent the body from being buried in state on the Campus Martius Pompey was one of those who opposed him and secured a state funeral for the late dictator.[7]

The chronology of events in 78 is uncertain and much disputed, largely because the accounts in the ancient sources are drastically abbreviated. The main point at issue is how soon it became clear that Lepidus was planning to put himself at the head of the discontented sections of the populace and lead an armed revolution against the Sullan faction. It is improbable that the speech which Sallust put into the mouth of Lepidus, attacking Sulla and urging a programme of reform, apparently while Sulla was still alive, has any value as an historical document. Lepidus' true colours were probably not seen before he had been allocated Cisalpine and Transalpine Gaul as his province for 77, and had been sent out with Catulus to put down a rising in Etruria. Here the people of Faesulae had taken up arms and attacked the Sullan veterans who had been settled on their land. Once in Etruria Lepidus encouraged the insurgents and clashed openly with his colleague to such an extent that the Senate made both consuls swear not to fight each other.[8]

Yet again Rome faced the danger of a Roman army commander advancing on his own city. But in 78 Lepidus did not feel that he had sufficient support to attempt a whole-hearted *coup*. Instead he announced a programme of reform, including the restoration of the rights of the tribunes, the return of confiscated property and the recall of political exiles. Earlier, it appears, he had tried to win popular support at Rome by means of a law providing for generous distributions of corn to all citizens, but now there were no massive demonstrations of popular feeling on his behalf. Rejecting the Senate's demand that he should return to Rome and preside over the consular elections for the next year (one of his duties as senior consul), Lepidus withdrew northwards into Etruria with the intention of recruiting more troops from his new province and making his bid for power in the following spring. The Optimates were thus given time to make their plans to counter this threat. In spite of a widespread inclination to negotiate with Lepidus the Senate was finally persuaded early in 77 by a speech from L. Marcius Philippus to pass a *consultum ultimum* and call upon the *interrex* Appius Claudius and the proconsul Catulus to take necessary measures to preserve public safety.[9]

The immediate need was for a general who could command support in northern Italy and Cisalpine Gaul while Catulus took steps to defend Rome against the threatened attack. The obvious choice was Pompey, and he was immediately sent northwards, no doubt once more with instructions to raise an army from his clients in Picenum and Gaul. His plan was to cut communications by land between Etruria and Transalpine Gaul and Spain and to prevent reinforcements from joining Lepidus' army.

In spite of his earlier connections with Lepidus, and the fact that he may have sympathised with some of his declared objectives, Pompey quickly accepted his commission from the Senate. The use of force to achieve reform was not to his liking, and in any case he must have realised, as we are told Julius Caesar did, that Lepidus was not a man likely to succeed in bringing about a counter-revolution at this stage. Also Pompey had his eye on a command against Sertorius in Spain. In the normal course of events such commands went to praetors or consuls after their year of office at Rome, but if Pompey could legitimately gain command of an army by other means and show himself once more a successful general, there was a greater likelihood of his persuading the Senate to waive the regulations in his favour again.

So, invested with the power of propraetor, Pompey set out once more for his ancestral estates. Lepidus' commander in Gaul was M. Junius Brutus, a Marian who could also call upon clients in that province. He had established his headquarters at Mutina, a town strategically placed on the *via Aemilia* just north-west of the point where the road branches south into Etruria and south-east to Picenum. Pompey moved up the *via Aemilia* with part of his army and blockaded Brutus at Mutina, meanwhile, if we can accept the account of Orosius, sending another part across country to Alba on the river Tanarus, where a second Lepidan garrison was guarding the road from Spain, under the command of Lepidus' son, Cornelius Scipio.[10]

Plutarch's account hints at successful operations against other pockets of resistance, but attention is concentrated on the lengthy siege of Mutina, which was finally brought to an end by the surrender of Brutus himself. With the town in his hands Pompey allowed Brutus with a small escort of cavalry to go free, but was soon informed that Brutus had merely moved on to the next town along the road, Regium Lepidi. Here he presumably began to whip up further support for Lepidus (the name of the town suggests that there were hereditary clients of his there), and Pompey was forced to send an officer, Geminius, to Regium to recapture Brutus and execute him.[11]

This episode, like the deaths of Carbo and Domitius earlier, was later used by his enemies to blacken the character of Pompey, but there is no more reason to suppose that it was the result of cruelty or perfidy on Pompey's part.

How long Alba held out before it was finally starved into surrender we are not told. Meanwhile Lepidus had been summoned from Etruria by order of the Senate. He obeyed, but brought with him the whole of the force he had mustered and encamped outside Rome, threatening violence and demanding a second consulship for himself. In the city the Optimates seem to have neutralised what support he may have had in the Senate by allowing the election of Mamercus Aemilius Lepidus Livianus and D. Junius Brutus, presumably relatives of Marcus Lepidus and Marcus Brutus, to the consulship. Catulus was able to raise an army to defend the city and occupied the northern approaches. Plutarch suggests that there was stalemate for a time until morale was raised in Rome by Pompey's despatch announcing the surrender of Brutus and the fall of Mutina. This may have been the factor which persuaded Catulus to attack Lepidus, and battle was eventually joined not far from the Campus Martius, on the Etruscan bank of the Tiber. The defenders of Rome were successful and Lepidus, with the remnants of his force, withdrew again into Etruria.

If the sequence of events suggested above is correct, Pompey must have set out for Rome very shortly after the execution of Brutus, probably with the intention of catching Lepidus in the rear and trapping him between the two loyalist armies. In fact he caught Lepidus in retreat near the coast at Cosa, but although he defeated him in another battle he allowed Lepidus to embark a force which was later reported as numbering fifty-three cohorts and to sail to Sardinia, where he hoped to bring pressure to bear on the government at Rome by stopping the shipment of corn to the city from the island. Lepidus met with firm resistance from the governor of Sardinia and died not long afterwards, but his legate M. Perperna Veiento took over command of his troops and sailed first to the coast of Liguria and then to Spain to join forces with Sertorius. Indeed it seems likely that the ships in which Lepidus escaped from Cosa were supplied by Sertorius or the Cilician pirates with whom he was in league, and possibly there was more co-operation between the two Marians than our sources have recorded.

With the defeat and death of Lepidus it might have been thought that the immediate threat had been averted. The Sullan faction were at pains to give this impression. Their new leader Q. Metellus Pius was in Spain with eventual prospects of winning military glory against Sertorius, and Catulus could fairly claim the credit for crushing the Lepidan revolt. It was important that the faction should be seen to be in control.

In fact, however, the escape of Perperna with a large force of Marians necessitated a more realistic assessment of the situation. His arrival in Spain would swing the balance decidedly in Sertorius' favour, and meanwhile it looked as if Rome's land links with Spain were still in jeopardy. Perperna's visit to Liguria may well have been connected with disturbances in that area, and it is possible that some of the fifty-three cohorts which Plutarch says he had when he joined Sertorius were recruited, after Perperna's departure from Sardinia, among the rebellious Gauls.[12]

With his considerable experience of fighting against the Marians, Pompey realised that much remained to be done. The difficulty lay in persuading the Senate to commission him to do it. Catulus, indeed, instructed him to disband his army, but Pompey disregarded the orders of his superior and remained with his troops under arms outside the walls of Rome. This move in itself will have reminded many of Pompeius Strabo's behaviour only ten years before. Moreover Pompey continued to make excuses for his apparent insubordination, and the similarity between the actions of father and son no doubt led many senators to fear that Pompey's loyalty to the Sullans was as ambiguous as Strabo's had been. Meanwhile Pompey's friends in Rome were breaking down senatorial resistance to the idea of a further command for the young general. Appian's statement that it was believed that Sertorius, reinforced by Perperna's army of Italians, intended to march against Italy itself probably stems from propaganda produced in Rome at the time to emphasise the threat which still remained. It was agreed that a new proconsul of the nearer province of Spain should be sent out with an army to join Metellus, the proconsul of the further province. The two consuls D. Junius Brutus and Mamercus Aemilius Lepidus both refused the command. Military inexperience may have been an excuse, but we have seen reason to suspect both of Marian sympathies. Pompey's old mentor, the senior statesman L. Philippus, seized the opportunity to propose that Pompey be sent out in spite of his technical lack of qualifications, and his jibe at the consuls that Pompey was going out not on behalf of the consul (*pro consule*) but on behalf of both consuls (*pro consulibus*) found its way into the collection of senatorial *bons mots*.[13]

The Senate accepted Philippus' proposal and within forty days Pompey had seen to the recruitment of new troops and the provision of equipment. The size of his army was given by the historian Galba as 30,000 infantry and 1,000 cavalry. This is a large force and was considerably greater than the one he had commanded against Lepidus.

Its very size is evidence of the seriousness of the threat presented by Sertorius, and the fact that it was led by a young man of twenty-eight with no senatorial experience behind him illustrates the weakness of the Sullan faction when faced by such a strong military challenge. Sulla's attempt to ensure senatorial control over army leaders was seen to have failed.[14]

On Pompey's staff were his old Picentine lieutenant L. Afranius, D. Laelius, M. Petreius, C. Cornelius, probably A. Gabinius and his close friend and adviser, the learned scholar M. Varro. His brother-in-law C. Memmius was already serving under Metellus and was to join Pompey as his quaestor on his arrival in Spain.

Although Varro produced for Pompey a naval itinerary describing in detail the sea route to Spain, the military situation demanded that he should take a land route through the Alps and along the coastal strip which at that time formed the province of Transalpine Gaul. Pioneering a new passage of the Alps, probably via the Mont Genèvre, Pompey defeated some hostile Alpine tribes, whom he later described as 'enemies already at the throat of Italy', and then moved down the valley of the Durance towards the great independent Greek colony and port of Massilia (Marseilles). This route brought him into the territory of the Saluvii, a tribe traditionally hostile to both Marseilles and Rome. A passage in Caesar's *Civil War* records that Pompey defeated this tribe in battle and assigned their territory to Marseilles, increasing the amount of revenue they were presumably already paying to that city. It follows that the Saluvii were in revolt at the time and one is forced to wonder whether this revolt may not be connected with the visit of Perperna to the Ligurian coast a few months previously. If Perperna had instigated a rebellion amongst the Saluvii and the Ligurian tribes of the Maritime Alps it would explain why Pompey did not transport any or all of his troops by sea or by the coast road, where they would have been in danger of attack from pirates as well, but took an arduous northern detour through a new pass, thus also gaining the advantage of surprise.[15]

We are not told any further details of this Gallic campaign of autumn 77. Cicero later described Pompey as leading his legions to Spain through a welter of carnage in a transalpine war. This expression is echoed by Lucan, and making allowances for exaggeration on the part of orator and poet we may conclude that it was only after much hard fighting that Pompey finally quartered his troops for the winter in or near the Roman colony of Narbo Martius (Narbonne).[16]

Final plans were now made for the coming campaign. Practically all the peninsula of Spain was in the hands of Sertorius except for the area of Andalusia, bounded roughly by the river Baetis (Guadalquivir) and the coast from Cadiz to New Carthage, and the towns of Lauro and Saguntum. Metellus was holding this area from his headquarters at Corduba, while Sertorius had made his own winter quarters at Castra Aelia on the middle Ebro, where he was busy organising the manufacture of new arms and equipment in the various cities allied to him, and distributing clothing and pay to his scattered troops.

Sertorius deduced that Pompey's plan would be to secure the coastal strip from New Carthage to the Pyrenees by winning over the tribes and cities there with a show of force. He would thus link up with Metellus and acquire a base from which it would be possible to penetrate up the main lines of communication into the interior. As well as securing his own supply lines by sea he could also hope to cut off Sertorius from his pirate allies by capturing his main supply depot at Dianium. One of Pompey's chief objectives would be the fertile plain of Valentia where he could expect good opportunities for foraging.

Sertorius disposed his forces accordingly. Perperna, who had been forced by his troops to put himself under Sertorius' command on the news of Pompey's approach, was sent with 20,000 infantry and 1,500 cavalry to join Herennius in the territory of the Ilercaones, with instructions to guard the crossing of the lower Ebro and try to lure Pompey into ambush. Hirtuleius was to keep Metellus penned in his province, if possible avoiding open battle, while Sertorius marched up the Ebro against the tribes of the Berones and Autricones. These had already solicited aid from Pompey. Sertorius wanted to establish a firm base of operations in northern Spain and to be in readiness to come to the aid of his subordinates if occasion demanded.

His deductions proved to be correct. Pompey rightly ignored the appeals of the Berones and Autricones since he did not want to be lured into the arms of Sertorius. Instead he crossed the Pyrenees by the Col de Pertus and received the submission of the coastal tribes of the Indigetes and Lacetani. Meanwhile C. Memmius, who had been sent to join him as quaestor by Metellus, accompanied by the able Spaniard Balbus, sailed with a force to New Carthage, under orders to secure that base and move up the coast to join his chief. In fact Memmius was immediately blockaded in New Carthage, probably by Sertorius' pirate allies, and was unable to play his part in the campaign.

At first things went well for Pompey. He managed to cross the Ebro unhindered by Perperna and Herennius and continued his advance, probably in several columns, towards the plain of Valentia. Here he came to grips for the first time with his main opponent. Hearing of his success in outwitting Perperna and Herennius, Sertorius marched rapidly south via Bilbilis and Contrebia to blockade the town of Lauro between Valentia and Saguntum. Here Pompey had collected his forces on the river Palantia, presumably with the intention of attacking Valentia, where the Sertorian commanders had taken refuge. The siege of Lauro successfully diverted Pompey's attention from this project and he was cunningly drawn by Sertorius into a deadly trap.

The battle of Lauro, described in some detail by Frontinus and Plutarch, is the best documented incident in the whole war and well illustrates Sertorius' tactical superiority over Pompey at this time (VB). Sertorius was ready for all his opponent's moves, indeed in several cases he deliberately created the openings for them, and brilliantly succeeded in frustrating Pompey's whole strategy at one stroke. With 10,000 men and all his transport lost Pompey had to give up any thought of joining forces with Metellus and re-establishing Roman control over the east coast of Spain. Retreating north of the Ebro he set up winter quarters near the Pyrenees and retired to lick his wounds.[17]

He was joined for the winter by Metellus, who had in August inflicted a crushing defeat on Hirtuleius at Italica, when the latter attempted to stop him breaking out of Andalusia and coming to the aid of his colleague. His victory had come too late, however, and the two commanders needed to plan a more closely concerted campaign for the next year. They also badly needed supplies and reinforcements, and although some of these may have been forthcoming from Gaul, the Senate at Rome seems to have been reluctant to comply with their requests.

The failure of the operation can be largely attributed to Pompey's inexperience, both of the geography of Spain and of guerrilla tactics, and to over-confidence leading to carelessness. Plutarch recalls the boasts Pompey is supposed to have uttered before Lauro, and his failure to insist on careful reconnaissance allowed his foraging party and Laelius' legion to be trapped. Again over-confidence may have caused him to call for Metellus' assistance too late. Although there is no really good evidence for failure to co-operate willingly with Metellus, Pompey clearly desired the glory that would come from defeating Sertorius single-handed, and this probably led him to take unnecessary risks. Memmius' failure to create a southern front also contributed to the frustration of Pompey's plans, but we have no evidence to enable responsibility for that failure to be attributed.[18]

Sertorius and his lieutenants spent the winter in Lusitania recruiting a new army to replace the 20,000 lost at Italica, and at the same time received an offer of help from a new source. Mithridates, who was once more expanding his influence and control in Asia minor, was persuaded by two Marian exiles, L. Magius and L. Fannius, to negotiate an alliance with Sertorius, and a deputation now arrived from the king with an offer of money and ships in return for Sertorius' recognition of Mithridates' right to his Asian conquests. After consulting his so-called 'Senate', which consisted of 300 of the leading Romans in his army, Sertorius refused to abandon Rome's claim to her own province of Asia, but recognised the king's possession of Bithynia, Cappadocia, Galatia and Paphlagonia. He also offered to lend him one of his own officers as a military adviser. As a result he received in the following year a gift of forty ships and 3,000 talents.

In effect Rome was now faced with a triple alliance of foreign enemies bonded by a large number of her own political exiles. For Marians had joined the forces of Mithridates and the pirates as well as Sertorius, and it was already clear that the Sullan government was going to have to fight major wars on two fronts without control of the seas. In addition it was having to supply money and troops for the current campaigns of first Appius Claudius and then Scribonius Curio against the Thracians in Macedonia and of Servilius Vatia against the pirates in Lycia and Pamphylia.

Orosius recalls that in this winter Pompey captured a city named Belgida in Celtiberia, and Sallust's reference to winter campaigns and the capture and destruction of certain towns suggests that Pompey decided to take advantage of Sertorius' absence in Lusitania to improve the fitness and experience of his comparatively raw troops by a campaign in the area where Sertorius had been so active the year before. In spite of early setbacks he was remaining on the offensive.[19]

In spring 75 the Roman commanders were ready to repeat their strategy of the previous year. While Metellus returned through the centre of Spain to the further province with the intention of finally crushing Hirtuleius, Pompey once more moved south towards the plain of Valentia. This time he met with no serious resistance until he reached Valentia itself and found Herennius and Perperna holding the line of the river Turia. Here he joined battle in the narrow space which separated the river from the city walls and heavily defeated the Sertorians. Herennius himself was among the 10,000 casualties. Valentia was taken and sacked.

Almost simultaneously Pompey must have received news that

Metellus had met Hirtuleius at the city of Segovia and won a decisive victory, killing both Hirtuleius and his brother. Perperna meanwhile had fallen back to join Sertorius at the next tenable line of defence, the river Sucro, some 30 km further south, and Pompey eagerly followed him.

The accounts of the subsequent battle in Appian and Plutarch are somewhat confused. The latter repeats the story that Pompey, elated by his victory at Valentia, was anxious to join battle before Metellus arrived, since he wanted to deny Metellus a share in the victory. Sertorius, too, wished to fight while Pompey was alone and numerically inferior and so launched his attack towards evening in the hope that darkness and ignorance of the ground would prevent Pompey from pursuing if he were victorious and hamper his escape if he were not. An alternative interpretation, which possibly does more justice to Pompey, is that he realised that Sertorius, with his known preference for guerrilla tactics, was unlikely to offer battle to the combined Roman armies. His only hope of defeating Sertorius in open combat was to risk a fight against larger forces before his opponent heard of Hirtuleius' defeat and Metellus' approach. In fact this is what happened on the morning after the battle and it had the effect of forcing Sertorius to revert to his plan of harrassing the armies by attacking their supply lines and foraging parties. Looked at in this way Pompey's tactics can be seen to have involved a carefully calculated risk and not the selfish desire for personal glory that his enemies later attributed to him.[20]

The risk, though, was too great. Pompey again under-estimated the skill of his foe, and although Afranius on his left wing managed to force his way through Perperna's resistance to capture the Sertorian camp, Pompey on the other flank suffered heavily at the hands of Sertorius. The recurring and probably exaggerated number of 10,000 casualties was reported. Sertorius deliberately weakened his own right wing in order to bring overwhelming force and his own inspiring leadership to bear against Pompey, and the latter was fortunate to escape with his life, after being wounded in the thigh and forced to abandon his richly caparisoned horse to divert the attention of his pursuers.

Sertorius' change of tactics on Metellus' arrival eventually caused the united Sullan forces to retreat reluctantly to the area round Saguntum. Here after continued attacks on Roman foraging parties Sertorius was again brought to battle and an engagement lasting half a day was fought near the river Turia. According to Appian, Sertorius, who again ranged his own troops opposite those of Pompey, defeated him killing 6,000 as against 3,000 losses, but this victory was outweighed by Metellus' defeat of the luckless Perperna with 5,000 killed. The following day a daring attack on Metellus' camp was thwarted by prompt action from Pompey. In the course of the battle Metellus was wounded and Memmius, who had been able to join Pompey in time for the battle at the Sucro, was killed.[21]

The ensuing movements of the two sides are uncertain. Sertorius' forces seem to have dispersed once more, leaving Pompey and Metellus no chance of winning a decisive victory on the battlefield, and Metellus eventually withdrew to winter quarters in Gaul. Pompey, unable to find enough supplies for his whole army in the territory of the Vaccaei, where he had some success in winning support among the Celtiberians, left his legate Titurius there with one-and-a-half legions and moved into the country of the Vascones at the western end of the Pyrenees.

During 75 the advantage had definitely begun to swing Pompey's way. Sertorius had lost his two best lieutenants, and although his guerrilla tactics had continued to bring success and he had twice personally outgeneralled Pompey in battle, he had been unable to inflict a decisive defeat on the Sullans, and his hold over his own troops and over many of the Spanish towns and communities was beginning to weaken. If Pompey could carry on wearing down the resistance of Sertorius and making him struggle continuously to maintain control over his allies eventual victory was in sight. Indeed, in spite of his losses in battle, Pompey deserves credit for not allowing himself or his soldiers to lose heart and for keeping up a relentless pressure on Sertorius in several areas. This ability when worsted at one point to strike at another is reminiscent of Philip of Macedon, father of Pompey's own hero, Alexander the Great.

However, such a war of attrition was impossible without more supplies and reinforcements, and during this winter Pompey sent a toughly-worded despatch to the Senate in which he complained bitterly of their failure to keep him properly supplied and threatened that if he was forced to abandon his campaign they might expect an invasion of Italy to follow. The despatch finally brought results and two new legions were sent out to Spain along with money and supplies.[22]

It is at this point that Plutarch's narrative of the war virtually comes to an end. We hear of no more fighting before Sertorius' murder and Perperna's final defeat at the hands of Pompey. The only coherent account is that of Appian, which briefly describes three more years of fighting in which Pompey and Metellus gradually won over more and more of the towns and tribes in the highlands of central Spain. Frontinus records a stratagem used by Pompey to secure control of the town of Cauca. He suspected that the inhabitants would be unwilling to accept a garrison of his soldiers, and so asked them to allow his sick and wounded to recover in the town. Being given permission, he sent in his strongest men disguised as invalids, and thus seized the place. Occasionally, as at Pallantia and Calagurris in 74, Sertorius was able to raise a siege and inflict considerable losses on his opponents, but the overall picture is one of unrelenting advance by the increasingly superior Roman forces as disaffection grew amongst both the Marian and Spanish adherents of Sertorius. After the proclamation by Metellus in 74 of a reward of 100 silver talents and 20,000 acres of land to any Roman who would betray him, Sertorius could no longer trust any of his Marian followers, and he exchanged his Roman bodyguard for a Spanish one. At the beginning of 74 he was faced with large-scale desertions from his army, and his own treatment of his men became harsh and even cruel. As Pompey and Metellus were now concentrating on the interior of the peninsula their supply routes will have been mainly through Gaul, which was now governed by M. Fonteius, a loyal Pompeian supporter. These routes will therefore no longer have been so vulnerable to attack by the pirates and Sertorius' new fleet.[23]

The conspiracy of senior officers led by Perperna, which resulted in the assassination of Sertorius at his capital of Osca, merely hastened his end. Its date is a matter of controversy. Appian's narrative, unfortunately interrupted at this point, puts it in 72, but the epitomator of Livy seems to place it a year earlier (in the eighth year of Sertorius' command), and this agrees with a reference in Appian's *Mithridatic Wars* to Sertorius' being dead by the winter of 73-2. Appian's chronology is not sacrosanct, and it may be justifiable to date Sertorius' death to the first half of 73. If this is correct Pompey might well have expected to be back in Rome by the end of the year, and this would explain why Sallust makes the tribune Licinius Macer, in a speech delivered in that year, look forward to Pompey's imminent return. Further, two of Pompey's friends and supporters at Rome were successful in the consular elections that summer. It does look as though the capital was preparing for a triumphant return.[24]

In fact this was not to happen till 71. Metellus, thinking that Pompey would soon dispose of Perperna, withdrew to his own now-peaceful province, and, rumour had it, to a triumphal welcome and a life of decadent extravagance. The contrast between this and Pompey's own simple and austere way of life was soon drawn, perhaps by Varro, and found its way into later histories. If we may place any weight on the evidence of a fragment of Sallust which mentions Perperna at a town called Cales, it seems that he shifted the theatre of war to the far north-west, to the country of Sertorius' earliest followers, the Lusitanians, and Pompey's pursuit of the new Marian leader will have cost him another year at least before he finally brought Perperna to a decisive battle.[25]

The account followed by Appian, however, ignores this time gap, if such it was, and stresses that after Sertorius' death, which it places in 72, both Pompey and Perperna were eager for an early encounter. The latter was rapidly losing support through desertion. If Perperna, an admittedly inferior leader, really did continue active resistance for a year or more, Pompey or his historian Varro may well have wanted to play this down, and so left the date of Sertorius' assassination deliberately vague in their account. No final certainty is possible.

The description of the final battle shows Pompey in a much better light as a commander than do the reports of his battles against Sertorius. Employing almost Hannibalic tactics he set a careful ambush into which he lured Perperna's army using ten cohorts as a decoy. He allowed these to be attacked while scattered over a wide area, perhaps foraging, and as they fled they drew the Perpernans between the hidden lines of the main army. As these rose from ambush the decoys also turned and attacked their pursuers from the front. The ensuing massacre was decisive.

After the battle news was brought to Pompey that Perperna had been captured hiding in a thicket, and that in an attempt to save his own skin he was offering to produce some incriminating letters from several consulars at Rome, which he had found among Sertorius' papers. With this information a number of secret Marian sympathisers could be uncovered. It is to Pompey's eternal credit that he refused even to see Perperna, but ordered his immediate execution and burnt the letters unread. His task was to bring to an end the civil war which had violently split Roman society for sixteen years, and a further round of political purges at Rome could have served no useful purpose whatever.

It is, indeed, in his treatment of his defeated enemies and his settlement of the war-torn province, as much as in his military achievements, that Pompey's greatest distinction lies. Cicero later recalled how he guaranteed the safety of the large numbers of

Sertorians who gave themselves up to him. Many were given safe conduct to start life afresh in Sicily or Africa, and others even returned to public life at Rome; some were settled at a new city on the Gallic side of the Pyrenees called Lugdunum Convenarum (Lugdunum, city of refugees: now St Bertrand de Comminges). This dispersal of those who had held out to the last against the Roman government ensured that trouble would not break out later between them and those of their countrymen who could claim loyalty to Rome, if only because they had come over to Metellus or Pompey during the war. As will be seen again in his treatment of the pirates, Pompey was at pains to reconcile Rome with her former enemies, and to give them a chance to adapt to the conditions of peace which he imposed. A further foundation was the city of Pompaelo (Pompey's town: today Pamplona) in Vasconian territory. Perhaps conscious imitation of Alexander can again be seen in the use of Pompey's own name for his new foundation, which would serve as a lasting reminder of his successes.[26]

For some time Pompey had been following a precedent set by Marius and his own father of granting Roman citizenship to certain Spaniards who had given loyal service to him and his party. In 72 these grants were ratified by a law passed by the two consuls L. Gellius Poplicola and Cn. Cornelius Lentulus Clodianus, no doubt in answer to a request from Pompey. Such was the structure of Roman politics that while serving the interests of his government Pompey was at the same time adding to the already considerable body of personal clients which had been growing for many years. More than twenty years later Caesar was to notice the affection in which Pompey was still held in Spain, and it is a great tribute to his generosity and moderation that provincials should remain so attached to a general whose armies had been fighting and foraging over their countryside during five years of bitter warfare.[27]

Even after Perperna's defeat, however, some cities still held out for a time, and the miseries suffered by the besieged inhabitants of Calagurris joined the grisly lists of horrors of notable sieges. Yet even these towns, it appears, were not harshly treated. Osca, Sertorius' old capital, retained its former status and had Calagurris put under its control. Although most of the details of the settlement of Spain elude us, it is clear that recrimination and punishment were kept to a minimum, and peace and stability restored in an imaginative and far-sighted manner, such as the Spaniards had previously had little cause to expect. With his love of efficiency and order and a soldier's respect for the qualities and rights of the provincials against whom and with whom he had been fighting, Pompey had proved an ideal choice for the task of ending the civil war. Although his attitude towards his fellow nobles at Rome always remained ambiguous and he appeared ill at ease on public occasions, he was later remembered as a man of great charm and approachability, who had the knack of bestowing favours without arrogance or giving offence. It is mainly in his dealings with provincials and subordinates who were his social inferiors that these unusual qualities can be seen.[28]

By the end of 72 the work of rehabilitation in Spain was under way, and Pompey will have been able to give thought to the situation which awaited him on his return to Italy. News had reached him of the slave revolution led by Spartacus, who had already defeated two consular armies in Picenum and was at the head of 100,000 rebels. He was being countered now by vigorous if not always effective action on the part of the praetor of 73, M. Licinius Crassus, probably the wealthiest man in Rome and an old colleague of Pompey in Sulla's army. Well-accustomed to sorting out the problems of the Senate, Pompey saw, perhaps with some relish, that his services would be required once again. He left Spain in the late autumn of 72 and wintered in Gaul, intending to cross the Alps into Italy at the first opportunity in the following spring.

His departure was marked by the erection of a triumphal monument at the summit of the pass over the Pyrenees. On it he recorded that from the Alps to the limits of further Spain he had brought 876 towns under Roman sway. No mention was made of his colleague Metellus, nor of Sertorius. It was best to forget that Romans had commanded and fought on both sides. Even if the number of towns was exaggerated the monument clearly emphasised the secret of Pompey's eventual success. It was not the set-piece battles which settled the issue in the long run. It was the painful, unspectacular fight for control of the hundreds of individual communities of Gaul and Spain. Unremitting patience, detailed planning, brilliant organisation and the ability to learn both from his opponents and his colleagues had been the keynotes of his victory.[29]

3 CONSUL AND PROCONSUL: ROME and THE PIRATES   70–66

At Rome the years of Pompey's absence in Spain had seen a considerable weakening of the power and control of those who were trying to preserve the reformed constitution of Sulla. This was matched by the growth of a movement agitating for the restoration of the powers of the tribunate, and for the breaking of the senatorial stranglehold over the courts for which such a restoration was seen as a prerequisite. After the failure of Lepidus' revolt and the death or exile of its leaders, the spearhead of the new popular movement was a younger and more moderate generation of politicians.

The early blows were struck in 77 and 76, when C. Julius Caesar brilliantly but unsuccessfully prosecuted the Sullans Cn. Cornelius Dolabella (cos. 81) and C. Antonius Hibrida. In 76 the tribune Cn. Sicinius attempted to get the powers of his office restored, but ran into violent opposition from the consul Scribonius Curio and lost his life as a result. The pressure continued in the following year, increased by the threat of revolution. This was due to a shortage of corn, aggravated, if not caused, by the requirements of the armies overseas. The consul C. Aurelius Cotta was forced to compromise and carried a law which allowed tribunes to stand for other magistracies. In 74, however, the consul L. Licinius Lucullus was made of sterner stuff, and firmly checked the agitation of the tribune L. Quinctius for the restoration of further powers. Nevertheless the movement continued to gain momentum and in 73 the standard was taken up by yet another tribune, C. Licinius Macer.

One of the highlights of the third book of Sallust's *Histories* was a rousing but responsible speech to the people which the author put into the mouth of Macer. In it he inveighs against the arrogant and oppressive despotism of the Optimates and introduces, possibly for the first time, the name of Pompey in connection with the popular movement. The Optimates had apparently been stalling, urging people to wait until Pompey's return for discussion of some of the burning issues, in an attempt to gain time. 'It is clear enough to me at any rate', Macer is made to say, 'that Pompey, a young man of such great renown, prefers to be a leading citizen with your support than to share in their tyranny over you, and that he will be in the very forefront of the movement to restore the powers of the tribunes.'[1]

Clearly all Rome was waiting to see what Pompey's intentions would be on his return. As always Pompey was careful not to broadcast these in advance, but it may be possible for us to make some deductions from a few fragments of evidence.

It is almost certain that towards the end of his Spanish campaign (say by 73) Pompey was giving thought to the lines on which he intended his career to develop. It was already clear that it could hardly advance on traditional lines. He had reached a position where in the provinces he acted with authority and enjoyed prestige equal to that of a consular of Metellus' standing. He had already held one triumph, and could confidently expect a second as a result of his recent successes. And yet at Rome he was not even a member of the Senate. Seeing that within ten years he was to become indisputably the most powerful and influential man in the Roman world, it is reasonable to consider the possibility that the moves by which he reached that position were both intentional and carefully planned.

Any such position of power required a solid body of support, a widely based *clientela*, and virtually a political party behind one. Pompey's rise had so far been largely due to his connections with the Sullan faction, and there were signs that these would no longer suffice. In spite of the fact that his alliance with the Metelli continued, the hard core of Optimate nobles, men like Q. Catulus, the brothers M. and L. Lucullus, and Q. Hortensius, would under no circumstances accept Pompey as their leader. However, there was another important group badly in need of a leader of Pompey's standing. This was the moderate reform movement, with whose aims Pompey was by nature in sympathy, and to whose help he could now bring his own great prestige and following among the *equites* and the common people.

His first objective was election to the consulship, a post which would guarantee his public standing at Rome, and in which he would be able to pass the legislation necessary for reform. Beyond the consulship his gaze was perhaps even now set on the East, where lay the glittering opportunity to display in still more glorious campaigns his abilities as a general and as organiser of Rome's overseas possessions. In 73 the big commands were in the hands of his Optimate rivals. In Asia and Bithynia L. Lucullus and M. Cotta were the proconsuls waging war against Mithridates, and in the Mediterranean M. Antonius had been given a wide-ranging command as proconsul against the ever increasing menace of the pirate fleets.[2]

At Rome senators were having to decide what their attitude would be towards Pompey on his return. In 72 the two consuls appear to have been friendly, and his supporters were also winning other magistracies. M. Pupius Piso held a praetorship and was appointed to the governorship of one of the Spains for 71. L. Afranius returned from Pompey's army to stand successfully for the praetorship of 71, as did C. Cornelius for the quaestorship, and the outstanding tribune of 71 was M. Lollius Palicanus, a voluble Picentine of little social standing who may well have owed his election to the influence of his powerful fellow-countryman. The value of Pompey's patronage could be clearly seen.

By March 71 Pompey was back in Rome, but circumstances conspired to see to it that his military duties were not yet complete. Marcus Crassus, who as praetor had been given command against Spartacus the previous autumn, was in difficulties to the south in Bruttium, where an attempt to blockade Spartacus' forces in the toe of Italy near Rhegium had failed. Spartacus had broken out of the trap and it was feared that he might march on Rome. To counter this threat the Popular Assembly passed a resolution that the recently returned Pompey should join his battle-hardened troops to those already ranged against the rebels. Further reinforcements were also expected in the shape of the legions of M. Lucullus, the proconsul of Macedonia, who was soon due to land at Brundisium on his return from a campaign at the western end of the Black Sea. Thus Spartacus' slave army would be trapped on three sides.

This resolution soon produced the required effect, though not quite in the way which had been intended. Galvanised into more positive action by the fear that Pompey might steal his thunder, Crassus defeated the divided forces of the enemy in three battles in Bruttium and Lucania, and in a very short time decisively crushed the revolt. Obviously he was aided by the fact that retreat to the north and east was cut off, and this may have led Crassus to claim later that it was he who had asked the Senate to send for the other two commanders. This latter version is found in Plutarch's biography of him, but is contradicted by the more convincing account of Appian.[3]

From Pompey's point of view the outcome, though not perhaps as pleasing as if he had himself defeated the main rebel forces, was still highly satisfactory. On his way south from Rome he met 5,000 fugitives who had escaped from Spartacus' defeat, rounded them up and had them executed on the spot. In his despatch to the Senate, in which he recorded the success of his mission, he stole a march on Crassus by claiming that while the latter had defeated the gladiators in open combat he himself had pulled up the war by the roots. The bitterness caused by this undignified rivalry between the two commanders for the glory of having saved Rome from the slaves was to last long. Indeed it is doubtful whether the two ever felt that they could really trust each other again.

Pompey could now return in earnest to his quest for a triumph and the consulship. For each he needed a dispensation from the Senate. He was well under the age required by the *lex annalis* for a candidate for the consulship, and there was a regulation that only a general who had held at least the praetorship could celebrate a triumph. Even so Pompey's extraordinary circumstances justified his claims that the regulations should be waived in his case. His enemies, though, would need powerful persuasion.

It was both politic and fair that Pompey should wait until Metellus had returned from Spain and that the two should hold a joint triumph. As Metellus was not due to return till late in the year Pompey had a good excuse to keep his army under arms until past the summer elections and to remain as a proconsul with *imperium*. We need not suppose that Pompey was averse to maintaining his army in this way. Its presence should be enough to persuade the Senate to grant his requests, even if he had no intention of using violence or making open threats. The ploy had worked in 77; there was every reason to suppose that it would work again.

Outside the Senate he was assured of massive support. He was the people's hero and he made it clear that he was sympathetic towards the aims of those *populares* who were seeking the restoration of the powers of the tribunate and the restriction of senatorial control over juries. Indeed Plutarch says that Pompey was asked to stand, and it would be very much in keeping with his character if Pompey allowed the first open moves to come from his supporters rather than from himself.[4]

Within the ranks of the Senate it is difficult to gauge exactly the extent of support and opposition. There was an antagonistic Optimate group, but we should not suppose that even all the Optimates were violently opposed to him. After all it was as leader of the Sullan army that he had just returned from defeating the remnants of the Marians. However, his own close supporters, men like Gabinius, Afranius and Varro, were not yet men of any weight in senatorial circles. But he soon found a collaborator who was. This was none other than Marcus Crassus, who, flushed with victory, was now also aiming at the consulship. Controlling his resentment in the interests of ambition,

Crassus offered Pompey an alliance. His wealth, rhetorical skills and influence in the Senate and among the *equites* combined with Pompey's own wealth and enormous popularity among both *equites* and people would be unbeatable. Both, moreover, had large armies at their backs. For the time being the demands of their combined election campaign outweighed the personal animosity created at the collapse of the slave rebellion.

The two generals had reached Rome with their legions still under arms. Large crowds ran to meet them, but a whispering campaign started by Pompey's enemies had suggested that, like his old patron Sulla, he was aiming at an armed *coup d'état*, and fear was alleged to have been as common an emotion as joy among his welcomers.

The Senate bowed to the inevitable. A decree was passed giving Pompey dispensation from the offending regulations. Many senators will, in fact, have recognised the reasonable nature of Pompey's requests; they had allowed him to reach his present position by irregular means, and should not now suddenly demand complete orthodoxy. Those who for various reasons did demand it were no doubt silenced by the sight of the Spanish legions.[5]

In his pre-election speeches Pompey pleaded Crassus' cause as well as his own, saying that he would be as grateful for Crassus as a colleague as for the consulship itself. Such evidence as there is suggests that he did not at this stage lay any programme of reform before the electors. Roman elections were almost always a choice between personalities rather than policies. However, he had already intimated to the *popularis* leaders, among them M. Lollius Palicanus, that he supported their aims, and he could thus rely on their help in bringing out the voters.

Whether any other candidates were foolhardy enough to present themselves we do not know. The two army commanders were duly elected, with Pompey at the head of the poll and therefore the senior partner.

His few months as consul designate were busily spent in making preparations for his triumph and his consulate. He delayed holding the former until the last day of the year, keeping his troops near Rome and giving as his reason that he was waiting for Metellus to return from Spain. After their joint triumph, of which curiously no description survives, Pompey disbanded his army, but we should not suppose that the soldiers all immediately left for home. Many had no homes to go to, and in any case Rome was the best place to spend some of the wealth they had acquired from the campaign. And their leader might still have need of their support.

For that leader some of the prospects for the new year were daunting. Without ever having attended a single meeting as an ordinary member of the Senate Pompey would be required to appear on 1 January as chairman of the first session of the year; to conduct the debates according to the complicated rules of the House; to observe strict protocol; and to be familiar with all the minutiae of organisation and procedure, before the watching eyes of several hundred sceptical and experienced senators. He could be very sure that any *faux pas* would be greeted with delight and derision, and it was in order to avoid this that Pompey got his friend Varro to write him a handbook of senatorial procedure, and tried to acquire in a few months knowledge which it had taken many half a lifetime to obtain.

As consul he would also be responsible for introducing some of the reforms which he and his supporters wanted in the form of bills, first before the Senate and then before the legislative assembly, and much time must have been spent with his advisers drafting these bills and preparing to counter the opposition they would have to face. Popular enthusiasm for these reforms was recalled by Cicero later in 70, when he referred in a speech to the first public meeting which Pompey addressed after his election. As he was still technically an army commander he could not legally enter the boundary of the city, and a meeting was called, probably by Palicanus, outside Rome, at which Pompey touched on the two major issues, much to the people's satisfaction.[6]

Plutarch in his life of Crassus claims that because of the bitter rivalry between them the consuls of 70 were politically ineffective and achieved nothing, except that Crassus made a great sacrifice in honour of Hercules and gave a feast to the people at which 10,000 tables were laid and each man presented with three months' allowance of grain. In fact the year saw a programme of legislation carried out which dramatically altered the balance of power at Rome and had a profound effect on the history of the late Republic. It is a commonplace to say that the reforms of Pompey and Crassus completed the dissolution of the political system of Sulla. Perhaps more important is the attempt to see the direction in which they now pointed Roman politics.[7]

The first reform was the restoration of the powers of the tribunes. With popular demand for this measure now at its height, and with two powerful consuls as sponsors, there seems to have been little active opposition in the Senate. Even the Optimate leader Q. Catulus appears to have conceded defeat, and valuable support for the bill came from the rising young politician Julius Caesar. The bill was presented to the people under the names of the two consuls and passed.

Another early measure was the reintroduction of the office of censor, which Sulla and his successors appear to have discontinued. This had three important results. First, the new citizens, whose rights Sulpicius Rufus had been fighting for as long ago as 88, could at last be enrolled in their tribes and centuries and take their full part at meetings of the assemblies. The census figures for 85 are given as 463,000 and for 69 as 900,000. Allowing for natural population increase and the fact that the figures for 85 are probably the result of a very imperfect count, this means that as many as one third of the citizens of Rome had been unable to exercise their rights for two decades. This was a grave social injustice, which no doubt reflected the uncertainty of Sulla and his successors as to their ability to control such a mass of new voters. The value of their votes to Pompey will, of course, have been enormous, but we should not assume that he was not also moved by the justice of their cause.

Secondly, it was now possible for unseemly behaviour by a senator to be punished by expulsion from the Senate, and thus the absolute freedom of the Senate from outside control was considerably weakened. Sixty-four senators in fact lost their seats. Thirdly, the machinery now existed for a reorganisation of the panel from which jurymen were chosen. The alternatives to senators as jurymen were the *equites*, and any transference of control from one order to the other required a prior definition and organisation of those orders. Such a thing had now been impossible for over a decade, and all lists must have been hopelessly out of date.

The new censors were the consuls of 72, L. Gellius Poplicola and Cn. Cornelius Lentulus, who had already demonstrated their support for Pompey. The highly honorific censorship was no doubt a reward. During their term of office, in addition to revising the list of the Senate and holding a general census of citizens, they celebrated the traditional review of the equestrian order, in which its members paraded in the Forum before the censors, and those who had completed their period of service as cavalrymen rendered account of their service and requested discharge. On this particular occasion Pompey himself appeared wearing his insignia of office and leading his own horse. With one of his favourite theatrical gestures he dismissed his lictors on reaching the censors and led his horse up to them. In a loud voice, audible to the whole crowd, he replied to Gellius' question whether he had served the requisite number of campaigns. 'I have served them all, and each time under my own generalship.'[8]

There still remained what was the most difficult and in some ways the most important reform, that of the system whereby the Senate had the right to try any of its members accused of extortion or maladministration in the provinces, or indeed of any criminal offence, in the courts. It could not be denied that the last decade or so had seen numerous cases of flagrant corruption and several scandalous verdicts, and this virtual guarantee that a governor could buy himself out of trouble had led to a terrifying outburst of rapacity in the provinces. The progress of the bill to reform the juries is hard to disentangle from the scattered references in Cicero's speeches against Verres (this trial was closely tied up with the political manoeuvrings in the summer of 70), but it appears that an early bill which proposed handing the jury courts completely over to the *equites* ran into determined opposition from the Optimates.

If the reform was going to be passed without recourse to violence, much hard and skilful bargaining was necessary, and Pompey probably realised that he had neither the time nor the temperament nor the political expertise required to pilot his bill through the Senate. This may be the reason why the job was given to one of the praetors, L. Aurelius Cotta, a moderate of considerable senatorial experience and a member of one of the leading noble families of the period.[9]

At the summer elections the hard-core Optimates won important successes with the election of Q. Hortensius Hortalus and another Q. Caecilius Metellus to the consulship, and of Metellus' brother Marcus to the praetorship. In mid-August, however, they suffered a set-back when C. Verres, some of whose ill-gotten gains had probably contributed to those successes, was forced by the brilliant prosecution of Marcus Cicero to abandon his defence on a charge of extortion in Sicily and retire to exile. Fairly soon afterwards Cotta got his bill passed, probably in late September. It was in fact a compromise, in that the composition of the new juries was divided equally between the Senate, the *equites*, and the *tribuni aerarii*. Exactly who the latter were, or how many there were of them is a matter of debate, but they were presumably of comparable wealth and social standing to the *equites* and shared their outlook and interests. The senatorial stranglehold over the courts was broken. Once again the way was open for the financiers and the business classes of Rome to make their voices heard.

Plutarch concludes his brief survey of Pompey's consulship with the story of his public reconciliation with Crassus, prompted by a well-meaning knight, C. Aurelius. The two may have been on opposite sides in the discussions on the jury reforms, and it seems clear that Crassus remained jealous of his more heroic colleague and resented his influence with and patronage of the equestrian order.[10]

One final measure was an agrarian law promoted by the tribune Plautius granting allotments of land to the Spanish veterans of Pompey and Metellus. This was the way in which the generals repaid their troops for their loyalty and made possible their peace-time return to civilian life. Presumably a commission was set up to deal with the purchase and distribution of the land, but such laws were notoriously unpopular with many senators, whose own estates were threatened, and the commission seems to have run into solid opposition and severe financial difficulties before very long.[11]

During 70 one of the most important problems in the field of foreign affairs was the steadily increasing menace of pirates in the Mediterranean. A year or so previously the ex-praetor M. Antonius had been seriously defeated by the pirates of Crete and forced to conclude a treaty with them, and in March 70 it seems that the Senate voted that Crete be allocated as one of the consular provinces. A resumption of the war on a larger scale was widely expected. Unfortunately for Pompey, according to a law of C. Gracchus (123) those provinces voted as consular in 70 would be drawn for by lot by the consuls of 69, and so there was little hope of his being able to secure this important military command in the immediate future.

Whatever provinces had been allocated to the consuls of 70, both Pompey and Crassus decided against accepting them, and retired on 1 January 69 to the life of private citizens. For Pompey this was his first release from arduous public duty for eight years, and it is hardly surprising that, as Plutarch tells us, 'he ceased his frequent appearances as a barrister, gradually abandoned the Forum, and seldom showed himself in public and when he did was always accompanied by a large crowd of followers'. He played the part, which seems to have come naturally to him, of the great Roman hero who was above the daily routine of normal, petty, political life, and seems to have been successful in avoiding the minor humiliations and embarrassments which so often befall great soldiers on their entrance into domestic politics.[12]

We need not, however, conclude that Pompey was idle. The mention of large crowds of followers shows that he was cultivating his clients and extending his patronage. He was also laying plans for the future. As so often happened, with the arrival of a new year and new colleges of magistrates, control of the Senate and assemblies had returned to the hands of the Optimates, whose grip on the machinery of Roman politics was rarely broken for long. It had been loosened when the two victorious generals had won the consulships of 70, but Pompey now no longer had his army, and in any case he was debarred by law from standing again for ten years.

The years 69 and 68 seem to have seen the formation of what amounted to a Pompeian party, designed primarily to protect the interests of its leader in opposition to the powerful combinations of the Optimates. With Pompey's support candidates would stand for election to the main magistracies each year and would, if successful, be expected to propose such legislation as Pompey required and protect him from any attacks that his enemies might see fit to launch against him.

This was no formal party in the modern sense of the word, with a constitution and a fixed set of policies. It was merely an extension of the time-honoured system of *amicitiae*, with the difference that one man rather than one family or set of families was at the centre of the grouping, and used it to establish his dominance in the Roman world. Though several members of leading noble families do appear as supporters of Pompey during the next two decades, the traditional abhorrence of the *nobiles* for the personal domination of one man made it inevitable that the main body of Pompeians should come from non-noble backgrounds.

In the years before Sulla it had been frequently demonstrated by Marius how valuable were tribunes in furthering the aims of a *'popularis* party'. Pompey had, no doubt, firmly in his mind at the beginning of 70 the uses to which he himself could put tribunes in the future, and indeed Plautius proved his worth early with his land law.

Pompey saw, more clearly than most of his contemporaries, where many of the faults lay in Rome's foreign policies. He disapproved of the arrogant attitude towards provincials shown most obviously by men like Verres but by all accounts common to the majority of provincial governors and their staff. A greater sense of justice and moderation and with it greater efficiency were required by Rome's administrators, and efficiency was not always easy to achieve in a system where ex-magistrates were sent out to govern strictly limited areas for a period usually limited to one or two years. Co-operation between governors was far from common and anything approaching continuity of policy virtually impossible. One answer, in Pompey's view, lay in 'extraordinary' commands, ones which lasted for as long as the circumstances required and where the geographical limitations of the normal provincial governorship were dispensed with. Such a concept was not new. An 'unlimited' command against the pirates had been given to M. Antonius in 74, but the man had proved incompetent. The difficulty lay in trying to ensure that the man who obtained command did so on merit and not by political intrigue. Pompey's solution was to take the appointment to those commands out of the hands of the Senate and put them into the hands of the popular assembly, and the machinery for this transfer lay, as Tiberius Gracchus had shown in 133, in the tribunate.

The year 68 brought a changed situation. L. Lucullus, who was governor of Bithynia and Cilicia in the Mithridatic war, had moved onto the offensive with an invasion of Armenia in 69. A great victory at Tigranocerta led to the liberation of eastern Cilicia and was followed in 68 by another victory over the Armenian king Tigranes and a further advance northwards, which was only halted by a mutiny in the army. So far from creating joy in Rome the news of Lucullus' successes only increased the jealousy felt by his enemies, amongst the Optimates as well as in the Pompeian camp, and a veritable campaign aimed at undermining Lucullus' position got under way. The *popularis* praetor, L. Quinctius, who as tribune had clashed with the consul Lucullus in 74, accused Lucullus of greed and ambition and was instrumental in securing the removal of Cilicia from his command and the discharge of many of his soldiers.

How far, if at all, Pompey was involved in these machinations we have no means of telling, although some historians claim that he employed the young P. Clodius Pulcher to tamper with the loyalty of Lucullus' troops as they quartered at Nisibis for the winter. The evidence for this rests on the statement of Plutarch that Clodius unfavourably compared the condition of Lucullus' troops with that of those whom Pompey had brought back from Spain.[13]

However, in July 68 Pompey had some success when his ex-quaestor Cornelius and his close supporter A. Gabinius were elected to the tribunate, and plans must have been soon under way for the moves which were to secure for Pompey his command against the pirates the following year. Not only that, but Pompey must have started planning his military strategy well in advance and selecting the men he wanted to put it into practice.

Many ancient historians, probably following the Greek Posidonius, describe in vivid details the growth of piracy in the Mediterranean during the late second and early first centuries BC and the threat thus presented not only to maritime trade and communications but also to life and property along every coast (VII, VIII). In 68 the gravity of the situation was brought forcibly home to the Senate and people when two praetors with their twelve attendant lictors were kidnapped on Italian soil. In spite of some minor successes in Crete it was clear that Metellus was getting no nearer to defeating the pirates as a whole than had any of his predecessors. The grain ships from Sicily, Africa and Sardinia either did not dare to sail or were failing to reach Italian ports, and the price of corn was rocketing. Rome faced the appalling prospect of a famine and rioting in the streets by starving crowds.[14]

By the end of 68 much of the required organisation must have been completed. Pompey will have needed to acquire as much up-to-date information as possible about the numbers and tactics of the pirates as well as about their main strongholds and the problems of conducting naval operations along their coasts. No doubt he made preliminary, if unofficial, arrangements for the equipping of ships and the rapid mobilisation of troops when the time came. In all this his many contacts in the provinces and in the recruiting grounds of northern Italy will have been invaluable.

Early in January 67 the tribune Gabinius published his proposals. He was fully aware that they would meet with strong opposition in a Senate controlled by Pompey's Optimate enemies, and so, following the notorious precedent of Tiberius Gracchus in 133, he decided to by-pass the Senate and take the proposals directly to the people. There could have been no clearer indication that the Sullan reforms were dead. At the first assembly Gabinius stated his proposals in deliberately general terms. The people should choose from among the ex-consuls a general to take command of the war against all the pirates. He should hold his command for three years, and his sphere of operations was to be the whole of the Mediterranean and Black Seas, and all the coastline for a distance of 400 stades (eighty kilometres) inland from the sea. He should have the power to appoint fifteen legates and to draw as much money as he wanted from the public treasury and from the funds of the tax-collecting firms in the provinces. He could raise as large a fleet and army as he required, and his authority in the various provinces in which he had to operate was to be equal to that of the provincial governors.

The assembly, realising that only Pompey could be intended for this command, enthusiastically approved the proposals. Whether or not Gabinius had intended to consult the Senate, that body soon debated this new law. Its attitude was quite different from that of the people. Of all the members present the only one recorded to have spoken in its favour was C. Julius Caesar. It was said that his motives were selfish — he wished to curry favour with the people. But Caesar had first-hand knowledge of the pirate menace; he had himself been kidnapped by them and taken savage reprisal for the insult, and must have realised that the situation called for firm and imaginative action and not for petty vindictiveness. Nothing, however, could calm the fears and jealousies of the Optimates. Gabinius was violently attacked in speeches from all sides and the consul C. Calpurnius Piso even hinted that if he could not see his way to abandoning his plans he might expect to meet a mysterious accident. 'If you emulate Romulus, you will not escape the same end as Romulus.'[15]

Gabinius managed to slip away from the Senate House and informed the waiting crowds of what had happened. Roused to fury by this news they stormed the House itself, routed the senators and seized Piso. They would possibly have lynched him there and then if Gabinius had not successfully pleaded for his life.

The Optimates, too, could call on a precedent from the tribunate of Tiberius Gracchus. As their predecessors in 133 had done they decided to pitch tribune against tribune, and found two men, L. Trebellius and L. Roscius, who were prepared to take the risk of opposing Gabinius. When a second bill, proposing Pompey for the command, appeared before the assembly for voting, these two were to use the various means at their disposal to stop it.

Pompey was clearly distressed by the bitter opposition to him personally that the proposals had aroused. We have already seen instances of his reluctance to bulldoze his way into positions of power and how he preferred to accept them in deference to popular demand. The accounts preserved in Plutarch and Dio of this episode well illustrate his attitude.[16]

When the second assembly sat, Pompey was called upon by Gabinius to address the people. We have no means of telling how accurate is the version of his speech which Dio gives us, but it is certainly in character and may be derived from a contemporary account. In it Pompey requested not to be subjected once again to the rigours of a major war and proclaimed his reluctance to incur the jealousy that the proposed command would bring upon him.[17]

Having made this public disclaimer of his own ambition Pompey left it to Gabinius and the people to overcome his reluctance. This was not difficult. Gabinius praised Pompey's modest attitude but maintained that the interests of the state must outweigh the personal feelings of one man, and that the present crisis demanded Rome's greatest general. He urged Pompey to set the friendship of the people against the jealousy of his enemies and to heed the call of his country.

Trebellius now attempted to speak, but failing to get leave from Gabinius he proceeded to exercise his right of vetoing the proposal. Once more the pantomime of 133 was re-enacted and Gabinius put forward a new proposal; that Trebellius was acting against the interests of the people and should be deposed. A vote was taken, and just before a majority was reached in Gabinius' favour Trebellius withdrew his veto. If the people were so firm in their support of Gabinius and Pompey, history showed that the Optimates had no card left to play except that of open violence. Their bluff was called. A feeble attempt by Roscius to propose that Pompey be given a colleague in order to put a check on his power was rejected out of hand, and Gabinius was now so confident of victory that he called upon the Optimate leader Catulus to speak before the vote was taken.

Dio puts into Catulus' mouth the standard Optimate arguments against an extraordinary command; the dangers of putting too much power into the hands of one man, and of by-passing the constitutional machinery whereby limited power was given to a large number of elected magistrates. In any case, it was impossible for one man to operate in such a vast theatre of war, and if concerted action by a number of commanders was necessary it was better for them to be responsible to the Senate than to a single generalissimo.[18]

After Catulus' speech and perhaps a supporting one from Hortensius, Gabinius postponed the taking of the vote. Maintaining his reluctant pose, Pompey withdrew to his country house for the day of the voting, so as to avoid any suspicion of having influenced the issue by his presence. Afterwards he was able to return and patriotically to accept the command which was pressed upon him. Moreover he seems to have been subsequently empowered to raise a force almost twice the size of that originally voted to him. The whole affair shows signs of careful planning and skilful stage management. Gabinius had done his work well, and Pompey was now in command of the largest combined forces Rome had ever put into the field, and had greater authority over

Figure 3: Map to illustrate Pompey's campaign against the Pirates.

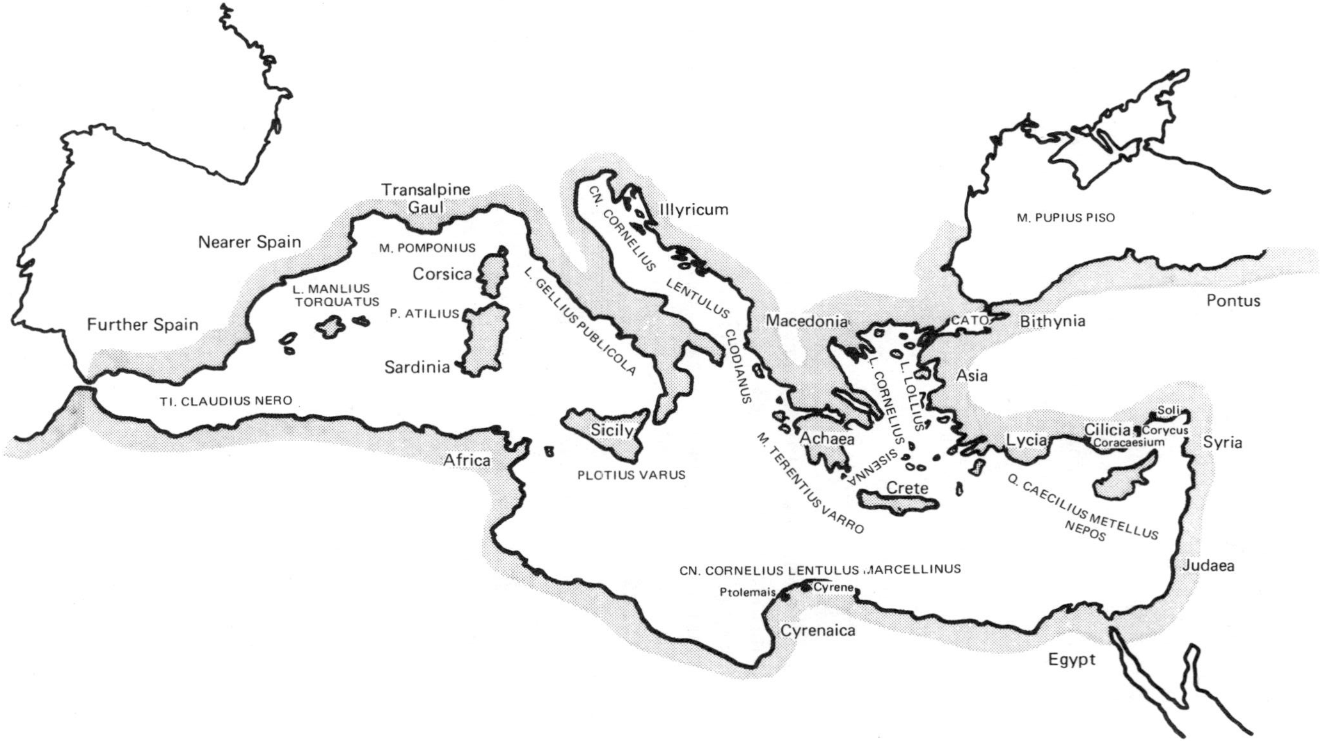

Rome's foreign policy than any previous politician except Sulla. The opportunities for extending his already vast patronage to the provinces and kingdoms of the East were virtually limitless. Once more general and tribune had combined to wrest control of the assembly and thus ultimately of Rome itself from the Senate.

The remaining weeks of winter were spent in mobilising the troops and ships which had been voted. The numbers are given by Plutarch as 500 ships, 120,000 soldiers and 5,000 cavalry. In early spring, even before the weather was considered suitable for sailing, Pompey was ready to move into action. As the pirates now controlled most, if not all, of the Mediterranean, and there was close co-operation between the various fleets, it was useless to concentrate the attack on any one area. Failure to realise this had accounted for the lack of success of Servilius Vatia in Lycia and Pamphilia, and of Marcus Antonius and Quintus Metellus in Crete. It was essential to keep the pirates split up, to prevent other fleets from coming to the help of one attacked, and to stop them from taking refuge among the numerous headlands and coves of the Cilician and Syrian coasts. Here ships could be effectively hidden from any prowling man-of-war, and crews had been able to hold out indefinitely in the many impregnable forts on promontory or mountainside.

Pompey's strategy was deceptively simple in concept and brilliantly executed. He divided the Mediterranean and Black Seas into thirteen areas, each under the command of one of his picked officers (see map, p. 69). Each officer had a flotilla of ships and some infantry and cavalry forces. He was to patrol his own area by sea and land, to attack the strong points and anchorages, to intercept any pirates entering his sector and to prevent any from leaving. Any pirate who put into harbour would be blockaded from the sea until troops arrived by land or he tried to break out. If he managed to escape he would immediately enter another patrolled sector. He could count on no safe harbour for the collection of water and food and could not rely on any comrades for help. Suddenly the whole sea, instead of being a limitless source of booty, became a hostile environment (VIII).[19]

Pompey's first concern was to get the corn ships once more sailing into Ostia, the port of Rome. Apparently the price of corn had dropped immediately upon his appointment. He had now to justify this expression of confidence. With his own flotilla of sixty ships he sailed first to Sicily, where he swept any blockading pirates into the waiting arms of Plotius Varus (possibly his helpful tribune of 70).

Crossing thence to the coast of Africa he cleared that before sailing north to link up with P. Atilius off the coast of Sardinia. These were the three main corn-producing areas. Cicero's account suggests that he next visited the areas off Further Spain (Ti. Claudius Nero), his old province of Nearer Spain (L. Manlius Torquatus), and Gaul (M. Pomponius). The combined operations of Pompey's mobile flotilla and the stationary forces of his officers were totally successful. Within six weeks the western Mediterranean was clear of pirates.[20]

Only in Gaul had Pompey met with any serious opposition, not from the enemy but from the consul Piso, who, as governor-designate of the province, carried his personal feud with Pompey to the lengths of interfering with Pomponius' efforts to raise troops there. Plutarch records that he was even discharging Pompey's crews.[21]

Sailing down the west coast of Italy Pompey landed in Etruria and proceeded overland to Rome, sending his ships ahead to wait for him at Brundisium. At Rome he found that Gabinius had already taken measures to check Piso and had a bill promulgated which would depose him from office. Pompey restrained his tribune from taking such drastic action, but presumably succeeded in first extracting a guarantee from Piso that he would not attempt any further sabotage.

The officers responsible for the seas either side of Italy were the most senior of Pompey's legates, the censors of 70. It is some measure of Pompey's authority that such men should be willing to serve under him. Florus' account suggests that Pompey gave his two young sons, Gnaeus and Sextus, their first taste of military service under Lentulus Clodianus on the Adriatic station, and the experience probably had a powerful effect at least on Sextus. He was later to become one of the most skilful naval commanders in Roman history, even if, in a time of civil war, his skills bore a closer resemblance to those of the pirates than of more orthodox sailors.[22]

For Pompey the most difficult part of his task still lay ahead. It was in the eastern Mediterranean that the majority of the pirate strongholds lay. His officers, however, had been doing their work well. Terentius Varro, who held the key station patrolling from the straits of Otranto to the island of Crete, and Lentulus Marcellinus, whose beat extended along most of the north African coast, had provided an effective barrier between the two halves of the Mediterranean. Varro had also maintained a barrage across the Otranto straits, thus trapping the pirates of the Illyrian coast in the Adriatic to be dealt with separately by Lentulus Clodianus. For these services Varro was decorated with the coveted Naval Crown by Pompey.

Only the coast of Cilicia had not been actively blockaded. Pompey's brother-in-law Metellus Nepos had been instructed to patrol only the coasts of Lycia, Pamphylia, Cyprus and Phoenicia, and the strategy was to allow those pirates who did not surrender or were not captured to escape to this one unguarded haven. This they would naturally do, as their main strongholds and store depots were situated in Cilicia, and Pompey planned to launch his full-scale attack there, once his officers, like sheep-dogs, had herded the remaining pirates into his trap.

Embarking at Brundisium he crossed to Athens and thence to Rhodes, picking up the allied fleets which had been instructed to rendezvous at those two places. While at Rhodes he took the opportunity to renew his acquaintance with Posidonius, and attended one of his lectures. On leaving the great philosopher's presence he asked him if he had any advice and was answered with a quotation from Homer's Iliad: 'Always be best, and pre-eminent above all others.' This was more, one would imagine, a confirmation of Pompey's existing philosophy than advice for the future.

As the plight of the pirates became ever more serious, they began to surrender to Pompey in increasingly greater numbers. Information about the secret hiding places of Cilicia no doubt came pouring in with them, and Pompey was able to lay detailed plans for his final *coup*.

He equipped the land forces with an elaborate siege train in anticipation of prolonged resistance, but in fact his own reputation and his merciful treatment of those who had already surrendered proved to be his most potent weapons. The details of this final campaign are unfortunately no longer recorded. Appian seems to preserve a memory of the capture and destruction of several castles, including that on the sheer promontory of Cragus, and some in the Taurus massif itself, before the final battle. This took place in the bay of Coracaesium (modern Alanya), where the pirates mustered all their remaining vessels for a last stand. This, however, was no desperate or hard-fought affair, for, if we are to believe Florus, the pirates soon realised that they were heavily outnumbered and surrendered without more ado. A brief siege brought about the surrender of the castle of Coracaesium and the end of the fighting. Seven weeks had elapsed since Pompey's departure from Brundisium.[23]

As yet, however, his task was only half completed. Plutarch records that more than 20,000 pirates surrendered to Pompey; most of them had been driven to piracy by the appalling difficulties of making an honest living in the places from which they came.

> He reflected therefore [Plutarch goes on] that man is not, nor does he become, wild or unsociable by nature, but is transformed by the unnatural practice of vice, and may be tamed by new customs and by a change of environment and way of life. Wild animals, too, often lose their fierceness and savagery when subjected to a gentler form of existence. So he decided to move the pirates from the sea to the land and give them a taste of civilised life by making them used to living in cities and farming the land.[24]

In Cilicia itself there were several cities which had recently suffered reduction in population, among them the old town of Soli, many of whose inhabitants had been removed by Tigranes of Armenia to people his new capital of Tigranocerta. Here, and in several other places in the provinces, Pompey settled his pirate captives. Settlements at Mallus, Adana and Epiphaneia in Cilicia, Dyme in Achaea, and even in Calabria are mentioned in the sources in addition to the refoundation of Soli under the name of Pompeiopolis. This city rapidly became the centre of Roman control for the new province of western Cilicia and in due course a magnificent port. Today an arch of the aqueduct, a few scrub-covered ruins and two lines of columns in an orange grove are all that remain of this monument to Pompey's victory over the pirates.

Recent study of a number of inscriptions from Cyrenaica has thrown more light on Pompey's activities in 67. Pirate activity on this stretch of the north African coast seems to have seriously threatened Roman control over the recently (*c.* 75 BC) annexed province of Cyrene. Following the defeat of the pirates by the legate Cn. Cornelius Lentulus Marcellinus, Pompey founded a settlement of non-Roman colonists at Ptolemais, including at least one man who appears to have been of Illyrian origin. Presumably, as in the case of a man from Corycus whom Virgil knew in Calabria, Pompey settled many of the pirates at considerable distances from their homes in order to make even more final the break with their past. In Cyrene one can also see Pompey making use of the wide powers granted him by the Gabinian law. It is possible, though the relevant inscription needs much restoration, that Marcellinus officially styled himself as 'propraetorian legate of the general Cn. Pompeius Magnus'. For a man who was virtually a provincial governor to act on the authority of a Roman general rather than the Roman Senate and people was unparalleled, and gives some impression of the control over Roman foreign policy exercised by Pompey under this command. The wider implications of this will be discussed later.[25]

One further incident of the war deserves mention. There was one independent commander against the pirates in 67, Q. Caecilius Metellus, who was still engaged in the Cretan campaign to which he had been sent in 69. The inhabitants of some of the cities he was besieging decided to offer their surrender to Pompey, whose sphere of operations included Crete, rather than to Metellus, and Pompey rashly accepted this invitation to interfere. L. Octavius was sent to Crete to negotiate with the pirates and the Cretans were told to ignore the authority of Metellus. The legate of Greece, L. Cornelius Sisenna, arrived with troops to persuade Metellus to see sense, and after Sisenna's death Octavius used his troops to oppose the activities of Metellus. There was a heated exchange of letters between the two generals, who in fact had equal authority in Crete, and eventually Metellus secured the removal of Octavius, and himself completed the subjugation of the island.

Octavius clearly acted tactlessly and perhaps treasonably in taking the side of the Cretans in a few engagements, and Pompey was probably lured by jealousy of Metellus to accept the cunning invitation of the islanders. Although he had the sense not to provoke Metellus too far the incident well illustrates the difficulties of trying to implement Rome's foreign policy through independent and frequently unco-operative proconsuls.

The remainder of 67 after the battle of Coracaesium was spent in organising the new settlements. If the number of 120,000 troops used in the campaign is correct, the majority of them must soon have been disbanded. Most will have been local levies with knowledge of their own coastlines, raised merely for the duration of the operations in their province. Cicero speaks of Pompey as present in the province of Asia with some troops during the winter but we can only guess as to the nature of his activities there.

Meanwhile plans were afoot to secure for Pompey the command of the war against Mithridates. Gabinius had, early in 67, continued the work of Quinctius in 69 by removing Bithynia and Pontus from Lucullus' control and handing them and the command of the war to the consul Manius Acilius Glabrio. Any chances Lucullus had had of bringing the war to a successful conclusion were now gone, and the opportunity was seized by Mithridates and his ally Tigranes of Armenia to recover their kingdoms. Lucullus' legate Triarius suffered a disastrous defeat in Pontus and the two new generals Glabrio and Marcius Rex (Cilicia) were unable to remedy the situation.

The Pompeians lost no time in putting forward the claims of their champion. Early in 66 the tribune C. Manilius proposed that Pompey should assume supreme command of the war against the two kings. He should take over control from the existing provincial governors in Asia Minor, have power to appoint more legates himself and the authority to make peace or war and conclude treaties at his own discretion.

Predictably the bill ran into opposition from Hortensius and Catulus, but it had overwhelming support from the people and from the *equites*, whose financial interests in Asia were once more in jeopardy. The threat of war and the collapse of confidence were as fatal to the commercial world in 66 as they are today. The new praetor M. Tullius Cicero spoke forcefully in favour of the bill, and it was further supported by such senior senators as P. Servilius Vatia (consul in 69 and a previous commander in Cilicia), C. Curio (consul 76 and an experienced soldier), C. Cassius Longinus (consul 73) and Cn. Lentulus Clodianus. Julius Caesar is also reported as having spoken in its favour.[26]

The threat of Mithridates and Tigranes was probably not quite as serious as Cicero made out. Mithridates himself was now sixty-five and had but recently recovered from a series of debilitating wounds. Tigranes' own position was threatened by internal troubles in Armenia. Nevertheless a strong hand was needed to control the poorly-disciplined and increasingly demoralised Roman troops, to bring the long-drawn-out war to a rapid conclusion, and, most important of all, to organise the provinces and kingdoms of the East on a basis of peace, justice and stability. The Pompeians had a strong case.

News of Manilius' law reached Pompey early in 66 as he was making a tour of the Cilician cities supervising his resettlement and rebuilding programme. He received it with an outward show of reluctance. 'Oh these endless tasks! How much better it would be to be one of the unknowns, if I am never to see an end to my campaigns, and can not put off this load of envy and spend my time with my wife in the country.' Few can have been convinced by it.[27]

Most, if not all, of Pompey's legates of the previous year retained their positions. In addition he appointed his old colleague from Spain L. Afranius, his second brother-in-law Q. Caecilius Metellus Celer, the stalwart A. Gabinius, and L. Valerius Flaccus, who had previously served under Metellus in Crete.

The troops at his disposal comprised the three legions of Q. Marcius Rex already stationed in Cilicia (about 15,000 men); the bulk of Lucullus' army, including two long-serving but mutinous legions (the Valerians) which had officially been discharged; levies from the Asian kingdoms still in alliance, of which the most important were the Galatian cavalry; and those of his own forces which still remained under arms. The total was in the region of 50,000 men. Mithridates was reported as having only 30,000 infantry, mostly Roman deserters or recently levied Asiatics, and two or three thousand cavalry — his main strength. Here again we can see Pompey's policy of operating with greatly superior numbers. This policy imposed serious problems of organisation and supply, but they were ones with which he was pre-eminently able to cope.

A diplomatic offensive preceded the military one. Pompey's immediate object was the final defeat and capture of Mithridates, whose position was somewhere near the Galatia-Pontus border. To ensure that the latter should not receive help from Tigranes, and to secure his own right flank in Cappadocia, Pompey sent representatives to the new king of Parthia, Phraates III, to confirm Rome's friendly relations with him and persuade him to reciprocate by invading the Armenian state of Gordyene and directing Tigranes' attentions wholly to his southern frontier.

He also realised that he might have to justify to his enemies in the Senate an invasion of Mithridates' kingdom. Lucullus, indeed, had already claimed to have brought the war to an end, and in 67 a senatorial commission of ten had arrived from Rome to organise the new province of Pontus (before its recapture by Mithridates), and ratify other measures that Lucullus had taken. Pompey required a cast-iron pretext.

He therefore sent Metrophanes, one of the king's ex-generals, to Mithridates in order to test his intentions, and offer him the opportunity of seeking terms. His overtures were proudly rejected by the king, who had no knowledge of the other negotiations which were going on behind his back. Accordingly Pompey set his invasion plans in action.

First, a naval blockade of the whole coastline of Asia Minor from Phoenicia to the Bosporus was established. Pompey was taking no chances that his communications might be cut, or that Mithridates might receive further help from any surviving pirates once Pompey's back was turned. Secondly he issued mobilisation orders for all the troops under his command, and summoned all the allied kings and potentates to join him with their own native units. Then with these and the three Cilician legions Pompey marched north through the Cilician

Gates pass towards Galatia, where a meeting with Lucullus and his army had been arranged. The three legions were instructed to secure the kingdom of Cappadocia, which had only recently been over-run and then abandoned by Tigranes, and to join him in Pontus when the occasion arose.

The uncomfortable conference between the outgoing commander and his successor at Danala in the land of the Trocmi (E. Galatia) has fired the imagination of ancient and modern historians alike. Relations between the two were already strained, to say the least, and although their formal greetings were courteous enough, rancour and recrimination soon broke out. Lucullus was in a highly embarrassing position. As a general his pride was shattered by the notorious ill-discipline of his troops; he had come close to victory only to see it snatched from his grasp by his own soldiers and by hostile politicians at Rome; he had long feared Pompey's threat both to his own power and to the domination of the Optimates, and he now had to stand by as his rival took over command and prepared to reap the rewards for which he had worked and fought for the past eight years.

Pompey made little attempt to soften the blow. He had already declared publicly that all Lucullus' arrangements were to be ignored. He re-enlisted the troublesome Valerian legions, making obvious the comparison between his own sure control and the precarious leadership of Lucullus, and he only allowed 1,600 presumably sick and wounded soldiers to return to Italy for Lucullus' triumph. How many of the accusations of greed for money on one side and greed for power on the other were made personally at that time or appeared in later 'smear' campaigns is not clear, but as Pompey turned east towards the valleys of the Halys and Lycus rivers in his search for Mithridates, Lucullus returned to Rome a broken and deeply embittered man.

4 CONQUEROR OF THE EAST: THE NEW EMPIRE 66–62

The full significance of the campaign on which Pompey now embarked has perhaps been lost sight of in many modern accounts, with their main emphasis on political and military history. Not only was Pompey about to defeat the king who had been Rome's most dangerous enemy since Hannibal and add vast territories to her empire; he was also about to emulate the achievements of his boyhood hero, Alexander of Macedon. As Alexander had spread Hellenistic ideas and culture from the Aegean to the Indus, so Pompey was to spread law and order, Rome's chief contribution to civilisation, to the Hellenistic kingdoms which were the successors to Alexander's empire west of the Euphrates.

Furthermore, as Alexander's conquest had been, so was Pompey's to be a journey of exploration, to extend the boundaries of knowledge in several fields, and to combine the interests of power politics with those of scientific research. The *Natural History* of the elder Pliny contains several references to botanical, geographical and medical discoveries made by Pompey in the East, and we know of at least two men who accompanied him for the express purpose of collecting and recording these discoveries. One was Lenaeus, a Greek freedman and teacher of rhetoric; the other Theophanes, an able politician and a leading citizen of Mitylene, who had probably met Pompey on his visit to that important naval base in 67, and who accompanied the expedition as official historian. Varro was another, combining outstanding skill as an admiral with an unquenchable thirst for knowledge.[1]

In spite of its military bias Pompey's education had also given him an enthusiasm for literature and for Greek ideas, especially for some of the views of the Stoic philosophers which seem to have influenced Alexander, and which were taught by the head of the Stoic school of Pompey's time, his friend Posidonius. Important among these views was the concept of the brotherhood of man. In Alexander's time this had challenged the deeply ingrained notion that Greeks were inherently superior to barbarians, and had found expression in Alexander's efforts to unite Greek and Persian in his new empire on equal terms. In Pompey's own outlook this concept affected his attitude towards provincials, whether in Sicily, Spain or Cilicia, and resulted in his humane and thoughtful treatment of enemies, be they

Sertorians or pirates. More than most Romans of his class and time he tried to understand non-Romans and to avoid the resentment and bitterness caused amongst provincials by the usual arrogant and profiteering representatives of his country. Illustrative of this attitude is the fact that he counted among his close friends a number of Greeks and freedmen, to whom he often turned for advice. He made it his business to know the problems and peculiarities of the communities with which he had to deal. This, combined with a careful attention to detail and a love of efficiency, accounts in no small way for his outstanding success as an organiser and administrator.[2]

It is notoriously difficult to disentangle the story of Pompey's eastern campaigns from the vague and often contradictory accounts of our main authorities, Plutarch, Appian and Dio. The few geographical references are often impossible to identify with certainty, and it is even harder than usual to draw the line which divides fact from fiction. There seem to have been at least two contemporary accounts, those written by Theophanes and Posidonius, but both are totally lost and we have no way of knowing how closely they were followed by the two extant writers closest in time, Livy and Strabo, or by the other three. This difficulty should be borne in mind when reading the narrative which follows.[3]

Mithridates was not long in learning of Pompey's alliance with Phraates. Alarmed also by his numerical inferiority, he sent to enquire on what terms Pompey would conclude a truce. Pompey was in no mood for such negotiations. A truce would only allow Mithridates to build up his own forces and give Tigranes time to reassert himself in Armenia. Pompey therefore demanded that Mithridates surrender both himself and the Roman deserters in his army, terms which were obviously unacceptable to both.

The king decided to withdraw into the centre of his mountainous kingdom, drawing Pompey after him, denying him supplies by burning the crops, and harassing him with his own superior cavalry. The early skirmishes and manoeuvres have been located near the upper reaches of the river Halys, where, according to Plutarch, Pompey seized an almost impregnable mountain stronghold which had been abandoned by Mithridates because of lack of water. The superior surveying skill of the Romans showed itself when, on Pompey's orders, the troops sank wells to reach springs, the existence of which he had deduced from the vegetation on the lower slopes. Mithridates then withdrew through a pass in the mountains to the north of the Halys into the Lycus valley, along which ran the main east-west trunk road of Pontus. Here he encamped on a well-watered hill called Dasteira, not far from the modern village of Pürk, with the intention of cutting Pompey's now extended supply lines and gradually wearing him down.[4]

Pompey, however, was not to be trapped. The three Cilician legions were now summoned from Cappadocia, and a division of the army was sent eastwards to capture the land of Acilisene, the plain of Erzincan near the upper reaches of the Euphrates. This move secured for Pompey a closer source of food and drove a wedge between Mithridates and his presumed ultimate refuge in Armenia. Meanwhile he began to construct a circle of siegeworks round Dasteira, about thirty kilometres in length, in order to starve the king into submission. It was probably during this blockade that Pompey struck a decisive blow when he lured the troublesome Pontic cavalry into an ambush, causing serious losses (VC). The siege lasted forty-five days. Mithridates' troops were reduced to killing and eating their pack animals, and in desperation he decided to make a break for it. Skilfully allaying the Romans' suspicions, Mithridates put all his sick and wounded to death and escaped by night through the Roman lines, heading for Armenia. The following day Pompey learnt of the king's escape and hurriedly set out in pursuit.

According to Dio, Mithridates continued his flight marching only by night and encamping by day, thus avoiding attack by Pompey, who was reluctant to charge a defended position or to risk battle by night in unfamiliar terrain. For the first two or three days Mithridates was far enought ahead to justify these tactics, but after he had gone some 80 kilometres Pompey, who had been marching by day, caught up with him before midday and managed to lead at least some of his troops past the Pontic camp unseen and set up ambush on either side of the narrow pass ahead (mod. Belgazi gorge). This time Mithridates was caught unawares. The following night, as his army entered the pass, the Romans on the heights above heralded their presence by a trumpet blast, the rattle of javelin on shield and the ring of bronze on stone. This alarming noise was followed by a hail of javelins and stones and a merciless charge into the now thoroughly confused ranks of the enemy. Trapped in the defile the Pontic troops put up little resistance, hampered as they were by panicking women, horses and camels and their own transport wagons. The moon, rising behind the Romans, so it was remembered, helped them by illuminating their victims and confusing their aim. In the ensuing massacre some 10,000 men, probably well over a third of the king's total force, were reported killed.[5]

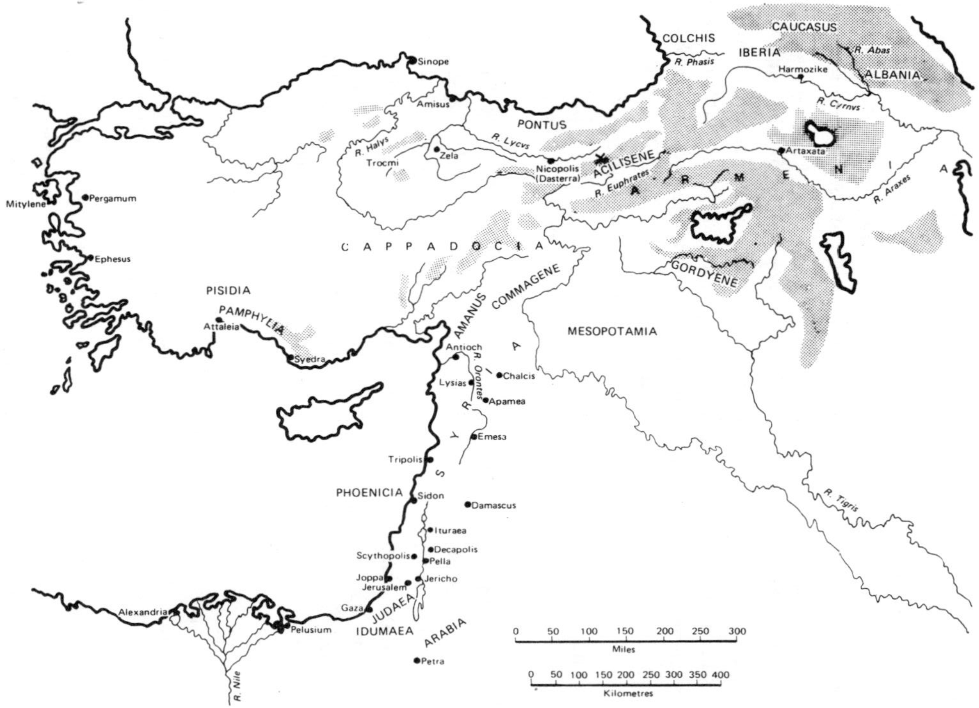

Figure 4: Map of Pompey's Eastern Campaigns.

Mithridates himself was not among them. This remarkable old warrior with a few companions and a concubine dressed as a man cut his way out of the trap and escaped. Joining up with 3,000 infantry and a troop of cavalry he made first for his great treasure store at Sinoria (probably on the upper Euphrates) sending messengers to king Tigranes to beg for refuge. At Sinoria he rewarded the loyalty of his followers, giving them each a year's pay and dividing the rest of the tresure among them to carry. The loyalty of Tigranes, however, was of a different sort. As soon as he heard of Mithridates' defeat he arrested the messengers and put a price on the king's head. It was said that he suspected Mithridates of turning his own son, Tigranes, against him; probably he saw that the old king's cause was now irretrievable. The only remaining escape route was to the north. From the source of the Euphrates Mithridates headed for Colchis, one of his old possessions at the eastern end of the Black Sea.

In fact Pompey had won the decisive battle of the war, but experience warned that the war could not be considered over while the king was still alive. A pursuit party was sent after him, but with no success. Pompey meanwhile prepared to advance into Armenia against his second enemy. Here he seems to have anticipated less spirited resistance, and he decided to reduce the numbers of his army. Granting some of his more long-serving soldiers their discharge, he settled them, along with the wounded, in a new city near Dasteira, which he named Nicopolis (city of victory).

He then moved the rest of his army up the Euphrates till he came to a crossing place near the source. Shortly after he crossed into Armenia he was met by the younger Tigranes. This prince had joined Phraates of Parthia in an invasion of his father's kingdom and had been left in charge of the siege of Artaxata. King Tigranes had succeeded in defeating him there, and after learning of the defeat of Mithridates, the prince had decided to throw in his lot with the victorious Pompey.

Led by Tigranes the Romans marched down the Araxes towards Artaxata in search of the king. The latter realised the hopelessness of his situation and at first tried to negotiate favourable terms through envoys. When this attempt failed he came to surrender himself to Pompey as the Roman army approached his capital. The self-styled King of Kings dismounted at the entrance to the camp, walked towards the tribunal of the Roman general, removed the tiara from his head, and prostrated himself before Pompey. Pompey accepted this act of submission, but was careful not to humiliate the old king too much.

He raised him from the ground, and with a symbolic gesture returned his tiara.

Pompey had already decided that it would be unrealistic and unprofitable to extend Rome's empire east of the Euphrates. Rome could not hope to conquer and hold the great oriental kingdoms of Armenia and Parthia. Instead she would have to exercise what control she could through her influence over the kings, whose power must be curtailed. Tigranes was allowed to retain Armenia, but not those lands which he had won by conquest during the war (parts of Cappadocia, Cilicia and Syria, and Phoenicia and Sophene). He was instructed to pay an indemnity of 6,000 talents. In return he was acknowledged as a friend and ally of the Roman people. Armenia was thus a buffer state between the power blocs of Rome and Parthia. Prince Tigranes was rewarded with the lesser kingdom of Sophene and the promise of the Armenian crown when his father died, but his refusal to allow Pompey free access to the treasure stores of his new kingdom resulted in his subsequent deposition and imprisonment.

The long Mithridatic wars had involved the peoples of the Middle East from Greece to the Caspian, and all the upheavals were not to be settled merely by the defeat of one king and the submission of another. As Pompey completed his preliminary settlement of Armenia in his camp outside Artaxata he knew that his attention was required to the north amongst the tribes of the Caucasus and to the south-east in the crumbling Seleucid kingdom of Syria.

Armenia was left under the military supervision of Lucius Afranius, the tested veteran of the Spanish war, and Pompey moved with the bulk of his army northwards into the valley of the river Cyrnus. Here he split his troops into three divisions and established winter quarters.

In December Oroeses, king of the Albani from the north bank of the lower Cyrnus, seized the opportunity to attack the divided Roman forces before, as he suspected, they could launch an invasion of his kingdom in the spring. He also wanted to rescue the imprisoned prince Tigranes. However, Pompey and his two divisional commanders, Metellus Celer and Lucius Valerius Flaccus, were more than a match for the tribesmen, and the three attacks, timed to coincide with the Roman feast of Saturnalia, were easily repulsed. Oroeses was forced to submit to terms.

The other sizeable kingdom south of the Caucasus, that of the warlike Iberians, was also obviously in danger, and their king, Artoces, adopted a more subtle strategy to defend himself. He sent a party of envoys to negotiate peace terms with Pompey, hoping to lull him into a false sense of security and then catch him off his guard. Thanks to the efficiency of the Roman intelligence service Pompey was ready for him, and before Artoces had completed his preparations he seized the narrow pass into Iberia and the stronghold of Harmozike which guarded it. He then pursued the elusive king into the centre of Iberia and brought him to battle near the river Pelorus. Artoces' main strength lay in his archers, but, using tactics reminiscent of the Athenians at Marathon, Pompey disabled them by a rapid infantry charge, which brought his swordsmen to close quarters before the enemy fire power could take effect. Nine thousand Iberians were reported dead, and 10,000 taken prisoner. Artoces himself escaped, and the Romans were hindered from pursuing by the flooded Pelorus. Eventually, however, Artoces was persuaded to agree to Pompey's terms. He sent his children to him as hostages, a practice which was to be an important part of Rome's method of dealing with oriental kings.

North-west of Iberia lay the small kingdom of Colchis through which Mithridates had fled the previous autumn. Crossing a southern spur of the Caucasus to the headwaters of the Phasis, Pompey advanced down that river towards the Black Sea, unmolested by the respectful tribesmen of the country. At the mouth of the river he met Servilius, the admiral of his Black Sea fleet. If it was part of Pompey's plan to continue the hunt for Mithridates, the information which now reached him made it clear that further pursuit would be both dangerous and unprofitable. Leaving his winter quarters at Dioscurias, Mithridates had continued his flight through savage tribes round the coast of the Black Sea towards the city of Panticapaeum in the Crimea. Pompey judged that Mithridates had now failed once too often, and that he could probably rely on disillusioned princes and subjects to administer the *coup de grace* to the aged king. Servilius was instructed to maintain a blockade of the Black Sea ports to ensure that Mithridates remained trapped in the north, while Pompey returned to deal with a reported revolt in Albania.

His line of march took him south of Iberia, where he no doubt feared serious hindrance from the inhabitants and a shortage of supplies due to the foraging of the previous campaign, and involved a hazardous crossing of the Cyrnus into Albania. Here Pompey used the device of shielding the infantry from the full force of the current by using the horses and pack animals as a sort of breakwater a short distance upstream. This crossing was followed by a long march through rugged desert terrain in pursuit of the Albanian army, a march made all the more difficult by unreliable guides and the fact that many of his thirsty soldiers fell ill after drinking too deeply of the chilly waters of the river Cambyses. This episode led Pompey to take more care over the provision of water and for the next stage of the march 10,000 water skins were procured and used.

The Albani were finally caught at the river Abas. Plutarch, supported by Strabo, gives their numbers as 60,000 infantry and 12,000 cavalry, but this must be an exaggeration, since Dio says that Pompey was at pains to disguise his own numerical superiority in order to induce Oroeses to attack. Such a move was necessitated by the thickly wooded terrain. If attacked by obviously superior forces the Albani would have retreated into the forest and embarked on a long-drawn-out series of guerrilla raids on the Romans. Pompey had learnt well the lessons taught him by Sertorius and saw that a pitched battle must be forced at all costs. He achieved this by placing his cavalry in the front line and instructing the infantry to keep out of sight by kneeling behind them with helmets covered. The Albani charged the cavalry, a thing they would never have done to the legions, and the cavalry after a brief resistance, withdrew in good order as the infantry rose from their kneeling positions, extended ranks to let their own horsemen through, and then fell on the pursuing Albani. The trap was closed by the Roman cavalry, who quickly wheeled to left and right behind their own lines and came round to attack the Albani from the rear. During the battle Pompey himself killed the king's brother, Cosis. Of those who escaped into the woods many were driven from their hiding places by strategically-started forest fires. The Romans took ample revenge for the treacherous attacks of the previous winter.[6]

The victory finally put an end to any threat of armed resistance in the north-east (it should be remembered that both Artoces and Oroeses had been allies of Mithridates) and the rest of the campaigning season was devoted to exploration and diplomacy. Many of the tribes of the Caucasus and Caspian sent envoys to conclude truces with Rome, among them the Elymaeans and the Medes. What was contained in Pompey's subsequent letters to the Median king, Darius, we do not know, but the terms of the truce were hailed as a victory for Rome, to such an extent that the imperial historian, Velleius, actually visualised an invasion of Media.[7]

More important, perhaps, were the negotiations with the Parthian, Phraates. In spite of the help Phraates had given him the previous year Pompey had decided that of the two great monarchs east of the

Euphrates Rome would do better to lend her support to Tigranes. How far Tigranes' lavish donations of money to the officers and men of Pompey's army had influenced this decision is not clear. During the summer of 65 Gabinius had been sent with part of the Roman forces into Mesopotamia *en route* for Syria and had advanced as far as the Tigris. Pompey's treatment of Tigranes and this invasion of the Parthian kingdom annoyed Phraates and he sent to Pompey at this time, protesting at the invasion and asking for a renewal of his treaty. Pompey replied by instructing Afranius in Armenia to annex the disputed kingdom of Gordyene for Tigranes, thus aggravating still further the hostility between the two monarchs. It was a classic example of the policy of 'divide and rule'.

Pompey followed his victory at the Abas by penetrating still further towards the east. How many of his soldiers accompanied him we do not know, but Theophanes was busy collecting information of all sorts about the geography and the peoples of the Caucasus, and Varro, among other researches, was examining the trade route from India to the Black Sea via the Caspian. The expedition was turned back when only three days' march from the Caspian (the edge of the known world) by the deadly snakes of that part of Albania. These few details happen to survive in the works of Strabo, Pliny and Plutarch, and there can be no doubt that Pompey did take the opportunity, while present in this remote part of the world, of encouraging a valuable programme of scientific research. Clearly he also added to his own fame by these discoveries, as do most explorers, but it would be wrong to criticise Pompey, as some have done, for picking up easy victories and gratifying the more dilettante members of his staff in trans-Caucasia while political and military problems of a more pressing nature remained to be dealt with in the south. Pompey's assessment of the military situation was based on more accurate knowledge than that of modern historians can ever be, and he, more than almost any other Roman, was aware of the need for efficient use of men, money and time.[8]

Largely due to the concentration of contemporary historians on the activities of Pompey himself, there has been a tendency to ignore the achievements of his many legates. In fact the forces with which he defeated the Iberians and Albani were a comparatively small proportion of the total number of troops under his command. We have already noticed Gabinius operating in Mesopotamia in 65, and Afranius engaged in the very considerable task of establishing Tigranes in firm control of Armenia and annexing Gordyene to his kingdom. Further south

Lucius Lollius and Quintus Metellus Nepos, who had been Pompey's admirals in the east Aegean and east Mediterranean sectors in 67, had clearly been operating against the numerous bands of pirates and brigands, both Jewish and Arab, which infested the coast and interior of Syria and Phoenicia.

Nominally Syria was under the rule of Antiochus XIII, the last king of the Seleucid line, who had been restored to his ancestral throne by Lucullus in 69. Antiochus, however, was at the mercy of the petty rulers of several city states east of the Orontes and of the Arab princes. For two years he was kidnapped and held prisoner by Sampsiceramus of Emesa and replaced by a pretender under the title of Philip II. In 67 the then-governor of Cilicia, Quintus Marcius Rex, had visited the city of Antioch and demonstrated Roman support for Philip, but quite clearly neither he nor Antiochus, who was restored in 65, could hope to control the kingdom, or ensure any sort of stability.[9]

Further south, beyond the Libanus range, control was divided between the Nabataean Arabs under their king, Aretas III, and the Jewish kingdom, whose queen, Alexandra, had died in 67 leaving two sons, Hyrcanus and Aristobulus. They were now in contention for the throne in a civil war in which Aretas was involved on the side of Hyrcanus.

In 65 it is unlikely that Pompey had yet formed any clear idea of the line he was going to take in settling this volatile and unruly part of his province. In the previous year one of his Asiatic protégés, Demetrius of Gadara, had been sent to Antioch on a fact-finding survey, and presumably Lollius, Metellus and Gabinius, who proceeded to Syria after his brief invasion of Mesopotamia, had instructions to check any obvious trouble-making and collect information. All we hear of their activities, however, is the capture of Damascus from the Arabs by Lollius and Metellus, probably in autumn 65. Two other legates were also detailed to move their forces into the area. Afranius, after securing Gordyene for Tigranes, moved across northern Mesopotamia to Osrhoene late in 65, and was fortunate to be rescued by the inhabitants of Carrhae from starving to death from lack of supplies. We next hear of him early in the following year operating against Arab units holding the mountain passes of the Amanus range on the northern frontier of Syria. Marcus Aemilius Scaurus, Pompey's quaestor and the brother of Aemilia, was sent to deal with the Jewish problem, and reached Damascus soon after its capture.

While these preliminary operations were under way some 1,000 kilometres to his south-west, Pompey withdrew from Albania, probably along the Araxes valley and over the Armenian plateau, into Lesser Armenia, on the right bank of the upper Euphrates. Here he spent the winter of 65-4 reducing a number of Mithridates' fortresses whose commanders had not surrendered after the king's escape more than a year before. Chief among these were Sinoria, which was captured by the legate Manlius Priscus; Symphorium, a treasury which had been left under the control of Stratonice, one of Mithridates' wives; Taulara, a storehouse whose vast treasure took thirty days to inventory, and the so-called New Fort. This remote and seemingly impregnable fastness was perched on the summit of a rock overlooking a sheer ravine and enclosed by remarkable walls. According to Strabo it contained Mithridates' most precious treasures, and it was here that Pompey discovered a collection of Mithridates' personal records and papers. These provided Pompey with a clearer insight into the character of his opponent, and were a valuable source of material for the scholars on his staff, giving *inter alia*, details of the king's dealings with wives, relatives and courtiers, and of the antidotes he took daily to secure himself from assassination by poison.[10]

From Armenia Pompey moved early in 64 to Amisus. This great commercial city on the Black Sea had been sacked and burned by Lucullus' troops in 71, and was still in the process of being rebuilt in accordance with the orders of the remorseful proconsul. There Pompey began the important task of creating the administrative framework within which the peoples of the eastern Mediterranean could live in peace and prosperity under the direct rule or the guiding influence of Rome. It will be convenient to leave detailed examination of the system till later, noting meanwhile some of the things he will have been thinking about during the winter of 65-4.[11]

He needed to know details of all the communities in the proposed new provinces which might be turned into self-governing city states. Decisions had to be taken about amounts of tribute to be levied; about concessions or loans which could be made to cities which had suffered devastation during the wars, or to impoverished rulers; about the qualifications of the various candidates for the thrones of the kingdoms and temple states which were to be left independent; about boundaries and frontiers and the positioning of garrisons; about local customs which ought to be kept and respected; about the legal principles and specific regulations to be incorporated in the *lex provinciae* (code of law for a province); and about the rewards for those who had deserved well of him during the past three years. These decisions were taken with the help of many advisers, both experts and officials on his staff and leading members of the communities, and although Pompey was well aware of the vast opportunities for personal gain in wealth, influence and power, he does not seem to have taken advantage of them to the detriment of those under his control.

In spite of Lucullus' previous arrangements it was clear to everyone that their destinies lay in the hands of yet another Roman general, who felt no inclination to abide by his predecessor's decisions. Twelve kings and petty rulers of all sorts flocked to Amisus to put their claims and offer their allegiance to their new overlord.

Whereas Lucullus had needed the advice and sanction of a senatorial commission for his arrangements, Pompey claimed that the terms of Manilius' law gave him the right to take these decisions on his own initiative, though he would have to seek official approval of them later. This is another example of the way in which, by the *popularis* technique of using a tribunician law to acquire an extraordinary command, Pompey managed to reach a position of unchecked power such as men relying on the traditional methods of appointment by the Senate could not reach. There had been no blatant use of force, no illegality which might leave him liable to prosecution by his enemies on his return.

Of Pompey's movements during the remainder of 64 we are given few details. Ordering the naval blockade of the northern Black Sea ports to continue, in the hope that famine and treachery would eventually do their work, he set out with his army for the final theatre of the war, Syria and Arabia. At Zela he came across the unburied corpses of a Roman army which had been slaughtered there three years previously. He buried them with due honour and ceremony.

Once across the Halys and into the wild and beautiful kingdom of Cappadocia, he had the opportunity of assessing the task of restoration which lay before its aged but loyal monarch, Ariobarzanes. Cappadocia had been frequently plundered during the wars and seems to have been seriously impoverished. It only boasted two cities worthy of the name, and clearly needed a large infusion of wealth from outside to restore its economy. This Pompey produced in the form of an enormous personal loan (estimated at 40,000,000 sesterces at least) to Ariobarzanes, or more probably to his son, to whom he soon bequeathed the kingdom, with Pompey's approval. This particular loan, known to us from a chance reference in one of Cicero's letters written fourteen years later, casts a gleam of light on the personal wealth Pompey had amassed by this time (there can be no doubt that he was by far the richest man in the Roman Empire, if not in the world), and on the ways in which he chose to invest it. Ariobarzanes was presumably not the only monarch to owe a vast financial debt to Pompey as well as his throne, and could literally not afford to neglect his Roman patron's interests. In the late fifties, so Cicero tells us, it paid Pompey to have 'hundreds' of agents in the east seeing to it that the monthly interest (legally 1 per cent but possibly more) was being paid on his investments.[12]

Another monarch probably visited at this time was Antiochus I of Commagene. This fertile and thickly forested country lay to the north of Syria, between the Taurus and the Euphrates, and guarded the important river crossing at Samosata. Antiochus offered formal submission to Pompey, as he had done earlier to Lucullus, and was confirmed in his kingdom.

From Commagene Pompey seems to have returned briefly to eastern Cilicia, and then crossed the Amanus range, where the passes had already been cleared for him by Afranius, into Syria. During the autumn and winter of 64, which he spent at Antioch, he had three main issues to consider. First there was the problem of what should be done with the remnants of the old Seleucid Empire. We have already seen how precarious was the position of Antiochus XIII, his authority threatened by pirates to the west, brigands within his own frontiers, and Arabs to the north, east and south. As a client king he had proved a failure, and Pompey had little compunction in refusing Antiochus' request to retain his throne, and claiming Roman sovereignty over the areas of Phoenicia and Coele-Syria by right of conquest. Along with eastern Cilicia they had been won from Seleucids by Tigranes of Armenia, and so legally passed into Roman hands at Artaxata in 66. Antiochus was probably allowed to abdicate, and the new province of Syria came into being.

Secondly there was the Arab problem. In the north the Arabs of the Amanus had already been defeated, and a loyal prince, Tarcondimotus, was found to rule over this remote and backward region. He was also given a stretch of the Cilician coastline from which his fleet could operate and provide much-needed protection from any piracy. South of Commagene the whole area between the Mediterranean and the western-most stretch of the Euphrates was annexed to the province of Syria, and the kingdom of Osrhoene to the east was entrusted to an Arab sheikh called Abgar, who had presumably negotiated with Afranius the year before. Emesa remained under her strong ruler, Sampsiceramus.

Further south, however, there was obviously a military threat from Aretas III, a king of wide-ranging influence, with his capital at the rock-bound city of Petra deep in the south. From here he controlled the important and lucrative incense road from South Arabia to the Mediterranean ports. His considerable wealth was based on the taxes imposed on the camel caravans. An expedition to Petra had obvious attractions both militarily and for propaganda purposes, and Pompey may have had an interest in exploiting the southern trade routes.

Aretas was also implicated in the third problem, that of the Jewish kingdom. When Aemilius Scaurus reached Damascus in 65 he found the following situation. Aristobulus, the energetic younger son of Queen Salome Alexandra, had, shortly after his mother's death, declared war on the High Priest and king, his elder brother Hyrcanus, and defeated him and his Pharisaic supporters at the battle of Jericho. Hyrcanus had agreed to abdicate in his brother's favour and retire into private life. He had subsequently allowed himself to become the tool of a powerful and ambitious Idumaean noble called Antipater. He was an enemy of Aristobulus and reckoned that he could use Hyrcanus to remove Aristobulus from the throne and establish himself as the real power behind the restored Hyrcanus. Using his very considerable powers of persuasion he got Hyrcanus to appeal for help to his friend Aretas, offering the restoration of twelve Arab cities now in Jewish hands in return for armed assistance. Aretas gathered a large force of Arab cavalry and some infantry (exaggeratedly reported as 50,000 strong) and in April 65 laid siege to Aristobulus and his supporters in Jerusalem.[13]

On Scaurus' arrival in Judaea both parties sent representatives to win his support for their cause. Both offered large bribes to the Roman commanders (variously given as 300 or 400 talents), but the forceful personality of Aristobulus and the difficulties of the siege if he supported Hyrcanus weighed most with Scaurus, and he instructed Aretas to withdraw his army from Jerusalem, on pain of being declared an enemy of Rome. He may also have lent Aristobulus some troops, for on Scaurus' departure to Damascus Aristobulus was able to pursue the retreating Arab army and inflict a defeat on it at a place called Papyron.

Thus, when Pompey reached Antioch, Aristobulus was the king of Judaea with Roman support. However, the arrival of the commander-in-chief prompted the two factions to try their luck again. Aristobulus sent an official deputation under Nicodemus with the gift of a golden extravaganza, variously described as a 'vine' or a 'garden'. For Hyrcanus, the indefatigable Antipater attempted to win the great man's favour. Aristobulus, fearing that the fortune he had already spent in persuading Scaurus and Gabinius might be wasted, accused these two of accepting bribes. Perhaps he hoped that Pompey, who was known to have more scruples than most Romans in such matters, might lower the price of Roman support. In the event he merely lost the support of the legates in Pompey's council. Pompey decided not to make any decision on this issue until he had met the rivals in person, and he instructed them to present themselves to him at Damascus the following spring.

During the winter Pompey was fully occupied with the complicated business of organising yet another new province, preparing for the next campaigning season and arbitrating in the countless disputes, both great and small, which were brought to him for settlement. Most important of these was the quarrel between Tigranes and Phraates, which had flared up once again. Phraates had not unnaturally been incensed by the loss of Gordyene and Gabinius' invasion of Mesopotamia. He was also smarting under the insult he received when Pompey, in his letters to him, had deliberately dropped his hereditary title of King of Kings. In an angrily worded despatch he forbade Pompey to cross the Euphrates frontier, and in 64 once more invaded Gordyene. Tigranes appealed to his Roman protector, and envoys from both kings arrived at Antioch. Pompey had no intention of subjecting his soldiers to yet more marching and fighting in the remoteness of Armenia, and instead sent three ambassadors to arbitrate a settlement.

Appian also reports the arrival at this time of envoys from Mithridates, who offered to submit and pay tribute to Rome if he were allowed to return to his old kingdom of Pontus. To Pompey it must have seemed either that the king's resistance was broken, or that he was up to his old trick of trying to lull his enemies into a false sense of security. In either case the proposal was unacceptable. After so long and, in many cases, so humiliating a war the Roman people would be satisfied with nothing less than the body of Mithridates, dead or alive. His reply was that Mithridates must make his submission and his plea in person. He can not have hoped that Mithridates would fall into the trap, but he remained confident that if he continued to pen him in on the far shores of the Black Sea other agencies would eventually complete his work for him.[14]

For the campaign of 63 we are more fully informed than for any other of Pompey's campaigns to date. Theophanes' full account of it was used extensively by the later writers, Strabo and Nicolaus of Damascus, whence it found its way into the works of Flavius Josephus, a Jewish historian of the reign of Vespasian (AD 69–79). In several places Josephus contradicts the very brief accounts in other authorities and is certainly to be preferred to them as the closest we can get to the official record, if not necessarily to the truth.[15]

At the beginning of spring the Roman forces left their winter quarters at Antioch and moved south. As he advanced up the Orontes valley Pompey took and destroyed two brigands' strongholds, Lysias, ruled over by a Jew named Silas, and the citadel of Apamea. The most serious trouble seems to have come from the robber gangs of the Libanus range and the coast north of Sidon. Strabo mentions the destruction of many of their hideouts up in the mountains or in rocky caves on the coast. We hear of the execution of one brigand chief, Dionysius of Tripolis, and the forcing of one of his relatives, Ptolemy of Chalcis, to pay an indemnity of 1,000 talents (24,000,000 sesterces). This vast sum was used by Pompey to pay his troops, and vividly illustrates the attractions of piracy and brigandage in this poorly controlled country.

Presumably leaving some troops to establish order firmly in Coele-Syria, Pompey crossed the anti-Lebanon and reached Damascus. Here, as planned, he listened to the cases of Hyrcanus and Aristobulus. The former stressed his own rights as the elder brother and Aristobulus' previous involvement in acts of terrorism and piracy. His arguments were supported by a thousand Jewish nobles, thoroughly briefed by Antipater. The other merely claimed that he alone could provide strong, effective, government, but the arrogance of his supporters did little to strengthen his case, and Pompey decided that Hyrcanus was likely to be the more satisfactory ruler from the Roman point of view. To proclaim his decision there and then would have been unwise, however, for his next objective was a trial of strength with Aretas and the Nabataean Arabs, and a thwarted Aristobulus in his rear would be likely to cause untold damage. He therefore postponed making his decision public, and merely ordered the brothers to keep the peace until he returned from Arabia.

Aristobulus, however, was no fool. He was *de facto* the ruler of Judaea, and the fact that Pompey had refused to confirm Scaurus' decision and acknowledge him as king made it very clear which way the wind was blowing. He rapidly returned to Judaea and prepared to resist the Roman advance. Pompey obviously had to deal with him before he could embark on his march to Petra, so he followed from Damascus with his whole army. He advanced through the now friendly Ituraea and the Decapolis to Pella, and then crossed the Jordan to Scythopolis in Samaria, continuing down the right bank of the Jordan until he caught up with his prey at the hill fortress of Alexandreion, just inside Judaean territory. War had not yet been declared, and the sight of the full Roman army persuaded Aristobulus and his followers to re-open negotiations with Pompey and Hyrcanus. His hopes were short-lived. Several visits to the Roman camp resulted merely in the command to surrender Alexandreion and to send signed instructions to the commanders of his other strongholds to do the same. Aristobulus' last hope lay in his strongly defensible capital at Jerusalem, and, abandoning Alexandreion, he resentfully withdrew there. This was an unmistakable act of defiance.

Pompey still followed him, marching down the Jordan valley to Jericho and then south-west to Jerusalem. As he approached the city, Aristobulus' nerve broke and he arrived once more at the Roman camp, this time with an offer of surrender and a further bribe to secure his own pardon. The offer was accepted, and Gabinius was detailed to take a detachment of troops to seize control of Jerusalem and lay hands on the money which Aristobulus had promised.

Aristobulus' partisans, however, refused to follow the example of their leader. Unlike him they could not buy their safety and the chance to fight another day. Even if they were spared by Pompey they could not hope for mercy from Hyrcanus and his supporters, so bitter and vicious are the reprisals to be expected in a civil war, especially when the parties are divided along religious lines. Gabinius was refused entry. Pompey immediately arrested Aristobulus and brought the full army up to the walls. Many of the citizens bowed to the inevitable and welcomed Pompey into the city, but the priestly aristocrats who formed the core of Aristobulus' party, with many thousands of supporters, barricaded themselves behind the deep ravines and high walls which surrounded the Jewish Temple.

The story of the ensuing siege, which lasted for three months, is told in detail by Josephus (IX). As a result of the hold-up, Pompey had to abandon his Arabian expedition, but before he ever reached Jerusalem something had happened to introduce an element of urgency into his planning and speed up his departure from Syria. While he was encamped near Jericho the news reached him that Mithridates was dead.

Pompey's plan had worked. From his new capital at Panticapaeum in Bosporus Mithridates had had the vision of one final and glorious campaign. He would muster one more army and march west over 2,000 kilometres up the Danube and cross the Alps into Italy itself. He was convinced that the barbarian peoples *en route* needed only a leader to march on Rome, especially when her army and her greatest general were tied down in the deserts of Arabia. By dint of ruthless commandeering of men and materials by his eunuch ministers, Mithridates had in fact succeeded in raising, training and equipping some 36,000 troops, organised, Roman-style, in sixty cohorts. His soldiers, however, were less sanguine than their king about the chances of success in this ambitious scheme, and when Pharnaces, one of the king's sons, raised the standard of revolt in spring 63, the mutiny spread rapidly through the army. An earlier revolt, started in the city of Phanagoria, had resulted in the secession of most of the cities and towns of Bosporus, and several of the king's daughters had been kidnapped by a detachment of troops who were supposed to be escorting them to prospective husbands among the princes of Scythia, and taken as hostages to Pompey.

After twenty-five years of war with Rome, Mithridates was at last unable to pull himself back, as he had done so often before, from the brink of disaster. Giving poison to the two daughters who were at his side at the last, he took what should have been his own fatal dose. But the antidotes which he had taken regularly during his lifetime proved too successful. The poison would not work, and Mithridates had to turn to an officer of his Gallic bodyguard named Bituitus to run him through with his sword.

For Pompey this was, of course, news of his greatest success. He had now defeated the last and most dangerous of the many enemies which had threatened the Roman people since the days of Marius and the Cimbric Wars. He had triumphantly carried out the missions laid upon him by the Gabinian and Manilian laws, but by his very success had brought an end to his own command. Whatever the temptations to make further conquests, Pompey knew that his enemies would be quick to seize on any attempt to prolong his 'extraordinary' command more than was necessary. The report of Mithridates' death and the end of the Mithridatic war was also sent to Rome, and a *supplicatio* or thanksgiving to the gods of ten days' duration was voted in Pompey's honour by the Senate, on the proposal of the consul Cicero.

After the fall of Jerusalem Pompey reinstated Hyrcanus as ruler and high priest of Judaea. But it was not the same Judaea that he had inherited from his mother. The cities of the coast from Gaza to Joppa, and many of the cities of Samaria and the Decapolis, whose citizens were not predominantly of Jewish descent, were given their autonomy and included in the new province of Syria. As a client of Rome Hyrcanus was under the supervision of the governor of Syria, and his most important task was the High Priesthood, for which he was temperamentally better suited. Much of the power in Judaea passed into the hands of the clever Antipater.

Josephus emphasises the ability of Pompey to win the goodwill of the inhabitants of Syria and Judaea. This was not only due to his personal moderation and concern with the building and rebuilding of cities, and the restoration of a comparatively settled way of life: he took pains not to antagonise people more than was necessary, but to respect their customs and traditions. This is seen most clearly in his treatment of Judaea, his regard for the sanctity of the Temple, and the fact that he allowed the religious basis of Jewish society to remain undisturbed. He also probably realised, as several emperors were later to discover, that the Jews would be a continual nuisance if brought within the Empire. The subtler methods of indirect control, through amenable high priests, were worth trying.[16]

The three months' delay at Jerusalem put any further campaigning in 63 out of the question. Pompey completed his preliminary arrangements for the organisation of Syria and left the implementation of them, along with the subjugation of Aretas, to his young quaestor, Aemilius Scaurus.

Before the onset of winter Pompey was back in Amisus and gazing at the coffin of Mithridates. Pharnaces had had it shipped across the Black Sea, sending with it a request to be reinstated as king of Pontus, or at least recognised as king of Bosporus. According to Plutarch Pompey refused to look at the body. The face was unrecognisable, since the embalmers had forgotten to remove the brain and decomposition had already started, but, after the body had been identified by its size and scars by men who had known the king, he ordered it to be taken to the burial place of the Pontic kings at Sinope and buried there with due honours. Pharnaces was rewarded with the kingdom of Bosporus and the title of Friend and Ally of Rome.[17]

This squeamishness is hardly to be expected from such a battle-tried soldier as Pompey, but it fits in with an often neglected aspect of his character. Cicero records that he was not a little affected by prodigies and the omens revealed by the inspection of entrails, and there is some evidence that he was fascinated by the practice of necromancy, a trait which certainly reappears in a number of his descendants, especially his son, Sextus.[18]

The winter of 63-2 and the spring and summer of the following year were spent in completing the organisation of his conquests and his return to Asia. The overall picture of the new system can best be seen

Figure 5: Map to illustrate Pompey's Eastern Settlement.

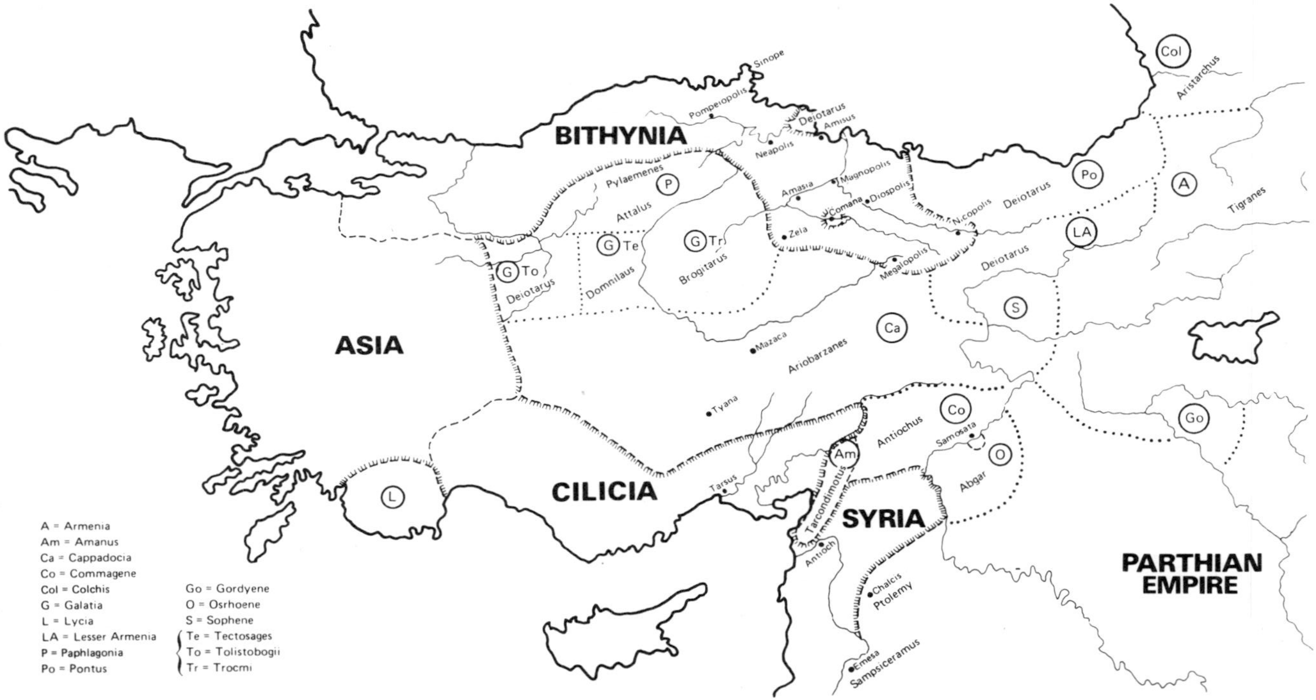

A = Armenia
Am = Amanus
Ca = Cappadocia
Co = Commagene
Col = Colchis
G = Galatia
L = Lycia
LA = Lesser Armenia
P = Paphlagonia
Po = Pontus

Go = Gordyene
O = Osrhoene
S = Sophene
Te = Tectosages
To = Tolistobogii
Tr = Trocmi

with the help of a map (p. 97). In Anatolia two existing provinces, Bithynia and Cilicia, were greatly enlarged to include much of the conquered territory. Broadly speaking, the area thus placed under direct Roman control was that nearest the coasts of the Black Sea and the eastern Mediterranean. Here the long existence of cities with Greek traditions had created a social system which could be fitted with reasonable ease into the Roman method of administration.[19]

Most of the cities were given a measure of internal independence. Their citizens elected their own local magistrates and council according to a pattern laid down by Pompey. The councils were responsible for the organisation of life in their cities and the surrounding *territoria* which were part of them. They also had to see that the stipulated taxes were collected and paid to the Roman governor, except in cases where immunity from taxation was granted. For this purpose they made use of the expertise of the Roman *societates* (tax gathering companies), a fact which cemented the bond that already existed between Pompey and the companies. The governor was responsible for the maintenance of law and order and the administration of justice in accordance with the code of law, or provincial charter, laid down by Pompey (*lex Pompeia*). This code was framed in such a way as to take local conditions and customs into consideration. It was mainly concerned with the establishment of constitutional law. For example, in Bithynia, Pompey had to ensure that all the cities had an equal chance to grow and prosper, irrespective of whether they were old-established Greek trading centres or new foundations on an inland village site. He therefore forbade the practice of dual citizenship whereby one city could offer honorary citizenship to a rich member of a less favoured city, and thus win his services and his wealth. Another stipulation allowed citizenship to be inherited from the mother in cases of mixed marriage, and increased the numbers from which citizens could be drawn. On questions of civil law the provincial charter recognised the existing laws of the cities, and these were administered not by the governor but by local magistrates, though the governor remained as the final court of appeal. It is not clear exactly what happened when new cities were founded. Perhaps they adopted the civil law code of some existing city, to which modifications could be made if necessary.[20]

There is still considerable disagreement among scholars as to the frontiers of the new province of Bithynia. Such references as can be found in Strabo's *Geography* are inconclusive, and, although he tells us that Pompey divided those parts of Mithridates' kingdom which he added to the old Bithynia into eleven city states, he does not give us their names. It is generally assumed, however, that they included Pompey's seven new foundations (Pompeiopolis, Neapolis, Megalopolis, Zela, Diospolis, Nicopolis and Magnopolis). It is probable that to start with these cities of the interior were little more than administrative centres and that there was no attempt to embark on impressive building programmes. Indeed it is unlikely that the cities would have had the necessary financial stability at this early stage. The development of city life, however, was invaluable in weaning the Asiatics away from an Oriental towards a Greco-Roman way of life.[21]

The interior of Anatolia, and indeed all the country up to the frontier with Parthia, was entrusted to numerous client kings and princes. Some of these, like Deiotarus of Galatia, who was given an extensive kingdom to the south and east of Bithynia, and Ariobarzanes of Cappadocia, were able and civilised men who had proved their good sense in supporting Rome during the Mithridatic wars. Archelaus, who was given the temple state of Comana on the upper reaches of the river Iris, was the son of one of Mithridates' generals, and had sought refuge at Rome and lived there for several years. He provided the ideal combination of qualities for a client, Pontic stock with a veneer of Roman manners, and a clear view of what a client owed to his patron. Other client rulers are unknown, or merely names. All owed their position to Pompey's recognition of their talents, and it is noteworthy how many were later to rally to his cause during the civil war of 49-5.[22]

South of the Amanus range we have seen a similar pattern emerge. The bulk of the province of Syria was the coastal strip from Gaza to the gulf of Issus with its many Hellenistic cities. Like the rocky coast of western Cilicia this had been the haunt of pirates and robbers and could not be entrusted for safekeeping to anything less than Roman legions under the command of a Roman governor. The situation of Judaea has already been described, and between Judaea and the lower Euphrates there was little but the Syrian desert. In 62 Scaurus advanced on Petra and forced submission and a blackmail of 300 talents from the helpless Aretas. The city of Damascus was returned to the Arabs, who thus guarded all the eastern approaches to the province.

There remained the question of Egypt. This wealthy but chaotic kingdom was precariously ruled by Ptolemy XII, nicknamed the 'Flute Player'. It was alleged that his predecessor, Ptolemy XI, a protégé of the dictator Sulla, had bequeathed Egypt to Rome in his will, but, by and large, the Senate was unwilling to add to Rome's overseas commitments and no positive move had been made to take over the kingdom. The question was in fact raised by Crassus in 65, perhaps because Pompey's presence in the East offered a good opportunity, perhaps because he felt that he could himself profit from the annexation, but nothing came of it. On Pompey's arrival in Syria Ptolemy sent him troops, money and clothing for his army, and, according to Appian, asked for his help in subduing riots in Alexandria. Pompey, eager though he may have been for further conquest, could not argue that Egypt lay within his allotted province and left it strictly alone, no doubt hoping that he might find a pretext to return later.[23]

The policing and protection of the new eastern empire was in the hands partly of the client kings, partly of five legions, of which one was stationed in Bithynia, two in Cilicia and two in Syria. Evidence seems to suggest that governors had difficulty in keeping the legions up to strength and tended to rely heavily on the native forces. Deiotarus, for example, had two legions of his own, trained and equipped in the Roman fashion.

As is shown by the activities of Gabinius when he returned as governor of Syria in 58, Pompey did not stay in the East long enough to dot all the i's and cross all the t's of his new organisation. None the less it forms the basis of his claim to the title of 'Empire Builder'. The pattern devised by Pompey and his advisers with some reference to the work of earlier senatorial commissions was basically that later adopted by Augustus. The main changes introduced by the emperors lay in the system of appointment and supervision of governors, and in the annexation of some of the client kingdoms as provinces. Pompey was in no position to do anything about the first, though his appointment of his own legates, such as Lentulus Marcellinus and Aemilius Scaurus, to *de facto* governorships was an important departure from the usual system of senatorial appointment. He also realised, as few other senators seem to have done, the vital importance of treating provincials with fairness and humanity, and later legislation which he introduced in 52 shows that he was concerned to check the corruption and exploitation which the republican system encouraged. Annexation of client kingdoms in later years was the result of a variety of changing circumstances, both social and political.[24]

The provincial charter for Bithynia, at least, remained largely unchanged until the early third century AD. The same may well be true of Syria, but the evidence is missing. The territory of Cilicia, which proved a rather unwieldy province, was divided between Asia and Syria by Caesar and his successors. The years 67-2 mark the real beginning of the Roman Empire in the East.

Before his final departure from Amisus Pompey paid off part of his greatest debt, that to his army. The sum distributed amounted, we are told, to 16,000 talents (384,000,000 sesterces), and it is clear that not only Pompey but also his senior officers returned home very rich men. A victory despatch to the Senate and people of Rome was followed by a slow homeward procession. This probably involved the seizure of some more strongholds and took the army past the new foundations of Neapolis and Pompeiopolis and through the old Bithynia to the coast. In honour of Theophanes and in recognition of his great services a crossing was made to Lesbos, where Pompey restored to the city of Mitylene the freedom which it had lost through its support of Mithridates, and publicly bestowed Roman citizenship on his friend. In the huge theatre he also attended a contest between poets. The theme for their compositions was his own exploits.

At Ephesus he rejoined his fleet, set up a permanent navy to patrol the coasts of the eastern Mediterranean, and probably took advantage of the time it took his army to embark to visit his old friend Posidonius on Rhodes. Here he refreshed his mind with philosophical discussions, giving a generous gift to the University, which was matched by similar munificence when he reached Athens. Much damage had been done to this city during Sulla's siege, and a grant of fifty talents was made towards rebuilding. Already Pompey was showing himself a generous patron of the Arts. This was a role familiar enough among Hellenistic monarchs, but may seem unusual in a Roman general. Among the marches and the battles and the triumphs it is easy to forget that Pompey was a man of many other accomplishments. If circumstances conspired to thwart any amibitions he may have had to become an established orator and a man of letters, he retained a lively interest in the Arts and counted numerous literary figures among his closest friends.[25]

In December he finally landed at Brundisium. He had to try to adjust once more to the demands of the domestic political scene, and to acquaint himself fully with the important developments of the last six years.

5 THE NEW CHALLENGE: POLITICS AT ROME 67–60

There had been no chance for Pompey during his absence in the East to take any active part in politics. It is important to understand the reasons for this fact, and its consequences. In the first place it was vital for the Roman politician to maintain personal contact, both with his fellows in the Senate and with his supporters and clients outside. Politics is a matter of reacting to rapidly changing situations, even if the politician is himself responsible for some of the changes, and the reaction in any given situation will depend on the parallel reactions of other politicians. These have to be known, or induced, quickly, whether in private discussion or public debate. Rome was where everything of political importance happened, and to be absent was to be irrevocably out of touch.

This was especially true, if, like Pompey, one was often 1,000 miles or more from Italy. Even when he was accessible by road or sea, news would take up to two months to reach him; when he was on campaign in the remote fastnesses of Armenia, Iberia or Albania he probably received no news at all. And by the time his reaction to any issue could be known at Rome, that issue would be long dead.

Nevertheless, even in his absence he was a factor to be seriously reckoned with. News of great successes and victorious marches to the furthest reaches of the known world kept his popularity very much alive among the masses, and his name could exercise magic at election time, still more his money, which members of his staff returning to stand for office could dispense generously in the right quarters. The *publicani*, and probably the equestrian class in general, would be increasingly grateful as the field for their own operations and investments widened with Pompey's conquests.

It would be meaningless to talk of a Pompeian party during the years 66-2; such a body required the continuous presence of its leader. But it is possible to identify a number of politicians who owed some sort of loyalty to Pompey, and, in the case of magistrates, probably owed him much of the money and support which won them election. Quintus Cicero, writing to his brother Marcus in 64, reminds him how important it is that the voters should know that Pompey is behind him (Marcus was a consular candidate in that year), and in

July 65 Marcus himself wrote to his close friend, the banker and backstage politician Atticus, to ask him to win the support of what he called the *manus Pompei*, the Pompeian group, the men on Pompey's staff who might be able to visit Rome before election time and canvass for him. He jokingly realises that the great man himself may not have the time.[1]

We should not think that men like Cicero or Gabinius or Labienus would always be working in Pompey's interests. Like most politicians they naturally put their own interests before those of any other, and if they felt that at any time they could benefit themselves by cultivating other men of influence, Crassus for example, they would not hesitate to do so. In any case it was notoriously difficult to know what supporting Pompey's interests would involve in any given situation. He was not a man who ever published his political philosophy or easily let people into his confidence. As Cicero, who knew him well, wrote later in 54, 'It is a hard job to know whether he wants something or doesn't.'[2]

In the meantime Pompey's rivals for popular support and his enemies amongst the Optimates were in a position to make up the ground lost in 67 and the early months of 66. In particular men such as Q. Catulus and Q. Hortensius continued to smart over their defeats by Gabinius and Manilius, and Q. Metellus, the conqueror of Crete in 67, and L. Lucullus harboured resentment at the treatment they had received from Pompey himself. After the brief *rapprochement* of 70, Marcus Crassus was growing increasingly jealous of Pompey's success and fighting hard to keep up with his younger rival. While his *amici* were busy guessing his wishes, his enemies were ready to seize any opportunity to weaken his position.[3]

During the mid-sixties it is possible to detect in Roman politics a movement for reform, fostered in many cases by men with Pompeian connections and probably enjoying general support from him. It was an offshoot or continuation of the movement which had been active in the years before Pompey's consulship in 70, and made use of the weapons created by Pompey in that year. Behind it lay the 'notion of a cleaned-up refurbished Republic, its grosser abuses checked, the machinery of administration improved, the tight grip of entrenched privilege loosened'. In the absence of that rare creature, a reforming consul, the movement relied on tribunes to prepare and pass the necessary legislation.[4]

The important tribunate of Gabinius and Cornelius in 67 has already been mentioned. In addition to the law giving Pompey his pirate command the reforms of these two were aimed at weakening Optimate control over the elections (especially by bribery) and at safeguarding some of the interests of provincials. The Optimates, however, were able to hit back. The Pompeian Lollius Palicanus tried to stand for the consulship of 66. His nomination was rejected by the consul Piso. The able soldier Gabinius escaped prosecution by being given a job on Pompey's staff in 66, but Cornelius ran into trouble when he was prosecuted for treason in the same year. Violent demonstrations by his friends caused the case to be dropped, but it was raised again in 65 and this time the biggest guns in the Optimate armoury were ranged against him. Manilius, too, was prosecuted by the Optimates towards the end of 66 for extortion during his earlier quaestorship, and in spite of devious attempts to rig the trial by the outgoing praetor Marcus Cicero and the breaking up of the court by a hired gang of rioters, he was finally condemned on another charge in February 65.[5]

A pattern thus emerges. In the popular assembly, which elected tribunes and in which tribunes could pass legislation, a movement for popular reform could make some headway. These gains, however, would usually be cancelled in the centuriate assembly, where consuls and praetors were elected and the voting system was heavily weighted in favour of the propertied classes, and in the law courts, where juries of senators and knights might listen favourably to cases brought against reformers. The balance was normally in favour of those who wanted to maintain the *status quo*.

The bitter and confused struggle for the consulships of 65 provides a good example of how dangerous it is to see Roman politics in terms of stable groupings. Of five known contestants four seem to have had Pompeian connections. L. Aurelius Cotta had co-operated as praetor in the reforms of 70; L. Manlius Torquatus was in all probability one of Pompey's legates in 67, and had married a girl from Picenum; P. Cornelius Sulla, nephew of the dictator, was a brother-in-law, having married Pompey's sister Pompeia shortly after the death of C. Memmius in Spain in 75; L. Sergius Catilina had served with Pompey's father at Asculum in 89 (I), switched sides to profit from Sulla's dictatorship in the late eighties, and was now a prominent, if somewhat unreliable member of the reform group. In the event Catilina's nomination was not accepted as he was threatened with prosecution for extortion, and after heavy bribery Sulla and another candidate, Autronius, were elected. They were successfully prosecuted forthwith, and Cotta and Torquatus were elected in their place.[6]

The story was later fabricated that the disappointed candidates, backed in some versions by Crassus and Caesar, formed a plot to murder the new consuls on 1 January 65, and seize power by force. This story has been shown to be a tissue of lies, woven partly by Cicero and partly by anti-Caesarian propagandists, and the truth is now irretrievably lost. Infuriatingly the impression persists that somehow Pompey was concerned, especially as one unlikely outcome of the whole business was that Crassus persuaded the Senate to send Cn. Calpurnius Piso, an enemy of Pompey but only of quaestorian rank, to govern Nearer Spain.

No certainty is possible, but it may be that behind the whole incident lay a move by Crassus, perhaps with Optimate connivance, to keep men with moderate views and Pompeian sympathies out of the consulship, and to whittle away some of the support that Pompey had established in Spain. P. Sulla's Pompeian ties may well have weakened since his marriage began (Pompey's own marriages show his own, not untypical, attitude to such things), and it is possible that Crassus' money paved the way for Sulla's and Autronius' initial success.

In fact the stalemate continued. Cn. Piso soon met his death in Spain, at the hands of some Spanish cavalrymen in his army. Rumour had it that they were loyal Pompeians and that Pompey had given them the nod. Neither of the consuls nor any of the tribunes made any reforming gestures, and such political activity as there was in 65 centred round the censors, Crassus and the staunch old Optimate Q. Catulus. Crassus' attempts to get moves started to annex Egypt and to grant full citizenship to the inhabitants of Transpadane Gaul, attempts which if successful would have brought him vast opportunities to increase his wealth and his *clientela*, were thwarted by his colleague.

Crassus' attitude towards reform was decidedly ambivalent. A man of the noblest ancestry and an unscrupulous capitalist, he probably had little personal inclination to improve the lot of the Roman *plebs*, the Italian peasant or the exploited provincial. But he was willing to support promising young politicians of any views if he thought they could be helpful to him. Such men of *popularis* leanings as Catilina, Caesar and Clodius all benefited from his generosity in paying their debts or bribing juries to acquit them of serious charges, and we must assume that he found most of them to be good investments.

In 64, however, things started to move. Spring brought with it reports of Pompey's victories in Albania and Iberia, and of successful operations in Armenia and Parthia. Back in Rome to stand for the praetorship were Q. Metellus Celer and L. Valerius Flaccus, heroes of the battles of the Saturnalia and presumably of the subsequent campaign. Both won election. In the tribunician elections there was a most unusual result. Ten tribunes of like mind were elected, with what appears to have been a fairly comprehensive programme of reform. Two of them at least, T. Ampius Balbus and T. Labienus, were Pompeians, and it is possible that a third, P. Servilius Rullus, was the man who had commanded Pompey's Black Sea fleet in 65. During the second half of 64, following their election, the detailed planning for the launching of their programme was under way. It had been hoped that there would be support from the consuls of 63; the strongest candidates were Catilina and C. Antonius Hibrida. Neither was ideal. Catilina was determined and magnetic, but extravagant and headstrong and seldom free from scandal; Antonius aristocratic but weak. Behind them stood Crassus' millions and the cautious support of Caesar. The signs were favourable for a repeat of 70, with consuls, praetors and tribunes working together in a programme of progressive legislation.[7]

In fact this was not to be. One of the other consular candidates was Marcus Cicero, fighting desperately to overcome his lack of *nobilitas* in a field full of *nobiles*. Following his brother's good advice he had carefully avoided taking a firm position on any issue during his candidature, and was not connected at the time with the reformers. Any earlier connections, and there were many, could conveniently be forgotten. Seizing the opportunity offered by Optimate fears of reform, he took a few sharp paces to the 'right', delivered a devastating speech in the Senate attacking the characters of his chief opponents and their disreputable pasts, and won the support of the Optimates and through them of their clients in the assembly. Antonius narrowly beat Catilina to win second place.[8]

During his consulship Cicero effectively crushed the reform programme. Antonius was silenced, one of the tribunes was induced to obstruct his colleagues, and Cicero's brilliant if unscrupulous oratory was used to deadly effect. But this is not the place to attempt yet another survey of Cicero's *annus mirabilis*. We are concerned, rather, with two questions: how much of a stake Pompey had in the ill-fated reform programme, and what his reaction was to Cicero's performance.

The main issues raised by the reformers were the following: a re-distribution of land in Italy so as to provide holdings for many of the poor and unemployed at Rome and in the rest of Italy (this of course could include retired veterans); an easing of the very serious problem of debt, which was causing misery, bankruptcy and even bondage to large numbers of people in all classes; the question whether the Senate had the right in times of crisis to suspend the normal rights of citizens by passing the Ultimate Decree (*consultum ultimum*); the restoration of full citizen rights to the sons of those who had been proscribed by Sulla. It can be seen that some attempt was being made to get to grips with the problems outlined earlier in Chapter 2 (p. 39). But how far was Pompey involved? Obviously he could have had no hand in drafting the proposed legislation or planning the strategy, but it is very likely that he was in sympathy with the aims. He himself sponsored an agrarian bill in 60 and again in 59. His reforms in 70 and his whole career demonstrated his attitude towards unlimited senatorial power. His treatment of Sertorians suggests that he favoured a policy of healing the wounds caused by the civil wars of the eighties.

There may be more than this. It has recently been argued that the agrarian bill proposed by Servilius Rullus in January 63 had a dual purpose — to provide land both for resettlement of the poor and for grants to Pompey's veterans on his return. When Rullus, on this view, was sent back to Rome in 64 the final settlement must have seemed not far off. Pompey did not know that he would be held up for so long by the siege of Jerusalem, and he knew from experience how important it was to have land available to give to his troops. His continued hold over their loyalties in peace-time would depend to a large extent on the way in which he rewarded them on demobilisation. Vast cash bonuses would be useless if they could not find land to buy with them. The danger to Italy's security of tens of thousands of unemployed soldiers was appalling.[9]

Rullus' proposal was that a special ten-man commission should be elected to organise the redistribution of the last remaining areas of state-owned land in Italy (in Campania) among poor citizens. More land should also be bought in Italy for the same purpose, and the commission should raise money for this by selling state property in the provinces, raising a special tax, earmarking the taxes from newly-acquired provinces, and using any booty which Rome's generals might win in future wars. The powers of the commissioners would obviously be very great. It would be up to them to decide which property could be sold and at what prices. They would have power to raise troops if necessary, if, for example, they were to annex Egypt. Vast sums of money could pass through their hands, possibly more than would be needed for the purposes of the bill.

However, the bill along with the rest of the reform programme was squashed, mainly through the determined opposition of Cicero. Moderate though he may have been in many ways, he reacted strongly to any threat to the interests of men of property, and any redistribution of land tended to be seen as such a threat. His speeches against the bill have been described as 'masterpieces of misrepresentation'. Rullus and his supporters were portrayed as a gang of villainous desperadoes eager to seize control of huge areas of land and sell them at inflated prices for their own profit. Behind them Cicero hints at the scheming presence of Crassus and Caesar, aiming once more to lay their greedy hands on the wealth of Egypt and build up an army against Pompey. In fact the bill specifically excluded Pompey's spoils of war from the possible sources of revenue for the commission.[10]

Most historians accept Cicero's hints as to the instigators of the bill, but this is not a necessary interpretation of the few unchallenged facts which emerge from the speeches. Their tone is typical of the almost hysterical reaction of the propertied classes at Rome to land reform. It remains possible that in its objectives the bill was a statesmanlike one. It could have been more carefully drafted — Cicero was able to tear the wording of it to shreds in some places — but it need not have been the cynical attempt to win unlimited wealth and power that its opponents suggested.

But if Pompey was behind the bill, why did Cicero pretend that it was aimed against him? Possibly Pompey realised Cicero's natural antipathy to such a measure and had not informed him. We know that Cicero was cold-shouldered by the tribunes when he learnt in autumn 64 that they were drafting a bill, and offered his help and advice. Quite possibly Cicero did not know who was behind it and felt all the more bitter against it for this reason. Such an interpretation would certainly explain Pompey's later coolness towards Cicero's achievements as consul and Cicero's ignorance of its cause.[11]

In fact most of the claims to respectability which the reform movement may have had were shattered in the second half of the year by Catilina. Thwarted for the third time in his attempts to win the consulship he followed the precedent of Lepidus fifteen years earlier and resorted to armed revolution.

The story of the Catilinarian conspiracy and its detection and defeat by Cicero is not directly relevant here and can be read in any standard history. It was ill prepared and poorly led, but the large volume of support for it from such places as Cisalpine Gaul, Picenum, Etruria,

Umbria, Campania and Apulia show how widespread was the social unrest in Italy which bills like those of Rullus were probably trying to help. There will have been men from all these areas in Pompey's legions and it is inconceivable that a general who won such devotion from his troops should have been unaware of their troubles and those of their families.[12]

One of the more unfortunate consequences of the conspiracy was that, by association, reformers became discredited in the eyes not only of senators but of *equites* and many of the *plebs*. For a time Senate and *equites* grew closer together than ever before or after. The class from which Pompey drew so much of his support had joined forces with his opponents.

In 63 one of the candidates for the tribunate was Metellus Nepos, who returned from Pompey's army in order to canvass. According to Plutarch Metellus was not only a powerful figure in his own right but also a stupid one, and we have no means of knowing whether he came with express instructions from Pompey or not. His appearance prompted the rival candidature of the man who was soon to emerge as the leader of the Optimates and to have an important affect on Pompey's fortunes, M. Porcius Cato. Both were elected.[13]

After entering office (10 December 63) Metellus' first actions included vetoing Cicero's delivery of his farewell address at the end of the year and criticising his having executed several of the ring-leaders of the Catilinarian conspiracy without a trial. Both moves perhaps suggest sympathy for the reform movement. In January, supported by the new praetor Julius Caesar, Metellus proposed that Pompey should be elected consul in his absence and recalled to suppress the remnants of the conspiracy, and that the privilege of dedicating the new temple of Jupiter on the Capitol should be transferred to Pompey from Q. Catulus.

We may well believe that Pompey, annoyed by Cicero's behaviour at the beginning of his consulship, encouraged Metellus to harass him, but hardly that he was behind the proposal for his own recall. The state of emergency was declared against Catilina on 21 October and there would not have been time for news to reach Pompey at Amisus and for instructions to get back to Metellus by the beginning of January. In any case, with events moving as rapidly as they did, it would have been foolish in the extreme to try to intervene at such a distance.

In fact Metellus' tribunate was a disaster. At the introduction of his

bill he brought armed thugs into the assembly to intimidate his opponents and the voters, but was completely outplayed at this game by Cato
and his colleague Thermus. He was made to look very foolish in public
and the ensuing riot resulted in the passing of the *consultum ultimum*
by the Senate. Metellus left Rome and returned to Pompey's army.

We may now review Pompey's position in Roman politics at the time
of Metellus' return with his news in the spring of 62. Pompey knew
that he could expect to find a predominantly hostile Senate led by
Cato, Hortensius and Lucullus, who had finally succeeded in holding
a long-delayed triumph for his victories over Mithridates and
Tigranes. The consuls appeared unfriendly and the now influential
ex-consul M. Cicero was also flirting with the Optimates. Full support
from the *equites* could no longer be guaranteed and bitter anti-
Pompeian propaganda was being disseminated among the people.
The strong following he had enjoyed before his departure for the
East had been whittled away. Hardly any of the men upon whom he
had relied to protect his interests had come up to scratch. One by
one the Optimates had succeeded either in silencing or converting
them. It must have been hard to know where to look for the friends
he would need on his return.

Marcus Crassus, his consular colleague of 70, had shown few signs
of friendship since, and was widely suspected of jealousy and of
attempts to win Pompey's early following for himself. In summer 62
he left Italy with his family, proclaiming that he feared for his own
safety when Pompey and his army arrived, but he sailed no
further than Asia, where he no doubt had business interests to
attend to. It has been suggested that he wanted to open negotiations
with Pompey there. If so, we have no information of their nature
or outcome.

Early in 62 there also arrived a long and somewhat high-handed
letter from Marcus Cicero, containing his own account and interpretation of the events of his consulship. Pompey's reply, which
may have coincided with his victory despatch to the Senate, was
cool and formal. There may have been a touch of jealousy for an old
ally who had managed to win the admittedly grudging support of
the *nobiles* and by his prompt action against Catilina acquire the
title of *pater patriae* — 'father of his country'. Probably Pompey
was also annoyed with the whole tenor of Cicero's consulship, which
had proved a turning-point in his own fortunes. Pompey was
genuinely interested in reform. He was a man who liked things to run
well, and saw dangers to the smooth running of the state in the popular

unrest in Italy. It has also been argued that Cicero's defeat of Rullus' agrarian bill had thwarted Pompey's hopes of having land available for his veterans when he returned.

He can hardly have been any more pleased to receive Cicero's second letter, written in April, in which he complained that Pompey had misunderstood the significance of his victory over Catilina and had failed to give him enough credit for it. He also rather patronisingly suggested that interests of state would bring the two closer together, and even hinted at an alliance in which the great soldier would be guided by the great statesman on the lines of the famous partnership between Scipio Aemilianus and Laelius eighty or so years previously. Pompey was not the man to welcome such gratuitous offers of advice from a former protégé.[14]

Thirdly there was Julius Caesar. A Pompeian in 66, he had been an active supporter of the reform programme in 63, in particular questioning the validity of the Senate's *consultum ultimum* and opposing Cicero's execution of the Catilinarians. He seems to have lent his support to Rullus' agrarian bill, and in 62 was closely associated with the proposals of Metellus Nepos, though far more adept than Nepos at restoring himself after the *débâcle*. He had also won a conspicuous triumph in being elected in 63 to the office of *Pontifex Maximus* against strong Optimate opposition.

It would be misleading to think of Caesar as a consistent supporter of Pompey during the sixties. He was a patrician and a *nobilis*, anxious to further his own career with help from any quarter, and was heavily in debt to Crassus at this time. However, he obviously had much in common with Pompey and would be a useful ally – he had many valuable connections, was a brilliant popular orator, and had built up a strong base of supporters at Rome. Unfortunately for Pompey he was due to follow his praetorship (62) with a tour as governor of Further Spain. For a while his influence and help would not be available.

There is a striking contrast between the scene Pompey was leaving and the one to which he was returning. In the East he was monarch of all he surveyed, with a vast army at his back, dictating terms and distributing favours to cities, kings and princes within a brilliantly organised system of his own creation. At Rome he would find himself once more working within a constitution hedged around with checks and restrictions against the growth of individual dominance, where every word of his would be scrutinised, every move opposed; where there were numerous rivals for position even among men who had been his friends, and advice was offered before it was asked for. If he was to adapt to the new environment, the mental adjustment required was enormous.

Such a position was not, of course, unique. Sulla had returned to march on Rome with his army, liquidate all serious opposition and establish his dictatorship. But that was not Pompey's way. Civil war was untidy, a negation of efficiency. He had in fact a deep regard for the Roman constitution provided that it could be adapted to suit his own requirements. It is part of our task to see what these requirements were and to discover the adaptations which Pompey devised and worked for during the decade which followed his return.

He saw clearly that this was no time to join a trial of political strength with the Optimates. For the time being, at least, he must aim at a compromise, while he settled the two most urgent problems which faced him. First he needed to pass a law setting up machinery for the provision of land allotments for his veterans, and secondly he had to persuade the Senate to ratify the settlement he had just completed in the East. It will be remembered that he had broken with tradition in acting on his own initiative without the usual help of a senatorial commission, and that he could expect bitter opposition from Lucullus and his friends.

His first requirement would be a helpful and conciliatory consul. For that purpose he chose to support the candidature of M. Pupius Piso, an old friend and legate of impeccable respectability, and a member of a family which had a tradition of hostility to himself. (One may recall the two Pisos, the consul of 67 and the quaestor of 65.) The Senate acceded to Pompey's request that the elections be postponed to allow Piso to reach Rome in time to submit his nomination, and he was duly elected along with the Optimate M. Valerius Messalla. At least one of the tribunes for 61, Fufius Calenus, was also briefed in Pompey's interest.

Pompey also decided that it would be worth his while to press for a marriage alliance with the Optimates. The political nature of his first three marriages has already been noted, and the advantages of the Metellan connections which Mucia had brought seemed now to be at an end. He had had trouble with Metellus Creticus in 67 and neither Celer nor Nepos had succeeded in giving him much assistance after their periods of service on his staff. In fact Mucia had collaborated with Cicero in an attempt to calm her brother Nepos the previous winter, and Pompey may have seen this as an act of disloyalty. Moreover rumour had it that she had been an unfaithful wife (Julius Caesar was, ironically, alleged to be the man involved) and when Pompey decided, shortly before his departure from Asia, to send Mucia notice of divorce, immorality was the charge he made. By the standards of Pompey's class and time the marriage had served its purpose. The children no longer needed their mother's influence, and it is unlikely that any close bond of affection remained after Pompey's prolonged absence from home. He can hardly have seen Mucia for more than five out of the last fifteen years. In a letter dated 1 January 61 Cicero says, 'Pompey's divorce of Mucia is strongly approved of.' This may reveal general disapproval of Mucia's allegedly adulterous behaviour, but it is more likely that Cicero is expressing satisfaction at the thought that Pompey was aiming at a new alliance, and at the cause for estrangement between him and Caesar.[15]

This proposed alliance was with Marcus Cato, himself the centre of a complicated nexus of Optimate families, and clearly emerging as a powerful force in politics in spite of his humble position in the Senate. Not long after his return to Rome Pompey, through the agency of his friend Munatius, offered to marry himself and one of his sons to two of Cato's nieces. Such an offer would have persuaded most, but Pompey had misjudged his man. Cato realised that this was an attempt to buy his support, or at least his silence, in the forthcoming negotiations over veteran allotments and the ratification of the Eastern settlement, and rejected the offer, much to the disappointment of his wife and sister. He had also opposed the postponement of the consular elections, and Pompey can have been left in no doubt about the firmness of the opposition he was likely to meet from that quarter.

Outside senatorial circles Pompey had done much to quell anxiety about his intentions and to counteract hostile propaganda by his prompt action on arrival at Brundisium. After a heartwarming speech to his army, assuring them of his gratitude for their long service and of his determination to protect their interests in the future, he dismissed them to their homes with instructions to return to Rome for his triumph in due course.

According to Plutarch, his arrival at towns and cities on his way to Rome was greeted with great celebration and rejoicing, and Appian adds that practically the whole population of Rome, including the Senate, came out to escort him on the last few miles.[16]

It is hard to tell whether this was the spontaneous welcoming of a national hero returning from his conquests or a measure of the relief felt at his refusal to copy Sulla or even repeat his own behaviour in 77 and 71. Probably both feelings were present amidst the cheering crowds.

How far a feeling of relief was justified is difficult to say. In ten years much had changed. As a young adventurer Pompey had needed the support of his legions in 71; now as the most powerful and famous figure of the Roman world he felt that he should be able to gain his requirements and maintain his position without resorting to unconstitutional methods. Within two years he was forced to change his mind.

The year that followed was one of strangely mixed fortunes. In the political field Pompey spent the first four or five months trying to win the confidence and support of the Optimates and to become familiar with the new issues and personalities in the Senate. It was only natural that he should wish to spend some time taking stock of the situation and avoid committing himself on issues whose full implications he did not, perhaps, understand.

Unfortunately such a wish was not easily granted. Rome was a place where, as we see clearly from Cicero's letters, everyone was agog to know not only everyone else's business, but also their thoughts on every problem, their friendships and their enmities. Shortly after his arrival Pompey made his first public appearance at a *contio*. As he was expecting a triumph he could not lay down his *imperium* before it had been held, and so could not enter the *pomerium* or boundary of the city proper, but there were many places of public assembly and even places where the Senate could meet outside this boundary. What he said we do not know, but Cicero gives a very scathing commentary on the speech. 'It held out no comfort to the poor, no hopes for revolutionaries; there was nothing to please the men of substance, nothing to impress the *boni*. It was a total flop.' In trying to avoid giving offence by taking sides Pompey had pleased nobody. Or perhaps Cicero and others had expected too much.[17]

At his next appearance Pompey was slightly more forthcoming. The burning issue of the moment was the prosecution of the young and brilliant P. Clodius Pulcher on a charge of sacrilege. It was alleged, on fairly good evidence, that he had attended the all-female rites of the *Bona Dea*, held at Julius Caesar's house, disguised as a woman. This was probably a harmless enough prank, though Caesar saw fit to divorce his wife, who had been hostess, to free himself of suspicion. However, Clodius' many enemies seized the opportunity thus offered to break his career by having him condemned, and were trying to get a special law passed which would enable the praetor who presided at the trial to hand-pick the jury.

This situation produced an unwelcome dilemma for Pompey. Clodius had been a helpful adherent of his in the past, and his two chief supporters in the Senate were Piso and Calenus. However, to lend his influence to the defence would automatically put him in opposition to those very Optimates whose help he most needed at the moment. Summoned in early February by Piso and Calenus to answer questions at a crowded public meeting in the Circus Flaminius, Pompey was forced to sidestep the whole issue. In reply to a question about his attitude to the jury selection problem he said, at some length, that he had always held the authority of the Senate in the highest respect in such matters and still did. Cicero adds that the tone of the speech was decidedly Optimate.[18]

The other consul, Messalla, was quick to spot Pompey's difficulty and to take advantage. At a meeting of the Senate shortly afterwards he put the same question and received a similarly guarded reply in which Pompey expressed his praise for *all* senatorial decrees. We may perhaps detect a note of exasperation in Pompey's aside to Cicero as he sat down — 'I think I've given quite enough answers on that subject.'[19]

Cicero's account of the rest of the debate is revealing. Pompey's speech was followed by one from Crassus in which he launched into an elaborate eulogy of Cicero's consulship. Cicero makes it clear that he felt that Crassus had scored a victory over Pompey by this speech, and that Pompey thought so too. Crassus had taken a specifically Optimate line, emphasising Pompey's studied vagueness, and winning widespread approval. What Cicero had missed in Pompey's utterances became apparent in his own speech later, in which he dealt with the theme currently dearest to his heart, that of the importance of unity, unity between the Senate and the *equites* and unity in Italy. This *concordia ordinum* ('concord between the orders'), as he called it, had been a reality in 63 when all men of property joined ranks behind Cicero to crush Catilina, and Cicero cherished the hope that it would remain, cemented by a firm alliance between Pompey and the Optimates. It was this hope to which he had alluded in his letter to Pompey the previous April, but so far Pompey had shown no sign of any interest in the idea.

His attitude towards Cicero was friendly, but cool. Cicero suspected jealousy and on 25 January had written some harsh words to Atticus: 'He's graceless and devious and politically unimaginative. There's nothing more honourable or courageous or frank about him.' – words more illustrative of Cicero's pique at Pompey's failure to fall in with his plans than valid as a description of the man,[20]

Anxious to avoid sitting firmly on either stool, Pompey fell between the two. By June at the latest it was clear that the Optimates were not interested in a compromise or an alliance. Cato's rebuff has already been mentioned and we may assume that Lucullus, Hortensius and the rest remained adamant. The Optimate ranks were swelled by the reversion to type of Metellus Celer, now front runner in the election campaign for the consulships of 60.

Equally seriously Pompey had won the hostility of Clodius. Sacrificed by Pompey in the hope of wooing the Optimates, Clodius had been brought to trial, and saved by Crassus, who successfully bribed thirty-one out of the forty-six jurors. Clodius never forgot, but Cicero was not long in burying his resentment. The willingness of a predominantly equestrian jury to acquit Clodius in the face of damning evidence and strong Optimate pressure marked the beginning of the dissolution of the *concordia ordinum*, and as Cicero saw his vision rapidly vanishing, his affection for Pompey as a man began to salve his wounded political pride. By July their close friendship was a byword at Rome. From Pompey's point of view Cicero's support became increasingly valuable. His skill as an orator was unrivalled and he had great influence among young senators, knights and people.

In spite of the comparative urgency of the legislation which Pompey wanted passed there is no evidence that he made any move in that direction in the first half of 61. As co-operators in winning senatorial or popular support Piso and Calenus proved dismal failures and by July Pompey had decided that he must make plans to introduce legislation early in 60. Once again he proposed to act through a co-operative consul and a tribune. With the aid of flagrant bribery (the flagrancy is perhaps a mark of growing desperation) he engineered the election of his trusted legate Lucius Afranius as Metellus Celer's colleague, and he secured the services of Lucius Flavius as tribune.

His running of Afranius, a *novus homo* with as little senatorial experience as himself, is a sure sign that Pompey had broken with the Optimates. The election of such a man was anathema to their prejudices and pride, and dismayed even the most recent *nobilis*, Cicero, to the extent that he felt the consulship itself was degraded by Afranius' tenure of it. It also illustrates well the disparity of outlook between Pompey and his fellow *nobiles*. He was remarkably free from the exclusiveness and snobbery which tainted so many members of his class.[21]

Towards the end of the year 61 two more events indicated that Cato and his allies were growing still more intractable and may have suggested to Pompey that the iron hand he had so far kept concealed might yet have to be used to overcome their stubborn opposition. A bill was proposed, with senatorial backing, providing for the investigation of the conduct of jurors guilty of taking bribes. It was not passed, but was seen by the *equites*, who produced two thirds of all jurors, as an attack on their order. Secondly Metellus Celer and Cato led firm opposition to a request from the tax company which had won the contract to collect the taxes of Asia that their price, which they had bid but belatedly found to be unreasonably high, should be reduced.

The result was the complete breakdown of the *concordia ordinum* in spite of the fact that the *equites* had no real cause for grievance. Pompey had lost his predominant patronage of the *equites* to Crassus during his absence, and must have felt the need to champion their interests once more, but he made no open move as yet. Inscrutable as ever, he was still biding his time.

Away from the complications of senatorial in-fighting, 61 brought more conspicuous success. Much of Pompey's time was taken up with capitalising on the fame and wealth he had won in the East, and in making the preparations for his triumph.

Part of his new fortune was spent on the building of a great palace, between the Alban Mount and Lake Albanus twenty-four kilometres south-east of Rome. Inspired in part by the *paradeisoi* or parks of oriental kings it was designed as a country retreat where Pompey could live in the grand manner and play the part of artistic and literary patron to which he was increasingly being attracted.[22]

It was probably at this time, too, that be bought the land on the Campus Martius and the lower slopes of the Pincian Hill in northern Rome which became the famous Pompeian Gardens. As an official dedication of his spoils he built a shrine to Minerva, significantly the goddess of learning and the arts as well as a goddess of war, and it may have been as early as 61 that he began the planning of the great stone theatre complex which was eventually dedicated in 55. Based, so it was said, on that of Mitylene it was Rome's first stone theatre and a landmark in the history of Roman architecture. Not since Sulla had Rome seen such a programme of city development. The general who had founded thirty-nine cities in the Eastern Empire had returned to apply his munificence to the beautification of the Empire's capital.

In September, probably, he addressed a public meeting at which he told the story of his campaigns, emphasising the sheer size of his conquests by the remark that he had accepted as his province Asia, the extremity of the Empire, which he now returned to the Roman people as the heart of their fatherland. On the last two days of the month he celebrated his third and greatest triumph (it is significant that we hear of no opposition to its granting by the Senate).[23]

As a public spectacle and an exercise in propaganda the triumph was a masterpiece. Rome's imagination was well and truly caught and for ever after, Pompey was referred to in speeches and in histories as the general who had triumphed over all three continents of the inhabited world in their turn. On his forty-fifth birthday Pompey had reached the pinnacle of glory, which, as events were to show, he could never attain again.

The text of his dedicatory inscription and Appian's full description of the triumph are given in the Appendix (IIIC and VI). Here we may note the enormous effect on the state income created by the conquests. The amount of tribute from the provinces was increased at one stroke by 70 per cent (200 million sesterces to 340 million sesterces per annum), and the value of the booty handed over to the treasury was a further 480 million sesterces. At Pompey's own personal fortune we can only guess.

Pompey's hopes that Afranius and Flavius would prove more effective than Piso and Calenus were soon dashed. Cicero had nothing but scorn for Afranius, whom he called idle and weak-hearted, and Dio remarks that he was better at dancing than coping with the complicated business of a consul. Clearly he was out of his depth in the job, and no match for his experienced colleague Metellus.[24]

The first proposal brought forward seems to have been that for the ratification of the Eastern settlement. It ran into difficulties from the start, for Cato insisted on prolonging the discussion of the Asian tax contract and there was little time available for anything else in the first months of 60. Then Lucius Lucullus, who had been recalled from semi-retirement to do battle with Pompey on this issue, insisted first that his own arrangements in Pontus which had been disregarded by Pompey should be discussed as well, and secondly that all Pompey's arrangements should be discussed separately. It was intolerably high-handed to expect the Senate to accept the package as a whole without the individual contents being carefully scrutinised.

Figure 6: Plan of the excavated remains of Pompey's villa at Albanum.

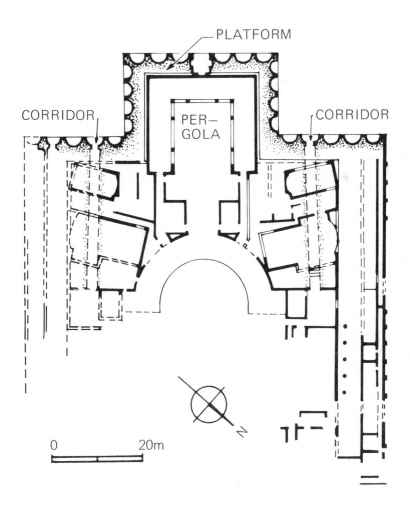

There was some justice in Lucullus' demands, for Pompey had so far dispensed with any senatorial advice, but the real purpose behind them was more sinister — to prolong discussion as long as possible and to delay final acceptance indefinitely.

Bound up with the fate of Pompey's proposals was the fate of every client king and prince in the East. No governor was bound to accept the arrangements until they had been ratified, and in theory any decision might suddenly be reversed with the approval of the Senate, though we have no evidence that any such action was threatened in 61 or 60.

More immediately serious was the reaction of 35,000 or 40,000 disbanded soldiers if their land allotments were not forthcoming. Their loyalty to their general was presumably not indestructible, and the large cash bonuses they had already been given would soon be spent.

Flavius introduced the agrarian bill in January. It provided for land allotments to veterans and needy citizens to be made from existing state land of various categories, and for more land to be purchased with the next five years' tribute from the new eastern provinces. Led by Metellus Celer and Cato the Senate rejected the proposals, partly through jealousy, partly because they suspected that Pompey was aiming at another powerful post on a land commission, partly through an inbred horror of any suggestion of redistribution of land. Flavius seems to have decided to do without senatorial approval, as on the *popularis* interpretation of the constitution a tribune was justified in doing, and prepared to take his bill to the people. Speeches against the bill continued, even from Cicero, who wanted considerable changes, and obstruction proved so successful that Flavius finally appealed to the tribune's ultimate weapon and had Metellus imprisoned. Nothing daunted, the consul made arrangements for a meeting of the Senate in prison. The situation was becoming farcical and Pompey eventually called Flavius off, not without difficulty. Metellus' resolute courage had won the day; the brinkmanship which had worked with Gabinius and Piso in 67 had failed.

The Optimates had used clever obstructionist tactics to which Afranius and Pompey were unable to find the answer. Indeed it is doubtful whether there was any answer short of violence. Yet that midsummer saw the return to Rome of Julius Caesar, flushed with success in a Spanish campaign and determined to win the consulship for the next year. Caesar was a candidate of quite different calibre from Piso or Afranius. There was no doubt about his political skill or energy or nerve. He was obviously the man Pompey was looking for.[25]

There has been much discussion about when the coalition between the two was formed, and who took the initiative. Most ancient sources date it to the time when Caesar was standing for election and give him the major role. But the negotiations were deliberately kept secret and there is no sure way of deciding. In any case it was an obvious move from both men's points of view, but as Crassus would naturally be supporting Caesar, Pompey may have been reluctant to approach him directly. Caesar, however, undertook the task of reconciling the two rivals, and the result was the coalition which has become known as the first triumvirate.

At the time of Caesar's return from Spain all three found their ambitions and requirements blocked by the solid wall of Optimate resistance. Pompey's situation has already been described. Crassus had taken a personal interest in the case of the *publicani* who were pressing for a re-pricing of the Asian tax contract, and stood to gain much if they were successful. Cato was working hard to deprive Caesar of a triumph for his victories, and Cato's son-in-law, M. Calpurnius Bibulus, was being run as a rival candidate by the Optimates and a large amount of money was changing hands. If Caesar won the consulship he could foresee bitter opposition to the legislation he had in mind and his attempt to win a great military command in Gaul.

By themselves Pompey and Crassus had so far failed. Together, with Caesar as a resolute consul, with Crassus' wealth and Pompey's veterans, and their combined following amongst *equites* and people, they could hope to outgun the Optimates.

It should also be remembered that, from Pompey's point of view, the coalition brought its dangers. The price that Caesar demanded for his help in passing the legislation that his colleagues required was their support in getting him a great military command similar to those which had brought Pompey to his position of power. In a sense Pompey was co-operating in the building up of a rival to his own supremacy, though at that stage no one could foresee Caesar's success in Gaul, and Pompey may well have thought that he could keep Caesar from getting too powerful. He may even have had ideas as early as this of using the threat of Caesar as a means of winning Optimate acceptance.[26]

The repercussions of the alliance, which Appian and Suetonius allege was sealed by an oath, were far greater than anyone could have envisaged at the time. In it were the seeds of the civil war which broke out ten years later. The next chapters will attempt to analyse Pompey's career during those years and trace the breakdown of his relationship with Caesar. But before that it is worth asking what Pompey hoped to gain from the triumvirate.

Essentially it was no more than the passing of his two pieces of legislation. There is no evidence that he now wanted to sponsor any new programme of reform. He was not a man with a Utopian view of an ideal society which he wanted to create. He accepted the basic framework of the Roman constitution, but was prepared to bring in changes in the way it worked as and when occasion demanded.

For example, foreign policy could, in his view, often best be implemented by long-term commands and large provinces, even though this meant putting great power into the hands of individuals. Provided that those individuals were responsible and efficient this was all right. His own successes against Sertorius, the pirates and Mithridates proved his point. As a soldier he took less interest in domestic politics and policies except where they affected him personally.

Government in the modern sense of the word, which needs a large bureaucracy, was almost non-existent. Even such things as the collection of taxes and tribute were in the hands of private enterprise, and the provision of public amenities depended very largely on the generosity and initiative of wealthy individuals. Where there was scope for decisive action by one man Pompey was ready to be active, but he had no taste for working within a ruling oligarchy. The reasons for this are probably very complex. There is no doubt that Pompey was proud, that he was ostentatious, rejoicing in flamboyant and even outlandish dress. He seems to have tried always to live up to the Homeric maxim 'continually to be best and to surpass all others'. Such an ambition was easier to fulfil on a *popularis* interpretation of the constitution than on an Optimate one.

There can also be no doubt that his experience in the East exaggerated some of these characteristics. Once he had acquired the taste for power and supremacy it is small wonder that he found it difficult to lay them down, and it was this position of supremacy that Pompey wanted to retain at Rome, to be, in the Roman expression, *princeps*, and to keep his *dignitas* and *auctoritas* without the constant struggle to secure magisterial office or pre-eminence in debate and at the bar which was the usual lot of the Roman noble.

This, then, would seem to have been his more long-term objective: to guide rather than help to govern the Roman state; to be there on call if crisis arose; and, almost like a Hellenistic monarch, to be acknowledged as the benefactor of his people.

Plate 1 The Asculum Inscription

Plate 2   Head of Pompey in the collection of Professor F.E. Brown

Plate 3   Head of Pompey in the Ny Carlsberg Glyptotek, Copenhagen

Plate 4   Model of Pompey's Theatre

6 THE COALITION WITH CAESAR: CORN COMMISSION AND SECOND CONSULSHIP 59–55

The purpose of the next two chapters is not to add another to the many existing accounts of the last decade of the free Republic, but to study the fortunes of Pompey's career during that period, his partial success in creating for himself a position of supremacy at Rome, and the dramatic and critical changes in his relations with Julius Caesar.

The political setbacks of 61 and 60 had finally convinced Pompey of the necessity of using open force or at least the threat of it in order to achieve his ends. In the first month of Caesar's consulship in 59 came the occasion. Caesar's agrarian bill, prepared the previous autumn, provided for the distribution of publicly-owned land in Italy to veterans and unemployed, and for the purchase of any further land that was needed at pre-59 valuation and without any compulsion on owners to sell. It was brought first before the Senate, and in spite of Caesar's care to avoid any threat to private property or to state finances (it was to be financed from the new revenue from Pompey's conquests), and his conciliatory tone towards the Optimates, it was not long before Cato's obstructive tactics began once more. After a futile attempt to silence Cato by the threat of imprisonment, Caesar abandoned his efforts to win the co-operation of the Senate and took his bill straight to the assembly.[1]

The pattern of future events was made clear at a public meeting held to explain and discuss the bill, when M. Bibulus, the other consul, declared that he would stop its passage even if the whole populace approved of it. Caesar then called upon Pompey to speak. He cleverly accused the Senate of petty jealousy and of inconsistency, for they had agreed in principle to the policy of land grants to veterans in 70, when one of the beneficiaries was Metellus Pius. But then there had not been enough money to implement the bill. Now there was a full treasury thanks to his victories, and it was right that the soldiers and the people should reap the benefits.

At Caesar's insistence the meeting called on Pompey to help the bill through the assembly, and Pompey ended his speech with the words, 'If anyone dares to raise a sword, I too will take up my shield.' It was astutely done. Any use of force could now be justified as being made in defence of the people's wishes.[2]

At the end of January the bill was ready to be put to the vote. Having failed to deter Caesar by the use of *obnuntiatio* and by declaring public holidays for all possible days on which the assembly could meet, Bibulus tried to interpose his veto at the actual vote. Pompey and Caesar were ready for the move. The place of assembly was full of armed veterans, specially summoned, and as soon as Bibulus started to speak he was forcibly removed. The *fasces*, his badge of office, were smashed, and a basket of manure was allegedly tipped over his head. Bibulus, two tribunes, and others of his supporters were wounded. The bill was subsequently passed.

February saw the ratification of the Eastern settlement. This was entrusted to Caesar's loyal tribune, the unscrupulous but capable Publius Vatinius. This time no violence seems to have been needed, but Vatinius must have put in a great deal of hard work, for, apart from getting general approval from the assembly for the statutes of the new provinces, he had to ratify separate treaties with numerous kings, princes and independent cities. We may suppose that Pompey's own staff was responsible for much of the paper-work involved.

One further loose end in the Middle East was also temporarily tidied up at this time, much to Pompey's advantage. The agents of king Ptolemy XII of Egypt arrived to try to win the Senate's recognition of their master on his throne. Persuasion was, of course, by bribery, and as the price for their support Pompey and Caesar squeezed out of the unfortunate monarch the promise of nearly 150 million sesterces. When it is remembered that this represented over 40 per cent of the total annual revenue of Rome from her overseas provinces one can get some idea of why Roman politicians were eager to get their fingers into the Egyptian pie.[3]

At long last Pompey had triumphed over his jealous and stubborn opponents, but he still had to fulfil his part of the contract and support Caesar in his next moves.

Cato and Bibulus had been temporarily neutralised by force. Lucullus, it seems, was silenced by threats, as many others must have been. But serious opposition could still be expected from the golden-tongued Cicero. True to his principles as a defender of the constitution, he had refused to join the three 'dynasts' at the end of the previous year, and, although he made no attempt to check the agrarian bill, he was a skilful creator of public opinion and a dangerous opponent. In March he delivered a bitter attack on the actions of Caesar in a speech for the defence of his old colleague C. Antonius, whose prosecution for treason and extortion in Macedonia was backed by the triumvirs.

The weapon used to silence Cicero was a subtle one. P. Clodius, the young noble whose trial for sacrilege had been one of the big political issues of 61, had a private vendetta with Cicero ever since he had broken his alibi at the trial. One of Clodius' aims was to pass a law exiling anyone who put to death Roman citizens uncondemned, and to prosecute Cicero under it. To do this he needed to win election to the tribunate, an office from which his patrician birth debarred him, and he had been trying since 60 to overcome this barrier by securing adoption into a plebeian family. Such adoption required a special enactment, and, apparently three hours after Cicero's speech for Antonius, Caesar as *Pontifex Maximus* and Pompey in his capacity as an augur had performed the necessary formalities. Henceforth the threat of prosecution lay heavy on Cicero, and it depended on Caesar and Pompey whether or not Clodius would be allowed to pass his law.[4]

This move was probably most distasteful to Pompey. Although Clodius was heavily indebted to Crassus, there was now little love lost between him and Pompey; and Cicero, for all his political differences, was a close personal friend.

In April we begin to learn from Cicero's letters of the growing unpopularity of the triumvirs, especially among the group of young senators and *equites*. Clodius, who was now a candidate for the coming tribunician elections, saw which way the wind was blowing and professed hostility to them as well. Pompey seems to have borne the brunt of the criticism, and we have a report of some of his replies to questions at public meetings:

Do you approve of Caesar's laws?

Yes.

What about their legality?

Caesar must take responsibility for that.

Yes, I approve of the agrarian law, but it is no business of mine whether a veto was possible or not.

Yes, I'm glad that the Egyptian king's position has been finally settled.

Was Bibulus watching for bad omens at the time?

It was not my business to enquire.

What is your view of the recent settlement in favour of the *publicani*?

I have been anxious to oblige that order.

What would have happened if Bibulus had come down to the Forum on that occasion?

I can't prophesy the answer to that one.

If Cicero's reporting is accurate, Pompey was clearly trying to shrug off any responsibility for illegality on to Caesar, and it seems that he was becoming increasingly embarrassed by the whole situation. He and his colleagues were being branded by their enemies as 'proud kings' aiming at a 'tyranny' — both well-worn political slogans designed to whip up emotions and blacken the character.[5]

It was at this point (the end of April) that three important events occurred. First, Caesar published a second agrarian bill to distribute the fertile public lands in Campania amongst veterans and poor citizens with families of at least three children. The bill was probably designed to speed up the process of resettlement by making enough land for 20,000 settlers immediately available, even if it did deprive the treasury of the rents from the land and spell ruin for some of the existing tenants. Secondly, Bibulus announced that he intended to postpone the elections for next year's magistrates (a move probably intended to hinder the triumvirs from rigging them in their own favour), and shortly afterwards retired to his house where he spent the rest of the year issuing a stream of edicts and propaganda pamphlets in an attempt to invalidate all legislation and heap every kind of abuse on his enemies. Thirdly, Caesar, in a determined effort to keep Pompey's support, offered him his daughter Julia in marriage.

Whether Pompey had been angling for this we have no means of knowing, but as things turned out it was a most successful match. Julia was probably thirty years younger than Pompey, but she was gay and talented and gave him the love and affection which must have helped him much at this critical time. By all accounts he was also deeply in love with her and devoted more time and attention to her than was usual for a Roman aristocrat.

Julia had in fact been betrothed to Q. Servilius Caepio, a legate of Pompey's from the days of the pirate war, and his natural disappointment at being robbed of this brilliant match was lessened by the offer of Pompey's own daughter Pompeia. Caepio seems, however, to have died shortly afterwards.[6]

For a time Pompey worked once more in close collaboration with his new father-in-law. On Vatinius' proposal Caesar was granted by the people a five-year command in Cisalpine Gaul and Illyricum, with the prospect of a campaign against the growing power of Burebistas, the king of Dacia, and at Pompey's instigation the Senate added the province of Transalpine Gaul, then threatened by an invasion from the Helvetii (modern Switzerland), and domination by the neighbouring German prince Ariovistus. It would be interesting to know whether Pompey had any suspicion that Caesar's new command would bring him wealth and victories to match his own. In any case it was the price he had agreed to pay.

On 13 May a warning note was sounded. Pompey received notice from Bibulus, of all people, that there was a plot against his life. Our sources are tantalisingly vague and ill-informed about this, and numerous interpretations were, and still are, put on the few indisputable facts which eventually came to light. The issue came to a head later in the summer when the consular C. Scribonius Curio informed Pompey that his son, who had distinguished himself as the vocal leader of opposition to the triumvirs, had been asked to join an assassination attempt by a notorious professional spy and informer, Lucius Vettius. Vettius was brought before the Senate, and after denying Curio's story got permission to turn state evidence. He then claimed that he was part of a plot organised by young Curio and several other junior senators and backed by a number of senior ones. The following day he was produced at a public meeting by Caesar and Vatinius and altered his story slightly, removing mention of Marcus Brutus and adding the names of several more leading Optimates, including a thinly disguised reference to Cicero. Before a full judicial enquiry could be set up Vettius was found strangled in prison.[7]

Cicero, not unnaturally in the circumstances, refused to believe in the existence of any plot and dismissed the whole episode as an attempt by Caesar to cast suspicion on young Curio. Most later historians have followed his cue, although opinions differ as to who put Vettius up to producing his accusations and what purpose was to be served by them. Nevertheless it remains possible that there really was a plot. We know that Pompey thanked Bibulus for his warning on 13 May. Presumably he did not merely leave it at that. It would be strange if he did not arrange a private investigation, and he had known Vettius ever since they had served together at Asculum in 89 (I). A well-tried way of finding out about a conspiracy is to join it, and that may have been Vettius' job. Curio's story sounds remarkably like an attempt to clear himself of suspicion once he realised that the plot had been rumbled, and it has often been wondered what Caesar could have stood to gain by murdering Vettius, as was rumoured at the time. If we look for Caesar's part in the episode it may be that he tried to capitalise on the situation by persuading Vettius to incriminate some of his more dangerous opponents at the second confession. This one, rather than the first set of disclosures in the Senate, is the one that Cicero said was obviously rigged. If Vettius had infiltrated into a conspiracy it is clear who benefited by his death.

So there is a strong possibility that Pompey scotched an assassination plot during the summer of 59. It is obvious from the few pieces of evidence that we have that the more hot-headed of the younger politicians were accusing the triumvirs of ambitions similar to those suspected of Caesar prior to the Ides of March 44. Then apparently respectable senators resorted to the dagger to preserve what they called 'liberty' from the hand of the 'tyrant', and the unscrupulous Marcus Brutus was at their head. It should not be forgotten that Pompey had been responsible for the death of Brutus' father at Mutina in 77, as well as for the deaths in the same year of the father and brother of another of the men who were implicated by Vettius, Aemilius Paullus.[8]

The existence of such a plot would explain another change of heart which is detectable from Cicero's correspondence during the summer. In June and July Pompey was largely occupied with his job as a member of the commission of twenty which was organising the redistribution and purchase of land under Caesar's laws, and with the task of founding a colony of Roman citizens at Capua. Such an appointment gave many opportunities for strengthening his patronage in an area which would in future provide a large number of voters and potential soldiers. While there he will have learnt of the growing hatred for himself and his partners at Rome and of the campaign which was fostering it, and we know of one letter from Caesar to Pompey at Capua which contained news of a hostile demonstration in the theatre during the games of Apollo in early July.[9]

For all his friendship, Cicero repeated to Atticus the accusations of 'tyranny' and voiced his fears that the tyrants would be forced to take violent reprisals. Part of the trouble was the way in which the triumvirs were trying to control the consular elections for 58 with the aid of lavish bribery. Their candidates were A. Gabinius, Pompey's tribune of 67 and a loyal friend and lieutenant ever since, and Lucius Calpurnius Piso, Caesar's father-in-law. Their co-operation would be essential if Caesar's position was not to be undermined during his absence in the North. It was characteristic of a 'tyranny' in political theory that it maintained itself by reserving the chief magistracies for itself and its supporters.[10]

About a week before the end of July Pompey was back in Rome, perhaps in expectation of the elections, only to find that Bibulus had fulfilled his threat and postponed them till 18 October. Cicero wrote a vivid account of Pompey's reaction to this edict and to the long campaign of hatred which preceded it.

So you can picture our friend. Unused to losing his reputation, always surrounded in the past by admiration and fame, he is now crippled in body and broken in spirit, and has no idea which way to turn. To carry on the way he is going would bring him to the edge of the precipice, to go back would brand him as a renegade, and he sees this. The *boni* are his enemies and their rascally opponents aren't his friends.

Look at my soft-heartedness: I couldn't control my tears when I saw him speaking at a public meeting on Bibulus' edicts on 25 July. In the past he used to play to the gallery so magnificently from that rostrum, before an adoring crowd, with everyone on his side. But this time he was so humiliated, so downcast, so dissatisfied with himself. The audience shared his opinion, but the only one who can have taken any pleasure from the sight was Crassus. Certainly no one else did. He has fallen from his rank among the stars, but it does look like an accident rather than his own fault . . .

Nobody thought that I ought to remain on friendly terms with him, because of that Clodius business, but my own affection for him was too great to be whittled away by some injury. Bibulus' Archilochian [scathing] edicts against him are so popular that you can't get past the place where they are posted for the crowd of people reading them, but they are such a bitter pill for him to swallow that he is visibly wasting away with unhappiness. I also find them unpleasant, because they cause too much pain to someone I have always been fond of, and I am afraid that he may lose all self-restraint and give in to his resentment and anger. He is an impetuous man and a fierce fighter, and he is not used to such insults.[11]

The most galling thing to Pompey must have been the loss of dignity and prestige that he was experiencing, due largely, as he must have realised, to the support he was giving to Caesar's measures. As the most prominent public figure of the three he was naturally regarded by many as their leader. If Cicero's diagnosis is correct many of the supporters of Crassus and Caesar (the *improbi* or rascally opponents of the *boni*) were turning hostile to him, and it is clear that neither Crassus nor

Clodius was prepared to do anything to help him.

In this predicament Pompey turned to the one leading politician whose friendship he always seems to have been able to win when he wanted it — Cicero. (It should not be thought that his other numerous personal friends, Varro, Lucceius, Theophanes, Afranius, Gabinius and the rest, deserted him, but their political influence among the *nobiles* was slight.) A matter of weeks after the disastrous public meeting Cicero wrote to Atticus again: 'The first thing that I want you to know is that our friend Samsiceramus is desperately unhappy about his situation and is most anxious to be restored to the position he held before his fall. He shares his distress with me and sometimes openly looks to me for a remedy, but I don't think any can be found.' The coalition, in Cicero's view, was beginning to crack up. It is usually thought that the remedy Pompey had in mind was a break with Caesar and a *rapprochement* with the Optimates, and that he hoped to use Cicero as a go-between.[12]

Shortly afterwards, however, the news of Vettius' 'conspiracy' broke, and it was clear to Pompey that there was no chance of doing a deal with the Optimates at this juncture. There was nothing for it but to ride the storm. For the rest of the year we hear little of him except that he added his weight to an appeal by Lucius Flavius to Quintus Cicero in Asia to grant some favour to his agents there. Such were the constant demands made on the patronage of the great.[13]

In October Piso and Gabinius won election to the consulship, as did Flavius to the praetorship. One incident suggests that the triumvirs resorted once again to strong-arm tactics to silence the opposition; Gaius Cato tried to initiate a prosecution against Gabinius for bribery, and, when faced by obstruction from the praetors, got up at a public meeting and called Pompey an 'unofficial dictator'. Cicero records that he was lucky to escape with his life.[14]

The expert at this time in the organisation of gangs and the use of rioting and violence to control assemblies was Publius Clodius. During his tribunate (58) and the years following he fully exploited the possibilities of mob control, first to pass a large body of reforming legislation, and then to establish himself as one of the most powerful politicians at Rome. He has often been thought of as the tool of the triumvirs left behind by Caesar to protect his interests, but recent studies suggest that he was an independent politician seeking power in his own right. The debts he owed to Crassus and Caesar were no guarantee that he was prepared to take their orders.[15]

Two of his measures are significant for this study. He made a strong bid for popular support by passing a law providing for the free distribution of corn to all citizens, and he made the organisation of gangs of thugs and gladiators easier by legalising the formation of *collegia* or political clubs, which had been banned six years earlier by decree of the Senate.

Certain of his control of the assembly, Clodius proceeded to remove two of his most dangerous rivals from Rome. He passed his law exiling anyone who had put Roman citizens to death uncondemned, and Cicero left for Macedonia. Pompey made no attempt to save him, in spite of appeals from Cicero and some of his influential friends. Cicero paid the penalty for his refusal to lend his support to the triumvirs the previous year. Whatever Pompey's private thoughts were on the matter, he felt that it was more important to humour Caesar, and Caesar was adamant that no one should be allowed to endanger the legislation of his consulate. Attacks had already been made on it, especially by two of the praetors of 58, C. Memmius and L. Domitius Ahenobarbus, and Cicero could certainly not be trusted to keep his mouth shut. Pompey's personal embarrassment can be seen from an anecdote in Plutarch. When Cicero came to visit him at his Alban palace, Pompey slipped out by another door in order to avoid the interview.[16]

Clodius' next rival to depart was Marcus Cato. He was forced to accept a commission to annex the island of Cyprus to the Empire, and was thus removed from Rome for a time. Pompey will have felt no dismay at that. But it is doubtful whether he was prepared for the savage campaign that Clodius next launched against himself. This took several forms. Personal abuse was combined with the prosecution of several of his friends and one particularly infuriating challenge to his prestige. This was Clodius' rescue of Prince Tigranes, who had been kept imprisoned at Rome ever since Pompey's return from Asia. He was held at the house of Pompey's friend, the praetor L. Flavius, and Clodius persuaded Flavius over dinner one night to have Tigranes sent across to his house so that he could have a look at him. Having thus got hold of Tigranes, Clodius refused to return him to custody, but put him on board ship, presumably for the East. Tigranes was blown back to Antium by a storm. Two parties set out from Rome to meet him. Clodius' reached him first but met the other, led by Flavius, about seven kilometres from the city, and a fierce battle ensued in which Clodius' mobsters had the better of it. Dio records that the consul Gabinius also intervened on Pompey's behalf but fared no better than Flavius. The government could raise no force to match the private army of Clodius. The need for a police force at Rome could hardly have been more forcibly demonstrated.[17]

The series of attacks on Pompey came to a head in August. When he attended a Senate meeting on 11 August there was an outbreak of violence in the Forum and one of Clodius' slaves was arrested in possession of a dagger. On interrogation by Gabinius he admitted that he was under instructions to assassinate Pompey. Once again we have no means of telling whether this was a genuine murder attempt. Pompey, however, was taking no chances and returned home, probably to one of his town houses. Here he was immediately besieged by a gang led by Damio, a freedman of Clodius. Flavius came to his rescue by trying to remove Damio, but the latter appealed to the college of tribunes for support. Unfortunately Asconius, who gives us the fullest report of this episode, does not reveal the outcome of the appeal, but according to Plutarch Pompey withdrew from public life entirely for the rest of the year.[18]

With the exception of his two allies Flavius and Gabinius, Pompey seems to have had little support from the Senate at this time. On the contrary, many senators were openly delighted at his discomfiture. He turned to his lesser friends for advice. One line of action proposed by the tribune Terentius Culleo he rejected. This was to break with Caesar completely and join forces with the Optimates. Quite apart from the fact that this would mean divorcing his beloved Julia, Pompey realised that there was no chance of his being reconciled with the Catonian group. His decision was to work for the recall of Cicero.

As always his motives were obscure, and probably mixed. It is tempting to conclude that because certain things happened as a result of Cicero's recall they were what Pompey intended to achieve by it. This is not necessarily so. Probably he felt that Cicero had learnt his lesson and would have less scruple in working in harness with him in future. Their common hatred and, be it said, fear of Clodius would be a strong tie, and although Cicero had little love left for the Catonians, who he felt had betrayed him, he still had much influence with the moderate Optimates.

Cicero and Atticus had been writing to Pompey and Varro regularly during the summer of 58 in the hope of getting things moving towards a recall. Pompey's replies had been vague, suggesting the possibility of action after the elections, but by September he began to work actively in Cicero's interests. This is not the place to catalogue all the moves and counter-moves which eventually led to Cicero's triumphant return in August 57. It was not easy to break Clodius' determined resistance, but Cicero's friends succeeded. Most of the tribunes of 57 were co-operative, and two, T. Annius Milo and P. Sestius, had considerable success in raising gangs of their own to counteract Clodius' continued use of violence. One of the new consuls, P. Lentulus Spinther, was a close friend of both Cicero and Pompey, and worked hard to achieve senatorial solidarity. Pompey finally persuaded Caesar to agree to the recall, and was tireless in his efforts in conjunction with Quintus to rally support for Cicero in Rome and in the towns of Italy, many of which he visited in person. He saw how important it was for an overwhelming majority in the assembly to sanction the recall and administer a sound slap in the face to Clodius.[19]

At this point it is worth asking what Pompey had been doing during the two years from his virtual retirement from politics in early autumn 59 to Cicero's arrival in Rome on 6 September 57. His only recorded political activity during that time is in connection with Cicero, and it seems unlikely that Pompey was content with the life of purely selfish extravagance to which several other leading *nobiles* (Lucullus, Catulus and Hortensius among them) retired at about this time.

Nor, like Cicero, did Pompey find recreation in writing. However, it has recently been argued that he was closely concerned with artistic activity, and that, encouraged and supported by the lively Julia, he became the centre of an important and productive literary circle. Such evidence as there is suggests that those writers who were indisputably connected with Pompey at this period fall into three main groups. There is a number of notable historians, L. Lucceius, Scribonius Libo, Theophanes, Voltacilius Pilutus and Terentius Varro being the most important, who included among their works the history of Pompey's exploits. Unfortunately none of their histories has survived. Another field of literary activity inspired by him seems to have been scholarly research into the writings of Pompey's great-uncle, the poet Lucilius. Varro himself, Lenaeus and Curtius Nicias of Cos, a gourmet and something of a hypochondriac, are all well attested as having combined friendship with Pompey with interest in Lucilius and the genre of satire which he initiated. It is suggested that Lucilius' papers may have passed into Pompey's possession. Curtius Nicias also provides a link with C. Memmius, nephew of Pompey's sister Pompeia and praetor in 58. He was a patron of the two greatest poets of the age, Lucretius and Catullus, as well as Nicias, and it may not be too fanciful to see Pompey and Julia providing support and encouragement to the 'New Wave' of poets which flourished in the gay, doomed period of the fifties.[20]

As the building of his new theatre also advanced, Pompey will have been concerned with the collection and commission of the paintings and statues with which he was decorating the covered walk attached to it. Pliny records the names of several Greek 'old masters' whose works were acquired, and there is evidence that Pompey patronised at least two contemporary Italian sculptors, Pasiteles and Coponius.[21]

Indeed the latter is thought to have been the sculptor of the fine Parian marble head of Pompey found at Rome (Plate 3). The description of it by Professor F.E. Brown may give some idea of the impression which Pompey created or wished to create among his circle of friends and admirers: 'The features . . . breathe a calm assuredness, a spirit of majestic and imperturbable benevolence. The eyes are wide and fearless, the mouth decisive and good-humoured. The only marks of age and greatness are the thoughtful corrugations of the brow and the firm wrinkles at the corners of the eyes and the edges of the cheeks.'[22]

The circle to which these writers and artists belonged has been briefly described by Professor Syme as 'a recognisable and raffish world – poets and scholars, gourmets, gamblers and musicians, financial experts and political agents'. It cannot be pure coincidence that so many members of it are known to have had close connections with Pompey, and it seems more than likely that, when rebuffed by the heads of aristocratic society at Rome, he chose to be the respected leader of the other society whose membership was largely of men of equestrian status or background like himself, of wealthy provincials and of talented and powerful freedmen.[23]

Caesar, too, had a following and friends from this large group (he probably succeeded Pompey as its leader), and it is important to note that it later provided the men who were the backbone of Augustus' new regime and the system of Empire which he devised. All three recognised its talents and its importance in a world where efficiency, energy and a breadth of outlook were beginning to replace in value the more traditional characteristics of the senatorial class.

It should be added at this point that our ignorance of Pompey's activities during 58 and the first half of 57 is largely due to Cicero's exile from Rome during that period. Cicero's letters are obsessed with his own problems during those months, and he seems to have taken little interest in anything not connected with them. On his return Pompey springs once more to the front of the political stage. As had happened so often before, it was a national crisis which provided the occasion.

For some months there had been an increasingly serious shortage of corn at Rome, with a corresponding rise in price. Our main authorities, Cicero and Plutarch, disagree as to the causes, but it would seem from the measures taken to rectify the situation that the trouble lay, as Cicero suggested, in the corn-producing provinces. For various reasons (inefficiency, desire to keep prices high, perhaps a poor harvest or two) those responsible for the shipping of corn to Rome were not getting their cargoes through. At Rome there was talk of famine; there had already been at least one serious food riot, and there were fears of more.

Pompey was the obvious choice to take control of the whole system of the shipping and distribution of corn. He had personal knowledge of the provinces and their problems, and had already successfully defeated one threat to Rome's supplies, that of the pirates. The position would give him renewed prestige and power, and a welcome success in his struggle with Clodius. Since his 'free corn' law of 58 Clodius had had control over the distribution to the populace and thus a considerable hold over public opinion. Here was a way in which Pompey could wrest this from him.

The post specially created for the occasion, that of Corn Commissioner or *curator annonae*, gave its holder complete control over corn supplies throughout the whole world for five years. He should have the rank of proconsul and the power to appoint fifteen legates to assist him in his task. Public opinion generally demanded that Pompey be given the post, and, following a proposal to that effect in the Senate by Cicero on 7 September (one day after his return), the consuls drafted a law which was passed by the assembly. Yet again Pompey had been called upon to save the state at a moment of crisis.[24]

Some problems, however, still remained. How far was the popular demand for Pompey spontaneous, or had it to some extent been engineered? Clodius, naturally, accused Pompey of creating the shortage, blaming the sudden influx of people to Rome to welcome Cicero for the rapid rise in price. It seems probable that news of Caesar's spectacular successes in Gaul had reawakened Pompey's ambitions and underlined for him the importance of a special command. His experiences during the last two years had demonstrated the difficulties of being a *princeps* at Rome while remaining a private citizen, but he also knew the dangers of staying too long away from the centre of affairs. The Corn Commission, with its opportunities for patronage and a display of his organising talents, and its five-year duration, was an admirable compromise.

Even so there were signs that what Pompey wanted was rather more than he was offered. A tribune, Gaius Messius, proposed that the command should include complete financial control, an army and a fleet, and superior authority (*maius imperium*) to that of the governors in all the provinces. This last provision would have removed the possibility of unpleasant clashes of authority such as Pompey had had with Metellus in Crete. Cicero reported that Messius' proposal, which introduced a revolutionary concept in *maius imperium*, was quite intolerable and that Pompey favoured the consuls' proposal. His friends, however, seemed convinced that Pompey really wanted the greater powers. Again doubt remains. Possibly Pompey did favour Messius' proposal but was unwilling to support it openly for fear of a rebuff; possibly the more extreme suggestion was merely put forward to be rejected, so that the still very considerable powers proposed by Cicero and the consuls might seem modest by contrast.[25]

The exact scope of the commission is not clear, but it seems from the brief reference in Plutarch that Pompey's task was to organise the whole chain of supply from sowing to final distribution so that it should not be at the mercy of greedy or incompetent middlemen. The provision of a reliable supply of corn had now become a priority of the highest order for the Roman government, owing to a steady increase in the city's population, and required a measure of state control. It thus fell to Pompey to initiate and devise a department of government which later became fully regularised under the Empire.[26]

Two of the assistant commissioners appointed by Pompey were Marcus and Quintus Cicero. Quintus, we know, was busy in Sardinia that winter, but Marcus' appointment seems to have been purely honorary, to mark his reconciliation with Pompey and as a token of gratitude for his proposal.

His vigorous activity on Cicero's behalf had gone some way towards strengthening support for Pompey among at least the more moderate senators. However, this new command resuscitated many old fears and jealousies, and in the months which followed his appointment it is possible to detect a very considerable hardening of the opposition to him. One notable feature of this opposition is the presence of certain *nobiles* who had supported Pompey during the sixties, among them such men as Lentulus Marcellinus, Metellus Celer, Metellus Nepos and Gellius Publicola. Renewed attacks came from his old enemies in the Catonian faction and from Clodius and Crassus, his two leading rivals in Rome for the control of popular support.[27]

It is in the light of this growing isolation that one should look at Pompey's activities during the last three months of 57 and the first half of 56. Cicero's help, valuable though it was, was not sufficient. If he was to maintain or even enhance the dominant position at Rome at which he aimed, Pompey began to realise that he needed the continued and active support of Caesar. He had learnt, however, from the events of 59 that Caesar was likely to demand a high price, and, probably remembering the bitter humiliations he had suffered as a result, Pompey decided that this time he would allow the pressure to build up on Caesar and place himself in a position where he could demand Caesar's assistance, not ask for it. The methods he used show that he had lost none of the cunning of his earlier career and had not taken long to adjust himself to the new political situation.

During November and at least the first half of December 57, Pompey was mainly concerned with his new task as Corn Commissioner. He personally visited the main corn-producing provinces of Sicily, Sardinia and Africa, and according to Plutarch he succeeded in 'filling the markets with corn and the sea with ships', with the result that he even produced a surplus which was used to relieve hardship in places outside Italy.[28]

At Rome he seems to have secured the services of several of the tribunes-elect for 56, and shortly after entering office on 10 December one of these, P. Rutilius Lupus, opened the campaign to put pressure on Caesar by raising in the Senate the question of Caesar's Campanian land law of 59. There was no debate, but clearly moves might be expected later in the year to repeal or amend the law, and by implication to attack the whole of Caesar's legislation. Apparently Lupus' speech included some complaints about the absent Pompey, so his name was not yet linked with the attack on Caesar.[29]

But before Pompey's return another issue had arisen in which he was to become very much involved. King Ptolemy of Egypt, whose recognition by Rome had cost him 36,000,000 denarii in 59, had had to impose heavy taxes on his subjects in order to pay his debts. The resentment caused by these taxes had been increased by his failure to prevent Rome's annexation of the kingdom of Cyprus, violent rioting had broken out in Alexandria, and Ptolemy had been forced to flee to Rome. There many of the king's creditors stood to lose large amounts of money if he did not get restored to his kingdom, and Ptolemy himself needed further loans to enable him to secure his return. At a meeting with a syndicate of bankers at Pompey's Alban palace these loans were negotiated and contracts signed. The Senate was prepared to listen to Ptolemy's pleas for help, and instructed Lentulus Spinther, now governor of Cilicia, to see to it that the king should recover his throne.[30]

This decision, however, was followed by the arrival in Italy of a deputation of 100 envoys from Alexandria, led by an Academic philosopher named Dio, with instructions to present the other side of the case, and the whole affair suddenly ballooned into a major political issue. Ptolemy took violent action to silence his opponents. Some he had murdered before they even reached Rome; others he tried to threaten or bribe into silence. At the instigation of M. Favonius the Senate ordered an official enquiry, but Ptolemy even managed to prevent this from taking place and secured the assassination of Dio into the bargain. Following the advice of an earlier African leader, Jugurtha of Numidia, who had discovered more than half a century before that at Rome everything could be bought for money, Ptolemy openly offered enormous rewards to the man who would effect his restoration.

It was a tempting prize, and by the time the Senate came to debate the question on 12 January 57 the various factions were already jockeying for position. Two names were openly canvassed, those of Spinther and Pompey, and Ptolemy was known to favour Pompey, at whose house he was being entertained while in Rome. For some reason a group of the king's creditors was by now strongly opposed to Spinther. It has been suggested that, following the Senate's granting him the commission, a second syndicate, with connections with Spinther, had raised a further loan for the king, and that the first syndicate suspected that Spinther would be primarily concerned to secure repayment for his own associates. Pompey, on the other hand, would have the interests of the first group at heart. The bulk of senior senatorial opinion favoured a commission of three, to be drawn from those who did not hold *imperium* at the time. Thus Pompey was to be excluded. Crassus, for reasons best known to himself, preferred not to limit the choice of commissioners in any way, and there was a body of opinion that the king should not be restored at all.

The issue was further complicated by the publication by C. Cato of some verses from the Sibylline books which proclaimed: 'If the king of Egypt comes requesting help, do not refuse his friendship, but do not go to his aid with any force; else you will have troubles and dangers.' This would appear to have precluded the possibility of a military command, and according to Cicero the Senate was unwilling to risk the unpopularity which would have arisen from the disregarding of such an oracle.[31]

As usual Pompey was reluctant to reveal his own feelings. In public, and in a private discussion with Cicero, he proclaimed support for his friend Spinther, but his own friends and confidants, led by the consular L. Volcatius Tullus and the tribune L. Caninius Gallus, were agitating strongly for Pompey to be given the job, and most people believed that they were acting with his full approval. Probably this is the correct interpretation. The commission would have given Pompey yet another chance to increase his prestige and wealth and to build up his *clientela* in Egypt as well as ensuring the full payment of his share of the king's bribe. On a less selfish level, the imposing of some sort of stability in Egypt might have led to a development of the corn trade with a country which was later to be the chief granary of the Roman Empire, and would have presented Pompey with the chance to complete the organisation of Roman control in the East.

The possibility nevertheless remains that Pompey was content to exercise his authority in Egypt through one of his own supporters, whether Spinther, or, as actually happened, Gabinius, who was then governor of Syria and busily employed in completing the pacification and organisation of that province. Pompey's followers in Rome may have been influenced more by Ptolemy's gold than their leader's wishes.

In fact, however, the Senate never came to a decision. The opponents of both Spinther and Pompey succeeded in prolonging the debate until the evening of 15 January, and further action had then to be delayed until the senatorial timetable permitted, at least until the end of February. Ptolemy eventually withdrew in despair to Ephesus, where he sought asylum at the temple of Artemis, and Pompey was left in no doubt as to the strength of the opposition to any plans he might have or devise in the future to secure a military command. In September 57 Messius' proposal to give him troops had been decisively rejected, and the recent publications of the Sibylline oracle had clearly been a move by the Optimates with the same purpose.

February 56 brought two important political trials. On 2 February, Publius Clodius began his impeachment before the popular assembly of T. Annius Milo, the tribune who had defended Pompey and Cicero from his attacks in 57. The charge, ironically, was one of illegal violence. Pompey was present as one of the counsellors for the defence. After preliminary speeches the hearing was adjourned to 7 February. The subsequent course of events was vividly described by Cicero in a letter to his brother.

On February 7th Milo appeared in the dock. Pompey spoke, or at least tried to; as soon as he got to his feet, Clodius' gangs started to shout at him, and this went on throughout his whole speech. It wasn't only heckling, but abuse and insults as well that he had to contend with. When he finished his peroration — for he was pretty brave in the circumstances, and wasn't put off. He said all he had to say, sometimes actually in silence, and completed his speech with authority — when he'd finished, up got Clodius. He was greeted with such a roar from our side — we'd decided to repay the compliment — that he lost complete control of his thoughts, his tongue, and his expression. Pompey had barely finished speaking at mid-day, and this barracking went on till 2 o'clock, with insults of all kinds and finally the filthiest of verses being chanted against Clodius and Clodia. Clodius was quite white with rage, and shouting above the uproar he asked his followers, 'Who is starving the people to death?' The gangs shouted back, 'Pompey.' 'Who is eager to go to Alexandria?' 'Pompey.' 'Who do you want to go?' 'Crassus.' Crassus was actually present, but not to help Milo. At about 3, as if at a given signal, the Clodians began to spit at our supporters. Tempers really flared up. They came over to try to push us out of the way. Our fellows charged them — rout of the gangsters. Clodius was thrown off the rostra, and we also took our leave then, to avoid any nasty incidents in the crowd.

The Senate was summoned to the House. Pompey went home. I didn't go to the Senate either. I didn't want to have to hold my tongue on such an important matter, and I didn't want to offend the *boni* by defending Pompey; for he was being criticised by Bibulus, Curio, Favonius and young Servilius. Anyway the debate was postponed to the next day, and Clodius adjourned the trial till the 17th. On the 8th the Senate met at the temple of Apollo, so that Pompey could attend. He treated the whole affair very seriously. No decision was reached that day. On the 9th, also in the temple of Apollo, a decree was passed that 'the events of February 7th had been contrary to the interests of the State'.

On the same day Cato violently attacked Pompey, and during his whole speech levelled accusations at him as though he were on trial. He also, to my great embarrassment, made many very complimentary remarks about me. He charged Pompey with treachery towards me, and our enemies listened to him in total silence. Pompey made a courageous reply, and passed some dark hints about Crassus, openly saying that he would take better care to guard his life than Africanus had done against C. Carbo who murdered him. It looks to me as if there are going to be serious repercussions. Pompey realises that there is a plot against his life; C. Cato is being backed by Crassus, funds are being provided for Clodius, and both are being supported by Curio and Bibulus and Pompey's other opponents. He has told me as much, and also that he is going to take careful precautions not to be beaten by that rabble-rouser. He has almost lost the support of the people; the nobility hate him; the Senate won't give him its support, and the younger generation of politicians is behaving disgracefully. So Pompey is making his own preparations and summoning men from the country. Clodius is also strengthening his gangs. Things are being got ready for a confrontation on the 17th. For that purpose we are far the stronger, thanks to Pompey's forces, and a large band is expected from Picenum and Gaul, so we can also oppose Cato's bills about Milo and Lentulus.[32]

The situation is reminiscent of that in 59, even to the extent that Pompey believed that he was once again the object of an assassination plot. Now, however, he was in a position to take more positive action. He summoned a large personal bodyguard and continued to let the pressure on Caesar grow.[33]

On 10 February the prosecution of Publius Sestius for riot during the previous year began. Like many another political trial this was one in which a powerful figure was being attacked through his subordinates. Failure on Sestius' part would lessen the *dignitas* and *auctoritas* of his patron, whose obligation it was to work for Sestius' defence. Pompey appeared in court to give formal evidence on Sestius' behalf, and he was present to hear Cicero's speech for the defence. This included a virulent attack on Vatinius, one of the prosecution witnesses, and on his work as Caesar's tribune in 59. In the full knowledge that a report of the proceedings would soon be on its way to Caesar, Pompey was quite content for his support of Cicero and acquiescence in the attack to be widely noticed.

Cicero himself was encouraged in the line he took against Vatinius, if not by Pompey personally, at least by the belief, which he shared with many others, that the members of the 'triumvirate' had now parted company for good. The bad blood between Crassus and Pompey was obvious, even if, as some historians have suggested, Crassus was cunningly fostering the ill-feeling in order to emphasise Pompey's isolation and thus prevent the *boni* from attempting to bid for his support against Caesar.[34]

Sestius was acquitted, as was Milo, but a further indirect attack on Pompey was not long delayed. On 3 April Marcus Caelius Rufus was brought to trial on a number of charges, among them the murder of

Dio, the leader of the Alexandrian deputation earlier in the year. Behind the prosecution was Clodia, Clodius' infamous sister and till recently Caelius' mistress. As we have seen, the part played by Pompey in all the dirty work that had gone on behind the scenes during Ptolemy's stay in Rome is obscure to say the least. People had their suspicions, however, and success in pinning responsibility for Dio's death on one of Pompey's younger associates would have left plenty of mud sticking to Pompey's reputation. Cicero and, interestingly enough, Crassus spoke in Caelius' defence, and he too was acquitted. In fact Crassus' behaviour should be a warning against accepting over-simplified accounts of the bewilderingly complicated patterns of friendships and hostilities in Roman politics. Politicians must have been influenced by a whole multitude of personal factors of which we have no inkling, as well as by their published attitudes to the great issues of the day.[35]

In spite of Caelius' acquittal, Pompey's own popularity seems to have continued at a low ebb, particularly in some quarters. In March Cicero wrote to his brother that the Egyptian issue was dead, that Pompey was being criticised for his opposition to Spinther, and that the lowest elements of the *plebs* objected to his support of Milo, and that the *boni* found fault with everything to do with him. This hostility was apparently reflected in the result of another political trial, that of one of Clodius' chief supporters, Sextus Cloelius. The solid opposition of the senators on the jury towards the prosecutor Milo (and therefore towards Pompey) managed to swing the votes of the whole jury in favour of an acquittal.

By April, however, Pompey had other problems on his mind, in particular the problems of the corn supply. More money was required, and on 5 April he managed to get a decree of the Senate passed allowing him to draw on the treasury for up to 40,000,000 sesterces. The debate was heated, for money was short and the price of corn was still too high. With this financial backing Pompey made prepara-tions to visit the provinces of Sardinia and Africa once again, leaving Rome on 11 April. But before he took ship at Pisa events had taken a dramatic turn. Caesar had been stung into action. According to Cicero the decisive point came during the senatorial debate on 5 April follow-ing the grant of funds to Pompey. Cicero himself had raised the question of the Campanian land allotments and suggested that a full debate be held on the subject on 15 May. The suggestion was accepted.

To many it seems to have appeared that this constituted an open and dangerous attack on Caesar's position. In addition there was now the threat from Lucius Domitius Ahenobarbus, Marcus Cato's enormously wealthy and influential brother-in-law, who was a candidate for the consulship of 55. Following his unsuccessful attempts to remove Caesar from his command in 58, he was now promising to have legislation passed to recall him in 55.[36]

Shortly after the debate on 5 April Crassus travelled north to confer with Caesar at Ravenna. What passed between them we shall never know for certain, but it seems likely that they agreed to try to win the active co-operation of Pompey once more. Quickly crossing northern Italy to the west coast they reached Luca, not far from Pisa, before Pompey left for Sardinia and invited him to meet them.[37]

In addition to his two former colleagues some 200 other senators are reported to have made the journey to Luca to see Caesar, no doubt with favours to ask and reports to submit on the state of Caesar's fortunes at Rome. However, the talks which have become known as the Conference of Luca were held in private between Caesar, Pompey and Crassus, and must have included some hard bargaining on all sides.

It seems that in many ways Pompey held the strongest cards. Caesar's need of his support was greater than his of Caesar's, but, on the other hand, Pompey was hardly likely to have precipitated an open split between them, especially as his own position at Rome was far from satisfactory, and there was still a strong bond between them in the person of Julia.

We should beware of assuming that what happened after Luca was necessarily planned there in detail. It is perhaps more likely that in return for guarantees of their support Caesar agreed to use his money, his influence and if necessary his troops to help Pompey and Crassus obtain the commands they wanted. As things turned out it was Pompey who emerged in the strongest position, and it is unlikely, to say the least, that this was accidental. The result of his apparent lack of concern for Caesar's interests since the beginning of the year was that Caesar (and Crassus) was prepared to pay a high price for his co-operation.

The man to suffer most was Cicero. There can be no doubt that in a sense Pompey had deliberately deceived him by letting him think that he approved of his attacks on Caesar. But it is possible that Caesar reacted more quickly and positively than Pompey expected. When Cicero visited Pompey on the evening of 7 April he was given no hint that Pompey was preparing for anything other than his voyage to Sardinia. Even allowing for Pompey's known preference for revealing no more of his plans than he had to, it may well be that he did not anticipate an approach from Caesar before his return. In fact when he did return he made it quite clear to Cicero that attacks on Caesar must stop, and that he would be well advised to use his talents on behalf of the now reconciled 'triumvirs'.[38]

There remains the problem of Pompey's real feelings towards Caesar at this time. Cassius Dio maintained that jealousy and resentment at Caesar's success caused Pompey to try to prevent Caesar's victory despatches from Gaul being read out by the consuls, and finally to ally himself with Crassus to force Caesar's hand. There is no hint in any of Cicero's letters of collusion between Crassus and Pompey prior to Luca, and Dio may be mistaken in ascribing to Pompey in 56 feelings which he certainly had five years later. To believe that in 56 Pompey was consciously planning to destroy Caesar eventually is to believe in a detailed long-term policy such as politicians can rarely, if ever, afford. In 56 Pompey was much more concerned with building up his own power once more than with cutting his potential rival down to size.[39]

When he returned from his tour of the corn provinces Pompey had to set his mind to taking control of the situation in Rome. Moves were already being made in the Senate to recall Caesar from Gaul by allocating his provinces to one of the consuls of the next year. These moves were checked by a speech from Cicero ('On the Consular Provinces') in which he lavishly praised Caesar's achievements and took the opportunity to press for the recall of two of his own enemies, L. Calpurnius Piso from Macedonia and A. Gabinius from Syria. Earlier Cicero had also been instrumental in getting the Senate to vote a thanksgiving for Caesar's victories and the grant of money to pay his troops.

Just when Pompey and Crassus made their decision to take the consulships of 55 for themselves remains in doubt. According to Dio they entered their nominations too late and the consul Lentulus Marcellinus refused to overlook the irregularity. This, and Dio's remark that they had earlier backed other candidates, suggests that the decision was taken after the talks at Luca, when it became clear that only they had any chance of defeating Domitius Ahenobarbus at the elections. The opposition of the determined and influential Marcellinus forced Pompey and Crassus to prevent any elections being held until the next year, when Marcellinus would be out of office and Caesar could spare some troops to give them armed support. With no doubt a handsome bribe they secured the services of C. Cato, one of the tribunes of the year, and his obstructive tactics had the required effect.[40]

The resistance of the opposition was strengthened by the return of Marcus Cato from Cyprus. It was he who persuaded Domitius to persevere with his candidature after the 'triumvirs' ' intentions became known. At one stage the Senate voted to put on mourning, a sign that they felt that the provocation against them was sufficient to justify the use of force, but they could not match the strength of their rivals' armed supporters and the gangs of Clodius. He, somewhat surprisingly, had also been prevailed upon, probably by pressure from Caesar and Crassus, to sink his differences with Pompey.

With the creation of an *interrex* to replace the consuls on 1 January 55 came Pompey's and Crassus' chances of election. Their names were accepted for nomination and they were duly elected, but not until they had used force to prevent Domitius and Cato from reaching the assembly, killing the attendant who was lighting their way through the dark streets on the eve of the elections.

Force, bribery and the flagrant abuse by Pompey of his position as augur were also needed to ensure that supporters of the new regime were elected to the other magistracies, and in particular to prevent Marcus Cato from becoming praetor. At the elections of the *aediles* the rioting was so violent that Pompey himself was spattered with blood. The shock of seeing his clothes brought into the house by a slave caused Julia to faint, and may have contributed to her subsequent miscarriage.

In the absence of any significant reforms it is probable that the main object of the two new consuls was to prevent their opponents from dominating the consulship for long enough to secure the necessary legislation to give themselves and Caesar important military commands for the next few years. The provinces they chose for themselves were the two Spains and Syria. The tribes of north-central Spain (an area largely untouched by Pompey in the Sertorian war) had risen in revolt under the leadership of the Vaccaei and had inflicted a defeat on the governor Metellus Nepos at Clunia. The uprising had subsided following Roman victories elsewhere, but the situation remained explosive. The danger to the rest of Spain justified the creation of a five-year command with four legions, and this was given to Pompey as the result of a law introduced by one of his tribunes, Gaius Trebonius. A pretext was also devised whereby Crassus was, as a result of the same law, given command of an expedition against Parthia, with the prospect of great wealth and glory at the end of it.[41]

In an enigmatic letter written from Naples on 27 April Cicero told Atticus that he had recently discussed the political situation with

Pompey, who had been staying at his country villa at Cumae. Pompey was apparently displeased with himself — possibly a reference to his having had to use force earlier in the year — but enthusiastic about the prospect of governing Spain. The fact that he seems to have played down the value of Syria suggests that the actual allocation had not yet been made and that the possibility of Pompey's going to Syria was being openly discussed.[42]

Stern opposition was offered to Trebonius' proposals, led by M. Cato and M. Favonius with help from two tribunes, C. Ateius Capito and P. Aquillius Gallus. In the face of superior force and the resolution of Trebonius it was of no avail.

The two consuls next honoured Caesar themselves by proposing a law extending his Gallic command for a further five years. Dio suggests that this measure was more or less forced on them by Caesar's supporters, but it is more likely that it had been agreed upon at Luca.[43]

The situation was thus a fascinating one for the historian. The military forces of the Republic were shared between three men for the next five years. With those forces went patronage, wealth, and the ability if necessary to impose their will upon the Senate and people. The danger to the peace of the Roman world should any of these three try to impose his will on the others is, and was, obvious.

For the moment, though, it looked as if the three were working in harmony. Cicero's letters in 55 suggest that Pompey and Crassus were on amicable enough terms, and Pompey actually succeeded in reconciling Cicero with Crassus for a short while before the latter's departure for Parthia. But if one compares the respective positions of the three, Pompey appears to have the advantage. While Caesar and Crassus looked like spending most of the next five years away from Rome, Pompey, claiming that his job as Corn Commissioner demanded his presence at or near Rome, took the unprecedented step of governing his province through legates. L. Afranius and M. Petreius, both loyal and experienced commanders, were sent out to Spain to take over command of the legions and deal with disturbances. The new levies which Pompey had been empowered to make, but which were bitterly resented by many people, remained in training in Italy.

The twelfth of August 55 saw the dedication of Pompey's new stone theatre in the Campus Martius. Containing seats for an estimated 10,000 spectators it had a temple of Venus (Pompey's patron goddess) constructed at the back of the *cavea* or auditorium in such a way that the tiers of seats formed the steps leading up to the front of the temple. Attached to the south-east side of the theatre was a great *porticus* or rectangular garden, some 180 metres by 135 metres with covered colonnades running round the sides, which provided shelter for spectators in the event of rain and a very popular place of recreation for citizens at all times. The walls of the colonnades were decorated with paintings gathered from the art collections of the Roman world. Either in the *porticus* or in the theatre itself were displayed numerous statues, the arrangement of which was entrusted to Cicero's friend Pomponius Atticus. They included fourteen statues representing the nations which Pompey had conquered, and one of Pompey himself was placed in a large hall attached to the *porticus*, where meetings of the Senate could be held. This great theatre complex which was to remain for centuries as one of Rome's finest amenities was a worthy symbol of Pompey's new position of power. Pompey's own personal comfort was not neglected either, for Plutarch tells us that at the time he built his theatre Pompey also built himself a house in the same vicinity, 'like a dinghy behind a yacht', more splendid than his old one on the Carinae, but not extravagant enough to excite envy. It was presumably only when he was away from Rome at his Alban palace that he felt free to play the part of the great grandee.[44] (Figure 6)

The dedication was accompanied by the production of a number of plays, musical performances and athletic competitions in the theatre, and five days of wild beast hunts and similar spectacles in the neighbouring Circus. In a somewhat critical letter to console his friend Marcus Marius for having missed the celebrations Cicero found the dramatic productions too lavish and the slaughter of the animals unenlightening, and, in the case of fights between eighteen elephants and heavily-armed warriors on the last day, thoroughly distasteful.[45]

Pompey admitted to Cicero personally that there had been some waste of time and effort, but the effect on the majority of the population seems to have been favourable. The production of extravagant displays of this sort was a well-tried method of winning popularity and of reducing popular tension. We have no way of telling just how far the building of the theatre affected the chronic unemployment problem in Rome, but it must have led at least to some temporary improvement.

Nevertheless a stream of anti-Pompeian propaganda continued to flow from the pens of his enemies. Accusations that the three dynasts were establishing a tyranny were repeated, and his responsibility for the deaths of Carbo, Domitius, Lepidus and Brutus a quarter of a century or more earlier was once again flung in Pompey's face (IVA). Cicero, however, was, outwardly at least, more reconciled to the situation than he had been in 59. Even allowing for the fact that he had been made to realise that his and Quintus' political future depended on their whole-hearted support of the regime, some of his justifications for that support have a ring of sincerity. Writing in January 55 to Lentulus Spinther, now on better terms with Pompey, he placed the blame squarely on the shoulders of those senators who had alienated Pompey and the *equites* from the Senate. That a man should fight hard when his *dignitas* and *auctoritas* were threatened needed no justification to a Roman. But Pompey and Crassus were no Sullas. There were no purges of their enemies, no reign of terror, and, in spite of a jibe made by Cicero in a private letter to Atticus, no rigging of the elections for 54. After the violence at the beginning of 55 and during the passing of the legislation granting the 'triumvirs' their commands, the rest of the year passed comparatively quietly and Domitius Ahenobarbus and Appius Claudius Pulcher were duly elected consuls for 54. This may reflect the strength of the Optimate opposition, but it also shows that Pompey was prepared to leave the usual machinery of government unharmed.[46]

On the domestic front Pompey seems to have paid careful attention to Julia after her tragic miscarriage. Much of the second half of the year he spent with her visiting the pleasure resorts of Italy, though this tour may have combined recreation with the fostering of his *clientela* in the Italian towns and with the overseeing of the recruitment for his new legions.

He was also keeping his eye on his interests abroad. In April the news came through that Gabinius, the governor of Syria, had succeeded in restoring King Ptolemy on the Egyptian throne. This was done, so Dio records, on the instructions of Pompey, who thus overcame the opposition of his enemies, at the same time taking upon himself a foreign policy decision which should have been by tradition the prerogative of the Senate.[47]

Gabinius also went a long way towards completing the thorough pacification of the kingdom of Judaea which Pompey had begin in 64. After Pompey's departure Alexander, the son of Aristobulus, had raised the standard of revolt and seized a number of important strongholds. A Roman victory over the insurgents near Jerusalem was followed by the siege of Alexandreum and a temporary truce during which Gabinius reorganised the government of Judaea, setting up five regional councils and restricting Hyrcanus' responsibilities to those of High Priest. The escape of Aristobulus from Rome led to a renewal of the rebellion, but both Aristobulus and Alexander were eventually defeated in costly battles. According to Josephus, Gabinius also made preparations for an expedition against the Parthians, who had raided Roman or allied territory west of the Euphrates. Probably there was a military justification for the full-scale expedition of Crassus, although hostile critics charged him with sheer avarice as his motive. In fact Josephus sums up Gabinius' governorship as one in which 'he performed great and glorious deeds', and it should perhaps be seen as the completion of Pompey's Eastern Settlement by one of his most capable lieutenants.[48]

It was during his second consulship that Pompey for the first time came near to achieving his ambition to be the undisputed leader of the whole Roman world. Cicero had already publicly called him 'The foremost man of all who are or ever have been', 'Of all races, of all generations, of all history easily the foremost man', and 'In the judgement of all by far the foremost member of our State', and the word *princeps* (foremost) denotes a type of primacy acceptable, if not welcome, to the majority of Roman *nobiles*.[49]

Abroad he controlled the army in Spain through his legates, and had shown by his restoration of Ptolemy that he could control policy in other provinces, especially in the East, through his friends and clients. The Corn Commission, too, gave him a great measure of official influence in Sardinia, Sicily and Africa. At Rome his authority and dignity were maintained by ostentatious munificence towards the people and by his Corn Commission, in addition to his already towering reputation. As consul he could secure the passage of such legislation as he thought necessary (for instance a law which tried to curb the bribing of juries by requiring jurymen to be drawn from those in the wealthiest census category). After his term of office he could hope to use tribunes as before, but it seems possible that he was by now toying with the idea of securing some more permanent post for himself.

As yet, however, there were two important areas where Pompey's predominance was not secure. One was in the Senate, where both Catonians and Caesar still exercised considerable influence; the other was in Gaul, where it must by now have been quite clear that Caesar was building up a power base for himself that would come seriously to threaten his own.

7 POMPEY'S 'PRINCIPATE': THIRD CONSULSHIP AND THE RIFT WITH CAESAR   54–50

In a curious way events at Rome during the years 54 and 53 now conspired to raise Pompey to a position of supreme eminence in domestic politics such as even he had never before enjoyed. The same events, however, were correspondingly damaging to the system of the Republic, bringing many of its institutions into disrepute, and exaggerating and drawing into the open the element of violence which was implicit in the framework of Roman politics.[1]

With control of the legions, the important provinces, and foreign policy firmly in the hands of the 'triumvirs', lesser politicians, unless they were prepared to serve their interests, were forced to turn their own ambitions exclusively towards the civil magistracies, and the acquisition of wealth in the peaceful provinces. Competition was more fierce and ruthless than for many years, and with it came bribery on an almost unparalleled scale. The most glaring example was the great scandal of the consular elections for 53. Of the four candidates two, Cn. Domitius Calvinus and C. Memmius, came to an agreement with the consuls of 54 that in return for assistance at the elections they would secure the provinces that the outgoing consuls wanted on the expiry of their term of office by producing rigged evidence that the necessary formalities had been completed. The pact was apparently drawn up on paper and the candidates guaranteed to pay 400,000 sesterces each if they failed to fulfil their part. All candidates had, moreover, offered enormous bribes to whichever century of voters voted first at the elections. Money became so hard to raise that on 15 July the interest rate doubled, from 4 per cent to 8 per cent.[2]

Of all the candidates Pompey seems to have favoured his old quaestor and Mucia's new husband, M. Aemilius Scaurus, while Caesar's support was for Memmius. According to Cicero Pompey was infuriated by the discovery of the arrangement and finally persuaded Memmius to reveal the details in the Senate at the end of September. The elections had still not been held, owing to prosecution of all the candidates, senatorial debates on the problem, and the use by interested parties of *obnuntiatio* to keep them postponed.[3]

Pompey's motives in having the scandal made public remain obscure, as does the nature of his hold over Memmius, though this may have been due to the fact that Memmius was Pompey's sister's nephew. Many thought that he wanted to prevent the elections in order to create a crisis in which he could be elected dictator. As early as June, Cicero mentioned to his brother that there was 'a suspicion of a dictatorship', and in other letters written in the latter half of October and November he mentions a 'sniff' or a 'rumour' of dictatorship in the air. In the third of these letters we hear that Pompey's own cousin, the tribune Lucilius Hirrus, was preparing to make such a proposal, but that Pompey himself denied favouring it. Nevertheless, Cicero says, he was not believed.[4]

The point at issue is whether Pompey deliberately engineered a political crisis in order to be called upon to save the state as dictator. It was an easy accusation for men to level at him, but not so easy to substantiate. It is almost absurdly cynical to suggest that in persuading Memmius to break the 'ring' Pompey wanted simply to make the situation worse. No doubt he watched the discomfiture of the consul Domitius Ahenobarbus with some pleasure, but it would have been quite irresponsible of him to remain in possession of the facts and allow the arrangement to go through. It could be argued that only someone strong enough to resist the combined pressure of the four parties concerned would have dared to take such action. Cicero, who knew of the pact in July, was not such a one.

Beyond that there was little Pompey could have done by himself to improve matters. He was not a magistrate and his *imperium* only empowered him to act in Spain or in matters concerned with the corn supply, and in fact he was absent from Rome for some time during October organising fresh supplies to replace those which had been lost when the Tiber broke its banks and flooded much of the low-lying part of the city including some of the store houses.

Two other preoccupations must also have weighed heavily on his mind during that autumn. In August Julia died in childbirth, to be followed shortly afterwards by the daughter she had borne. Plutarch records that Pompey was greatly distressed by the death of the wife he had loved and with whom he had found real happiness, but historians tend to concentrate on the effect of Julia's death on the relationship between her father and her husband. By all accounts her influence had preserved a personal friendship which political rivalry had not overcome. Now, however, there was little except political expedience to keep them together.[5]

Pompey had plans to bury Julia in the grounds of his Alban palace, but these were thwarted by the Roman mob, which took matters into its own hands and, after a memorial ceremony in the Forum, carried Julia's body to the Campus Martius where it was given a public burial, in spite of protests from the consul and tribunes. This was presumably a demonstration of the affection with which Julia had been regarded by the people rather than of support for either Pompey or Caesar.

The second problem concerned Gabinius. On 19 September he returned to Rome from Syria to face a hostile reception and prosecution on at least three different charges: treason, extortion and bribery. Pompey saw the first of these charges as a thinly veiled attack on himself, for it was known that he had sanctioned, if not ordered, Gabinius' restoration of Ptolemy, and he took great pains to get Gabinius acquitted. Although, according to Dio, Pompey was away from the city organising the corn supply before the trial for treason, and got back too late to attend it in person, Cicero's letter to Atticus written shortly after the trial on 24 October states that it was Pompey's personal entreaties to the jury and the fear that he was likely to become dictator in the near future which secured Gabinius' acquittal by thirty-eight votes to thirty-two.[6]

At the second trial, for extortion, he was not so successful. Cicero was with difficulty persuaded to defend Gabinius, a letter from Caesar requesting acquittal was read in court, and Pompey himself gave lengthy evidence on his behalf. Nevertheless, the jury, responding to the public outcry which had followed the first trial and to the presence of the resolute M. Cato as praetor in charge of the court, this time found Gabinius guilty, and he retired into exile.

Rome seems to have been a sad and dangerous place to live in during these months. To the uncontrolled political bribery, the destructive floods and the shortage of corn already mentioned there was added a marked increase in the level of violence and gang warfare on the streets as government began to give way to anarchy. For example, in September the quaestor Faustus Sulla was attacked by the rivals of his half-brother Aemilius Scaurus and resorted to moving in public only with an armed bodyguard of 300 men. There certainly seems to have been some demand for a dictatorship, recorded in a passage in Appian, but Plutarch states that Lucilius Hirrus' proposal (late December 54 or early 53) was attacked by Cato and that many of Pompey's friends said that he had neither need nor desire for the post.[7]

Among leading politicians the name of dictator had an unsavoury ring about it, recalling the dark days of the Sullan proscriptions. Yet, curiously, it was the tribunes, men who had saddest memories of Sulla, who seem to have resorted to the proposal, while opposition to it came mainly from Optimate quarters. After the opening of the new year (53) without consuls, the tribunes in fact took over much of the control of affairs, but for reasons which are not recorded prevented successive *interreges* from holding consular elections. For the first half of the year Pompey was not at Rome. Unfortunately our sources are silent about where he was or what he was doing, and it is impossible to be sure whether he was engaged on his proconsular duties or replenishing the city's food supplies, or merely withdrawing from the forefront of politics. A letter of Cicero's, telling Atticus that he has been appointed one of Pompey's legates and will thus be away from Rome after 13 January 53 rather suggests that Pompey had official duties to perform, although Cicero in the event took no part in them.[8]

However, by midsummer he was back. Once more he was offered the dictatorship and refused it. He did, though, use his influence to get the consular elections held and, several months late, Domitius Calvinus and Valerius Messalla were elected. Again we are not told how Pompey succeeded in restoring some sort of order; unworthy motives are imputed to him. According to Plutarch he was shamed into it by Cato; Dio emphasises the belatedness of the action; Appian accuses him of deliberately overlooking the disorder. But these are all secondary sources, probably reflecting hostile propaganda, and from the contemporary Cicero we hear not a word.[9]

There can be little doubt that the Senate as a body should bear much of the blame for this sorry state of affairs, and in particular the leaders of the Senate. But they were too preoccupied with personal ambition and factional rivalry to exercise the necessary authority over magistrates and people. Pompey, it must be emphasised, was not a senatorial leader and here lay the root of the problem: the power to control law and order lay elsewhere than the authority to do so. It was a serious flaw in the Roman constitution that there was no police force in the city under the control of the civil magistrates. Individuals had to rely on their own resources for protection (in the case of the wealthy often armed bodyguards of slaves or gladiators) and the state looked to its armed forces — always a dangerous solution. Troops owed their allegiance first and foremost to their commanders and could never be trusted to stand aloof from factional politics.

The election of new consuls might have been expected to stabilise the situation. Instead attention merely shifted to the struggle for the magistracies of 52, and even worse violence developed as the gangs of supporters of the several candidates clashed in battles in the streets and murder became an almost daily occurrence. The consul Domitius Calvinus was wounded and consulars of the standing of Hortensius and Cicero narrowly escaped death.

Four candidates in particular were concerned: three rivals for the consulship, T. Annius Milo, P. Plautius Hypsaeus and Q. Metellus Scipio, and one of the praetorian candidates, P. Clodius Pulcher. Plautius and Scipio were running together against Milo, and Clodius, who still continued his bitter feud with Milo and realised that his own chances of achieving anything as praetor if Milo were consul were slight, was supporting them and apparently advising them on the tactics of their campaign.

In many ways Milo was a strong candidate. He had won popular favour through largesse and the promotion of extravagant games, and he enjoyed the support of most of the Optimates. Pompey, however, in spite of the help Milo had given him in 57 was lending his support to the other two. Plautius was an old quaestor of his from the days of the Mithridatic war, and Scipio was the father of the girl Pompey married as his fifth wife, probably late in 53. She was Cornelia, the widow of Publius Crassus, who with his father Marcus Crassus had been killed during the disastrous Roman defeat at the hands of the Parthians at Carrhae in June. Young and beautiful, Cornelia also displayed talents for literature, music and geometry, and an intelligent interest in philosophy, and combined with these accomplishments, freedom from what Plutarch called the usual 'objectionable officiousness' of the bluestocking.[10]

Cornelia was thus eminently suitable to take the place of the unfortunate Julia, but her marriage also seems to mark a significant point in Pompey's relationship with Julia's father. Although Caesar had tried to renew the alliance by offering Pompey the hand of his sister's grand-daughter Octavia, and asking to marry Pompey's own daughter, Pompey had rejected these overtures and instead had chosen to ally himself with Scipio, who provided a link with two of Rome's greatest aristocratic families, the Scipiones and his adopted family the Metelli. Whatever his personal preference may have been as between Cornelia and Octavia, Pompey must have known that his choice would be seen as a political one and made his decision accordingly. A further link with the Optimates and their leader Cato was provided by the marriage, perhaps as early as 54, of Pompey's elder son Gnaeus with Claudia, the daughter of Appius Claudius Pulcher. Claudius came from the very heart of the Optimate nobility and had married another daughter to Marcus Brutus, Cato's nephew. The contrast with the situation in 62 is very marked.

As a result of the rioting and bloodshed the year 52 also opened without new consuls being elected. This time Pompey does seem to have contributed to the disorder. According to Asconius, whose full and vivid account is our chief source of information on this troubled period, Pompey, through the agency of a friendly tribune T. Munatius Plancus, vetoed the appointment of an *interrex* at the beginning of 52. Thus there was no one at Rome with the necessary *imperium* to hold the elections. If Asconius is correct the reason would appear to be that Pompey and his friends were afraid that Milo's candidacy would be successful.[11]

If so, we have no idea what their plans were for improving their own chances. Fate took a firm hand in altering the situation when on the afternoon of 18 January Milo and Clodius, each attended by a retinue of armed slaves, happened to meet on the Appian Way near Bovillae. A scuffle as the parties passed broke into a fight; Clodius was wounded and sought refuge in an inn, from which he was extracted on Milo's orders and murdered.

The details of the riots and demonstrations which followed the arrival of Clodius' corpse at Rome are fully recounted by Asconius and Dio. Inflamed by the tribunes Plancus, Pompeius Rufus and Sallustius, the mob cremated Clodius in the Senate House, destroying not only that building but adjoining ones as well. In an attempt to make capital out of the sudden wave of indignation against Milo his opponents not only allowed the appointment of an *interrex* but tried to force him to hold an election before it was legally allowed, besieging his house and actually stealing the *fasces* from his care.[12]

On the day of Clodius' murder Pompey was at yet another of his country houses, at Alsium in Etruria. On his return he found that the cry for him to assume the dictatorship had been renewed. Milo, however, had also returned and with the aid of another tribune, M. Caelius Rufus, was busily swinging popular opinion round to his side again. On 22 January Milo tried to obtain an interview with Pompey at his home on the Pincian, apparently with a positive suggestion to improve the situation by withdrawing his candidature if Pompey agreed. Pompey refused even to see him, on the somewhat curious grounds that it was not up to him to take such a decision for Milo and that he was not going to interfere with the prerogative of the Roman people on such a point. We are left with the impression that Milo had proposed some unacceptable deal, the full terms of which Asconius had been unable to discover.

On the next day (23 January) at a *contio* the Clodian tribune Pompeius Rufus hinted that Milo's violence threatened even Pompey's life. Probably the tribunes were taking advantage of Pompey's well-known fear of assassination to turn him actively against Milo and also alienate popular sympathy for Milo.

However, at last the Senate took action. Recognising a state of acute emergency it passed the *consultum ultimum*, urging the *interrex*, the tribunes and Pompey to take steps to see that the Republic suffered no harm, and instructing Pompey to levy troops in Italy for that purpose.

He responded to the call with his usual rapidity. Collecting a personal bodyguard he set about levying troops with which to restore order in the city. He probably returned to Rome before the levy was completed, for we are told by Asconius that on his return he took firm precautions against an assassination attempt, posting guards round his estate and actually moving to a house in his 'upper gardens' which could be more easily protected. He also appeared at a *contio* held by the Clodian tribunes and announced that information had been given him of a plot against his life instigated by Milo, and that a man who had tried to tamper with a key witness had been imprisoned. However flimsy the evidence may seem at this distance of time Pompey was taking no chances. He even refused to attend a meeting of the Senate specially held in the *porticus* of his own theatre (in order that he might be able to attend without contravening the law which forbade holders of *imperium* from entering the city proper) unless Milo was excluded.[13]

In spite of the senatorial decree which had urged them to co-operate in protecting the safety of the Republic, the tribunes appear to have made little constructive effort. Asconius merely records frequent *contiones* held by the supporters of both sides mainly in order to stir up feelings against their opponents. None of a succession of *interreges* was able to get elections held, and pressure for the appointment of a dictator mounted again.[14]

Cato and his followers, who had long resisted all such pressure in the Senate, finally agreed that some such solution was inevitable, and that the only man with the ability and standing to hold such a position was Pompey. A dictatorship, however, was still objectionable, and Cato eventually came up with what appears to have been a compromise. At a meeting of the Senate four days before the end of the intercalary month which had been inserted in the calendar between February and March the issue was discussed. The ex-consul Bibulus was the first to be asked his opinion and he proposed that Pompey should be elected consul without a colleague. The proposal was supported by Cato and passed.

In many ways it was a most ingenious compromise. The hated title of dictator was avoided; the position was subject to the usual checks on a Roman magistrate except for that of a colleague with equal power; the uniqueness of it could be expected to appeal to Pompey's vanity. And yet it was quite unconstitutional. Consul without a colleague was almost a contradiction in terms, and, besides, Pompey was legally debarred from holding the consulship for ten years after his last tenure in 55, or for that matter while he was still proconsul. In the heat of the crisis such niceties were forgotten or ignored. The *interrex* Servius Sulpicius was given his instructions and Pompey was created sole consul. None of our sources indicate whether any form of popular assembly was held. Probably in the absence of rival candidates no election would have been required and any nominations from Milo, Plautius and Scipio would not have been accepted.

This latest assignment was not one for which Pompey's experience really suited him. The control of bribery, anarchy and gang warfare in the streets of a great city was very different from the defeat of Sertorius, the pirates or Mithridates. But with the aid of his advisers Pompey soon had his plans ready. Two things were to be done: troops were to be brought into the city itself in sufficient strength to control the rioting; legislation was to be passed enabling those who were guilty of instigating the bribery and violence to be brought swiftly to trial with no opportunities for further bribery or intimidation of witnesses or jury.

The first laws were drafted and brought before the Senate two days after Pompey's appointment. One set up a court of enquiry into the events of 18 January and the subsequent disorders; the other allowed for prosecutions for bribery to be brought against any magistrate who had held office since 70, and granted immunity to anyone convicted of a minor offence if he could secure the conviction of anyone else on a more serious charge. A thorough purge of leading politicians was in prospect.

Strict regulations were also laid down for the selection of the presidents of the courts and the juries, and time limits established for the hearing of witnesses and for the speeches of prosecution and defence. Irrelevant but often compelling evidence in the form of testimonials of character by influential supporters of the defendant were banned. Punishment on conviction was to be harsher than before.

Needless to say the proposals ran into opposition from Milo's supporters and others. We hear of three lines of argument. Q. Hortensius agreed that there was a state of emergency, but argued that the existing laws were sufficient. Combining both points as one proposal he tried to move an amendment to Pompey's bill. The Pompeians were wise to his tactics, forced him to submit his points separately, and got a tribune to veto the second. Cato, who had rejected a request for co-operation and advice from Pompey, objected to the retrospective element in the second bill, and was supported by several Caesarians who saw in it a threat to their own patron. Pompey replied that his own two earlier consulships were also under scrutiny, but may in fact have agreed to a compromise. The day after the Senate's meeting to hear the proposals Caelius raised objections at a public meeting, claiming that Milo was being discriminated against and that not enough time was being allowed.

Somewhat exasperated Pompey threatened to use his troops if tribunician obstruction continued, and the laws came into effect. By all accounts they enjoyed considerable success. On 4 April Milo was the first to be prosecuted under the new system. L. Domitius Ahenobarbus was elected as president of the court; the list of jurymen was drawn up by Pompey himself. Troops were introduced, allegedly to protect Milo and his counsel, but seem strangely to have intimidated Cicero, who broke down during his final speech for the defence. Milo was condemned by thirty-eight votes to thirteen and went into exile at Marseilles.[15]

A whole spate of further prosecutions followed, in many of which a condemnation was secured. In two cases we hear that Pompey (quite contrary to his own regulations) intervened personally in an attempt to affect the verdict, once unsuccessfully when he put in a personal appeal on behalf of Munatius Plancus, once successfully when, according to Plutarch, he summoned all 360 jurymen who were about to hear the trial of Metellus Scipio to his house and asked them to acquit him. The case was dropped.

In fact Pompey's relations with Scipio were probably closer than with any other senator at this time. In about July, in accordance with a provision in the decree making him sole consul, Pompey nominated his father-in-law as his colleague for the rest of the year, in spite of suggestions from Caesar's supporters that he should share the consulship with Pompey. Plautius, however, paid the penalty for his violent and corrupt candidature, as did another of Pompey's close adherents, Aemilius Scaurus.

In Plutarch's account this abandoning of such men to their doubtless well-deserved fate won Pompey nothing but criticism, but Plutarch seems to be reflecting the opinions of a hostile source at this point, and we may perhaps rather believe Appian, who says that Pompey speedily restored the ailing Republic and caused neither offence nor trouble to anyone during his term of office, winning the goodwill of the Senate.[16]

Appian, however, also says that the Senate's goodwill towards Pompey was due to their jealousy of Caesar, and this remark raises once more the question of the relationship between the two surviving 'triumvirs'. Caesar himself, probably somewhat alarmed by the news of the anarchy early in the year, and preoccupied with the Gallic revolt which that news had precipitated, seems to have been relieved by Pompey's success at restoring the rule of law. But at least two of Pompey's measures gave him some cause for concern. Apart from the threat of Pompey's law on bribery, which may have been a hare started by Caesar's supporters, Caesar was beginning to think seriously about his future position at the end of his proconsulship of Gaul.

At the beginning of 52 the situation must have seemed as follows. Caesar knew that on his return from Gaul he could expect his enemies to receive him in a way similar to that in which Gabinius had been welcomed in 54: with a series of prosecutions leading almost inevitably to conviction, exile and an end to his career. To avoid this he needed to return, not as Gabinius had done as a private citizen but to a consulship, to which he would have to be elected in absence. The excuse for this privilege, which was given him by a law supported by the whole college of tribunes in 52, would be his tenure of *imperium* which excluded him from the city. As the earliest he could legally hold the consulship again was 48 he needed to retain his command in Gaul till summer 49. It appears that under the terms of the *lex Licinia Pompeia* of 55 no successor could be appointed by the Senate before 1 March 50, and as that successor would be by law one of the consuls of 49 it looked unlikely that he would be replaced before he was ready.[17]

But in 52 the situation changed. In an attempt to remove one of the major causes of bribery, which was the knowledge that a successful candidate for consulship or praetorship could expect to govern a province after his year of office and there make sufficient profit to repay the loans he would have had to raise in order to offer his bribes, Pompey passed a further law concerning magistracies and provincial governorships. Under it there was to be a five-year gap between one and the other. Not only would money lenders be less willing to part with loans for six years or more, the appointment to a province would now be a direct appointment by the Senate instead of the almost automatic consequence of election to a magistracy. Furthermore it was specifically restated that candidates for office must submit their nominations and appear before the assembly in person.

Caesar's position was thus doubly affected. His right to stand in absence had been removed and any successor appointed on 1 March 50 could now proceed immediately to take over Gaul. But was it any part of Pompey's intention to achieve this? Caesar's supporters pointed out how the nomination regulations affected him, and Pompey agreed to a last minute alteration in Caesar's favour, but it remains uncertain whether the alteration had the force of law. It was later claimed that it had not. Suetonius ascribes the 'oversight' to forgetfulness; pre-occupation with other issues might be more accurate. As to the other regulation, it was the putting into law of a senatorial decree of the previous year, and can hardly be counted as a deliberate attack by Pompey on Caesar.[18]

In fact the two had not yet split, although as we have seen they were drawing further apart. Pompey, partly through force of circumstances, partly through clever opportunism, had reached a position of almost total dominance at Rome by the end of 52. The Catonians were still not reconciled to it, though they had been forced to accept, even propose, the sole consulship, and Caesar had many supporters among the lower ranks of the Senate and elsewhere; but in so far as any individual could establish his own supremacy without appeal to the naked use of force in support of himself Pompey had done so.

Once there, as everyone soon realised, he would brook no rival. With Clodius —and, be it said, Milo — out of the way, the threat came from Caesar. But Caesar's enemies at Rome were many and powerful and Pompey knew that there was no need for him to add his weight to their attack, and perhaps increase his already unfortunate reputation for faithlessness. All he had to do was to revert to the tactics which had proved so successful in 56 and allow the pressures on Caesar to build up. If Caesar wanted his help this time he would have to pay a higher price — the acceptance of a subordinate position. He had not yet learnt that this was the one price that Caesar would not pay.

Caesar's two main bargaining strengths were his wealth and his army. If necessary Pompey could probably match the first. To ensure that he could match the second, before the end of 52 he had his own command in Spain extended for a further five years. The army under his command seems to have now consisted of seven legions in Spain, some troops stationed at Ariminum in north-east Italy, and some recent levies. In addition he had lent a legion to Caesar at the end of 54 to help make up for some of Caesar's losses in that year.

The consuls for 51 were the slow and ineffectual M. Claudius Marcellus and the indecisive Ser. Sulpicius Rufus. The former was an avowed enemy of Caesar, and it was he who led the attack on Caesar during this year. This took two forms. The first, an attempt to undermine Caesar's authority in the Transpadane region of Cisalpine Gaul, included the flogging of a man from Novum Comum. If, as the man claimed, he was a Roman citizen, such treatment was quite illegal, but Marcellus' view was that his citizenship depended on an illegal grant from Caesar and was therefore invalid. The second was a series of attempts to persuade the Senate to vote a successor to Caesar in Gaul, mainly on the grounds that the war there was over and Caesar's task done. After a succession of postponements Marcellus eventually raised the issue on 1 September, but as the necessary quorum of senators failed to appear no decision was taken. Finally on 29 September action was possible and Marcellus achieved the approval of four motions designed to break Caesar: (i) that as a matter of first priority the question of Caesar's successor should be raised on 1 March 50; (ii) that the tribunician veto should be invalid on such an occasion; (iii) that the Senate should discuss the retirement of some of Caesar's soldiers; (iv) that only Syria and the two Gauls should be available for allocation to ex-consuls on 1 March. The last three of these motions were in fact vetoed by Caesarian tribunes, but the attack had been well and truly launched.

Pompey's position throughout the year had been sturdily non-committal. He had probably disapproved of Marcellus' flogging of the man from Novum Comum — a particularly barbaric way of proving a point — as he had many interests in that area himself, but for some time he was occupied with problems concerning his provinces in Spain. Indeed it was commonly thought during the summer that he would go to Spain in person, but Cicero and presumably many others felt that the security of Rome demanded his continued presence and he was prevailed upon to stay. One is left with the impression that in dropping the hint through his legate Varro, and personally to Cicero, that he might be going to Spain Pompey was 'flying a kite' in order to be able to justify his remaining in Italy in response to popular demand.[19]

During much of May Pompey was at his estate near Tarentum, and there on 19, 20 and 21 May he entertained Cicero who was on his way to take over the governorship of Cilicia. His knowledge of the province will obviously have been valuable to Cicero, and we know that they spent much time discussing the political situation. For once Cicero thoroughly approved of what Pompey said to him, and wrote to Atticus, 'It was an outstanding citizen I left behind, and one fully prepared to ward off those dangers we are afraid of', by which Cicero presumably meant the dangers of anarchy and mob rule. He later repeated these sentiments to Caelius, who had asked for his impressions, with the warning, 'He [*sc.* Pompey] has a way of thinking one thing and saying another, though he is not subtle enough to conceal what he really wants.'[20]

On 22 July Pompey was back in Rome *en route* for Ariminum, where he had a visit to pay his troops. In order to let him attend, the Senate met outside the *pomerium* at the temple of Apollo to discuss the question of pay for his army. The question also arose of the standing of the legion Pompey had lent to Caesar, and under pressure from his critics, probably those who wanted him to take a harder line with Caesar, he agreed to recall it. He was also requested to return by mid-August so as to be present when provincial appointments were discussed. On his own thoughts he kept quiet, merely remarking at one point that everyone ought to respect the pronouncements of the Senate.

What happened at Ariminum we do not know. On his return there was no important meeting of the Senate until 1 September, when Pompey urged postponement of any decision on the provinces. He expanded this a little on 29 September when he said that it would be quite wrong to come to a decision before next 1 March. After that he would have no hesitation. Caelius reported the cross-questioning that followed:

What will happen if someone imposes a vote on that day?
It makes no difference whether Caesar intends to disobey the Senate's decree or to put up someone else to prevent the Senate passing one.
What if Caesar wants to be consul *and* retain his army?
What if my son wanted to lay into me with a cudgel?

This was a characteristically enigmatic reply presumably meaning, 'An unlikely situation, but I would have to take the necessary action.'[21]

Pompey was being scrupulously legalistic, putting Caesar in a position in which he would have to defy the Senate openly in order to survive, and hinting that he would be prepared to back the Senate. Historians have surmised that there were secret negotiations between the two men at Ariminum; if so, Caesar had failed to produce another agreement similar to the Luca one, and he soon had other plans under way.

The year 50 saw significant changes in the situation. Instead of being able to watch while pressures built up on Caesar, Pompey began to feel pressure being applied to himself and the initiative slipping from his hands. It was taken, of course, by Caesar, who now dramatically stepped up his campaign to win support in all possible quarters. To ensure the loyalty of his army he doubled the pay and made distributions of grain and personal slaves. Early in 50 he was busy drumming up support in Cisalpine Gaul with conspicuous success, and on his return north he left his senior commander T. Labienus there to enable him to canvass for the coming consular elections. He strongly backed his quaestor M. Antonius as a candidate for a vacant augurship and for the tribunate in 49, and he partly neutralised his opponents' successes at the elections in 51 by purchasing the support of Aemilius Paullus, one of the new consuls, with a bribe estimated by Appian at 1,500 talents.[22]

Caesar's money was also at the disposal of many another politician (and there were few who were not in financial difficulties), and his task was made easier by the activity of Appius Claudius, one of the censors of 50, in expelling large numbers of senators and *equites* from their respective orders, allegedly for behaviour unbecoming to men of their position. Most of these, we are told, flocked to Caesar's side.

However, the most important political figure to emerge in 50 was one of the new tribunes, C. Scribonius Curio. By a strange accident of fate he only stood for election because of the disqualification of one of the originally elected ten, and in the latter half of 51 it was commonly assumed that he would act in the interests of the Optimates and Pompey. This was a sad under-estimation of the man, and of his independence. In 51 he had two grievances against Caesar: he had been refused financial aid, and Caesar's supporters, including M. Antonius, had opposed his candidature. However, in February 50 Caelius reported to Cicero that Curio had changed sides and was now speaking for Caesar. Later historians are almost unanimous in detecting a bribe of enormous proportions. Admittedly Curio did not lose financially by his action, but his motives were almost certainly more complicated, and probably undiscoverable at this distance of time.[23]

Dio records without details a number of bills early in the year aimed against the Optimates and Pompey, adding that Curio knew that they would be rejected but wanted an excuse for changing sides. Caelius, on the other hand, ascribes his actions to infuriation at his fellow *pontifices* who refused to agree to the addition of an intercalary month in 50. He probably wanted more time to act before the critical senatorial meeting on 1 March.[24]

It remains possible that Curio saw the threat to Rome as much in the attitude of Pompey and the Optimates as in that of Caesar, and began by attempting to find a compromise. This has been suggested as the motive for his Road Bill introduced in February, which would have set up a commission to supervise roads. The commissioners would have had *imperium* for five years, and Curio could have intended to have Caesar appointed to the commission on his departure from Gaul, thus overcoming the now all-important problem of the time gap.

The bill was obstructed by the consul C. Marcellus, cousin of M. Marcellus, and apparently one of Pompey's men. In return, when 1 March arrived, Curio succeeded in preventing Marcellus from getting the allocation of Gaul discussed, and when the proposal was finally made, probably some time in April, Curio produced his own counter proposal. This was that Pompey should give up his command at the same time as Caesar. The idea was rejected, whereupon Curio vetoed the proposal that Caesar should be replaced.[25]

Caesar's tactics were clear. He proposed to use Curio to veto any proposal to replace him (ironically this was now possible under Pompey's law, whereas it had not been under the old Sempronian law), while taking the fight into Pompey's camp and trying to undermine his position. In April 50 the Senate was not prepared to consider releasing Pompey from his responsibilities. On the contrary it looked as though yet another command was about to come his way. In the East the provinces of Syria and Cilicia were threatened by a Parthian invasion across the Euphrates. The previous winter Pompey had written to Cicero in Cilicia that he might have to bring an expedition himself to deal with the situation, and in May the Senate decreed that two legions should be got ready for action, one each from Pompey's and Caesar's armies. Pompey took advantage of this to reduce Caesar's strength by two legions by seconding to the expeditionary force the legion he had previously lent to Caesar.

Following Curio's veto of the proposal to replace Caesar Pompey had lent his support to an apparent compromise, namely that Caesar should give up his provinces on 13 November. Exactly why that date was chosen is not clear, but Pompey claimed that it was fair. But it was obvious to most people at Rome that Pompey was now determined that Caesar should not retain his command until he was elected consul, and Curio refused to accept the offered compromise.

On top of all this Pompey fell ill. For several weeks around mid-summer he was confined to his bed in his house at Naples and there were reports that his life was in danger. Appian records a letter he wrote from his sick bed to the Senate. It was full of praise for Caesar's achievements, but reminded the readers of all his own exploits as well, and the fact that his third consulship and his present provinces and army had been pressed on him when he was summoned to the service of the Republic. 'I will willingly hand these powers back to those who wish to take them from me, without waiting for their full term to be completed.'[26]

Appian, with some justification, sees this as a cunning way of calling Curio's bluff, written with no intention of fulfilling the offer in an awareness of his indispensability to the Republic. Yet it could be the letter of a man weakened by illness and suddenly eager to drop his arduous responsibilities. If this was so, the feeling was short-lived. Several of the Campanian cities had offered prayers for Pompey's safety (a Hellenistic custom which illustrates the almost royal position held by Pompey in the eyes of many, especially in the Greek cities of southern Italy), and Pompey's full recovery was greeted with unprecedented displays of joy, not only in Naples but throughout Italy. His return to Rome is described as a 'progress', with torch-lit and garlanded processions escorting him through the cities on his route.

Such adoration seems to have had a marked effect on Pompey's outlook and on his judgement. Plutarch records a growing arrogance and over-confidence, as if, perhaps, the gods had just proved their goodwill towards him. In view of Pompey's known tendencies towards superstition we should not reject such interpretations out of hand.[27]

Plutarch and Appian also state that when Appius Claudius with the two legions for the Parthian expedition arrived in Italy his report of low morale and disaffection in Caesar's army had a similar effect on Pompey. Remembering the loyalty and affection his troops actually displayed to Caesar we should not be surprised that Appian adds that the troops and their commander may have been paid to make this report, recalling that on the departure of his own legion (the XV) Caesar gave each man a donative of 250 denarii. It would not have been beyond Caesar thus to lull his opponent into a false sense of security, and such a sense is surely indicated by Pompey's smiling reply to questions as to where were the forces to meet Caesar should he decide to march on Rome: 'Wherever in Italy I stamp my foot there will spring up forces of infantry and cavalry.'[28]

But it should not be forgotten that ever since Curio's intervention (and Curio was an old enemy from as far back as 59) Pompey's own position had been under attack and he was fighting to maintain his supremacy. On his return to Rome after his illness he apparently repeated his earlier offer to resign saying that he knew Caesar would also be happy to do so. This time his insincerity was patent, and Curio immediately called upon him to disarm.[29]

Pompey's determination that Caesar should be made to give up his provinces was thus clear to all by August, and Caelius wrote then to Cicero that the prospect of a full-scale civil war was drawing rapidly closer and that firm attitudes were being struck by the two protagonists; the Senate had not yet made up its mind, though Caelius saw most of the 'establishment' as likely to side with Pompey. There was, however, a strong swing towards Caesar. His quaestor Antonius not only won election to the tribunate for 49 but also defeated the leading Optimate L. Domitius Ahenobarbus for the vacant augurship. Another tribune-elect, Q. Cassius, was also on Caesar's side, and in October Cicero wrote to Atticus to tell him of his dismay at hearing that even the consul-elect Lentulus was supporting him.[30]

Pompey's reaction was to threaten to leave the city to its fate. As Cicero was later to remark, the Senate had taken a very feeble line with Curio. It had upheld the validity of his veto and protected him when he was threatened with expulsion by the censor Claudius. No doubt his distinguished family background helped him, but he certainly had succeeded in thwarting every attempt to exercise the Senate's authority over its proconsul in Gaul.[31]

During the late summer and autumn of 50 Pompey must have had two main preoccupations. The Parthian threat had receded thanks to competent action by Cicero in Cilicia and C. Cassius Longinus in Syria, and Pompey will have been giving thought first to gathering forces and making plans for the possible conflict with Caesar, and secondly to fighting the battle of words which would precede it. As always in a civil war it was important to be seen to have right on one's side.

Early in November Pompey was at Naples, where he received a visit from Atticus enquiring about his current attitude towards Cicero and the latter's request for a triumph on his return from Cilicia. Pompey was full of praise for Cicero's upright conduct in his province and seems to have been in favour of a triumph. The good news was soon on its way.[32]

The thirteenth of November came and went with Caesar still firmly in his province, and the movement towards war gathered momentum at the critical Senate meeting on 1 December. C. Marcellus tried once more to get the Senate to come out firmly against Caesar. Taking the earlier proposal of both Curio and Pompey he astutely divided it into two motions. There was a majority for sending successors to Caesar, and a majority against removing Pompey from his command. But Curio sensed an even greater majority in favour of peace, and put his own proposal once more, that both commanders should resign. The resulting vote produced highly significant figures: 370 in favour of the motion, 22 against. The size of the hard-core opposition to Caesar was apparent. Marcellus' reaction was to call for a declaration that Caesar was a public enemy, claiming that news had arrived that Caesar had crossed the Alps with his army. Curio's was to announce the verdict to the waiting assembly. At the thought that war had been averted the people responded with loud applause and showers of garlands and flowers.[33]

But fear, distrust and hatred had gone too far. It was this apparent victory for Curio and Caesar that drove the Catonian clique, for that it was which provided most of the twenty-two diehards, and Pompey at last into close alliance.

During the debate, which seems to have lasted two days, Pompey was at his house just outside the city. The first he knew of the result was the arrival of the consuls and their entourage, which included the two consuls-elect. At Marcellus' insistence they had taken it upon themselves to make a positive move. With a now famous gesture Marcellus thrust a sword into Pompey's hand. 'I and my colleague here instruct you to march on your country's behalf against Caesar. As an army for this purpose we give you the troops at Capua and elsewhere in Italy and whatever other forces you wish to raise.' Non-committal as ever, Pompey replied, 'If there is no better way.'[34]

Once again Rome had turned to Pompey in an hour of crisis and called upon him to defend her. But Caesar was no Lepidus or Sertorius, and it was clear to Pompey as to everyone else that if Caesar was prepared to use his legions in defiance of the Senate's will then they must expect a civil war on the scale of that which had followed Sulla's return from the East.

It has often been noticed that ancient sources make no mention of any strategy for this war that Pompey devised before its outbreak, and it is clear from Cicero's letters that for several months he and most of his fellow senators were not let into Pompey's confidence. It seems likely, however, that Pompey believed some time before the end of 50 that if Caesar invaded Italy it would be impossible to defend Rome with the forces at his disposal. His great strength lay in his own seven Spanish legions, his navy, and the enormous forces he could muster from the provinces and client kingdoms of the East. He would have to abandon Italy, maintain a naval blockade to prevent Caesar from following him or receiving shipments of corn from the provinces, and then bring his armies back from west and east to trap Caesar in Italy. It was, to say the least, an ambitious and imaginative plan, demanding the organisation and deployment of troops over a vast area, but one which was not, in theory, beyond the capabilities of a general who had cleared the Mediterranean of pirates and organised Rome's Eastern Empire.[35]

But the greatest difficulty lay in persuading the Catonians and others who now looked to Pompey for leadership of the wisdom of his plans. To most of them the very idea of abandoning Rome, let alone Italy, to Caesar was virtually unthinkable. On the contrary, their strategy seems to have been one of holding northern Italy against Caesar and forcing him to an early battle, should he decide to march against the capital. To decide finally between the merits, militarily speaking, of these alternatives we should need not only to be able to assess the value of the forces on each side taking into account such factors as weapons, training, skill, loyalty and morale, but also to know what assessment each side had of the other's forces, and for both of these requirements the evidence is inconclusive. We have already seen reason to believe that Caesar tried to mislead his opponents with regard to his troops' morale, and although Pompey several times affected to belittle Caesar's strength some of his actions suggest that he retained in reality a very healthy regard for it.

The whole problem was further complicated by a political issue. Pompey was fully aware that his new alliance with the Catonians was based on nothing more than expediency. While they remained in control of the Senate at Rome he would be no more than a proconsul obeying senatorial instructions, and if Caesar were defeated in Italy it would be a senatorial victory. Away from Rome, however, the senators would be deprived of their constitutional powers, and in the East Pompey's control over all his forces and the conduct of the war would be unchallenged. Success would bring a Pompeian rather than a senatorial victory and for the future Pompey's personal supremacy would be unrivalled. In a sense the question was whether Pompey would help the Catonians to crush Caesar or the Catonians would help Pompey. Since Caesar's bid for the consulship could be defined as a threat to the constitution, the Catonians and Pompey might stand as defenders of the constitution, as staunch republicans against a would-be tyrant, but if it came to open civil war there could be no doubt that the losers would be the Roman people, the mass of the inhabitants of Italy.

On 7 December Pompey left Rome for Capua to visit the two legions in winter quarters there, and possibly to make arrangements for the further levying of troops in southern Italy. Three days later he met Cicero, who had reached Campania on his return from Cilicia. Cicero described the meeting thus:

> I saw Pompey on 10 December. We were together for perhaps two hours. He seemed to me to be greatly delighted by my arrival, to be encouraging about a triumph, to be offering his assistance, but to be warning me not to enter the Senate House until I had finished my business in case I should alienate one of the tribunes in giving my opinion in debate. In short, as far as what he said went, nothing could have been more obliging. On the political situation, however, he spoke as if we had a certain war on our hands and held out no hope of agreement. He had had recent confirmation of his earlier view that Caesar had broken with him. Hirtius, a very close friend of Caesar's, had come from him without calling on Pompey; he had arrived on the evening of the 6th and Balbus had arranged to visit Scipio before daybreak on the 7th to discuss the whole situation, but Hirtius set off back to Caesar late the same night. This seemed clear proof to Pompey of a rift between them.[36]

During the next few days Cicero gained the impression from those he met that the over-riding desire of most people was for peace, and that it was generally agreed to be preferable to concede to Caesar's demands than to provoke war. We learn of Pompey's attitude from a letter recording a further meeting on 25 December.

> He overtook me near Lavernium. We went together to Formiae and had a private discussion from two o'clock in the afternoon till evening. You ask whether there is any hope of a settlement. As far as I could see from Pompey's long and detailed discussion of the situation there is not even any desire for it. He thinks that if Caesar

becomes consul, even after dismissing his army, there will be an overthrow of the constitution, and he also believes that when Caesar hears that careful preparations are being made against him he will abandon hopes of the consulship for this year and prefer to retain his province and his army. But if he should go mad, Pompey is full of contempt for the scoundrel and has confidence in his own forces and those of the Republic. Well, even though that quotation about 'the impartiality of Mars' frequently came to mind, I was relieved of worry when I heard a man of courage and experience and enormous influence discussing the dangers of a hollow peace in such a statesmanlike fashion. We had before us a speech of Antonius delivered on 21 December which contains an attack on Pompey since his boyhood, complaints about those who had been condemned, and the threat of war. Pompey's reaction was: 'What do you think the master will do, if he gains control of the state, when his wretched and impoverished quaestor dares to say this?' In short he seemed not only not to be looking for peace but actually to be afraid of it.[37]

Antonius had entered on his tribunate on 10 December, and his speech was no doubt made with Caesar's approval, for the latter had heard of recent developments from the outgoing tribune Curio, who had met him at Ravenna as soon as possible after the expiry of his office. If we are to believe Appian, Caesar also instructed his friends at Rome to try to effect a settlement on the terms that Caesar would give up his provinces and his army except for Illyricum and Cisalpine Gaul and two legions until he should be elected consul. If Pompey could be made to agree to this, Caesar was well on the way to splitting him away from the Catonians. It was apparently acceptable to Pompey, but was rejected by the consuls. Perhaps, however, we should not accept Appian's date in the second half of December, but a date of a few weeks later as Plutarch and Suetonius suggest.[38]

On 1 January 49 came the next move. Shortly before the first senatorial debate of the new year Curio arrived with an ultimatum from Caesar. He would lay down his command if Pompey would do the same; otherwise he would march quickly to avenge his own wrongs and those of the state. Presumably Caesar was aware that Pompey would never accept these terms, but remembering the support there had been for a similar proposal in the Senate a month earlier, he was taking the opportunity to put the blame for the outbreak of war on Pompey's shoulders. The new consuls, C. Claudius Marcellus (brother of the consul of 51) and L. Cornelius Lentulus Crus, realised the effect that this ultimatum might have on the majority of senators and at first refused to read it to the House. Eventually the Caesarian tribunes forced them to do so, but they did not put the terms to the vote, merely initiating a general debate on the state of the Republic.

A summary of the debate is given by Caesar in the first two chapters of his commentaries on the Civil War. Pompey had returned to the neighbourhood of Rome a few days previously, with some of his troops, and the proximity of these and the threateningly belligerent attitude of the consul Lentulus and others in the Senate whom Caesar vaguely calls 'Pompey's friends' frightened the vast majority into voting for a proposal of Pompey's father-in-law, Metellus Scipio, that Caesar should disband his army before a fixed day (possibly 1 March); otherwise he would be counted as plotting to act against the state. In the propaganda campaign Caesar was once more saddled with the responsibility for the war. However, the motion was promptly vetoed by Antonius and Cassius.

During the two days of the debate Pompey had been in his suburban mansion to which, on the evening of 2 January, he summoned all the senators in an attempt to harden the opposition to Caesar. The methods, according to Caesar, were largely those of intimidation, and they seem to have been successful. On 5 January the debate continued in the Senate. The attack on Caesar was led by Lentulus, Scipio and Cato, but it would appear from Plutarch that an attempt was made with the help of the recently arrived Cicero to achieve a last-minute settlement on the terms which had perhaps been suggested a few weeks earlier. The number of legions Caesar was prepared to keep was reduced to one, a condition said to be acceptable to Pompey, but the Catonians would have none of it. Possibly Pompey was made to see that if he appeared ready to compromise with Caesar he would lose all credibility with and all the support of the Catonians. An offer made by the censor L. Piso and the praetor L. Roscius to ride at full speed to Ravenna to inform Caesar of the situation was rejected, as was the suggestion that other legates be sent to him.[39]

The climax of the long debate, according to Livy's account, came when the Senate voted to send out a successor to Caesar in the person of L. Domitius Ahenobarbus. Clearly all attempts at negotiation had failed. Antonius and Cassius immediately interposed their veto, and by so doing exasperated Lentulus into making a most injudicious move. He warned the two tribunes that if they did not leave the Senate they could expect violent reprisals. Once more a consul had been driven to resort to force in the face of obstinate tribunician tactics. The machinery of the constitution had finally broken down, and there was no possibility of a solution short of civil war. In recognition of this the Senate passed the *consultum ultimum*: 'The consuls, praetors, tribunes of the people, and those proconsuls who are near the city shall take measures to ensure that the Republic suffers no harm.' That night, 7 January, Antonius, Cassius, Curio and Caelius Rufus escaped from Rome and headed north to join Caesar.[40]

The narrative of the Civil War can be followed most easily in Caesar's own commentaries, with some invaluable corrections and many additional details from Cicero's correspondence. There are also Lucan's long epic poem *Pharsalia*, and briefer accounts in Plutarch, Appian, Dio and Suetonius, which sometimes draw on other no longer extant sources. It is not the purpose of this study to retell the story at length, but rather to concentrate on the actions of Pompey himself up to the time of his death.

During the days following the passing of the *consultum ultimum* there were frequent meetings of the Senate outside the city boundary which Pompey was able to attend and at which plans for combatting Caesar were made. Whatever his real opinion was about Caesar's forces, Pompey expressed confidence in his own ten legions (of which seven were in Spain) against the allegedly disaffected legions of his opponent. The decision was taken to levy further troops in Italy and to make a grant of payment for Pompey's army from the treasury. In spite of opposition from the consul Marcellus, King Juba of Numidia was granted the title of 'Ally and Friend of the Roman People' in expectation of his support, but a move to send Pompey's son-in-law Faustus Sulla to win over the princes of Mauretania was vetoed.[1]

The allocation of provinces was also made. In addition to Domitius Ahenobarbus' governorship of Transalpine Gaul, Metellus Scipio was appointed to the important province of Syria (virtually to the command of the Eastern Army), L. Aelius Tubero to Africa, M. Considius Nonianus to Cisalpine Gaul, M. Porcius Cato to Sicily, and P. Sestius to Cilicia. In the eastern provinces the task was to raise as much money and collect as many soldiers and ships as possible, and in Africa and Sicily to secure control of the corn supply. In Gaul it was important that Caesar should have been legally replaced, though unlikely that either of his successors would be in a position to take over their new posts.

In Italy commanders were allocated to the important regions and garrison towns. Etruria and the roads from the north which ran through it were guarded by Pompey's associate and adviser L. Scribonius Libo, Umbria by Q. Minucius Thermus at Iguvium and C. Lucilius

Hirrus at Camerinum, and Picenum by Lentulus Spinther at Ancona and P. Attius Varus at Auximum. These commanders no doubt all had instructions to levy troops as fast as possible, as had M. Cicero in Campania and Domitius Ahenobarbus, who established himself with a force of some 4,000 men at the important stronghold of Corfinium.[2]

Pompey meanwhile remained in Rome. He probably did not anticipate an immediate invasion by Caesar, hoping, as he had earlier said to Cicero, that the measures they had taken would deter him from using force. Within a week, however, of the passing of the *consultum ultimum* news reached Rome that on the morning of 12 January Caesar with one legion had occupied the Italian town of Ariminum, and that refugees were already beginning to stream southwards towards Rome. By 17 January it was also learnt that he had occupied Pisaurum, Fanum and Ancona, the next three towns along the Flaminian Way, and that M. Antonius had captured the town of Arretium and thus controlled the Cassian Way. The uproar and panic which greeted this news is vividly described by Appian, Plutarch and Dio. Portent-mongers announced a whole host of ominous occurrences, rumour had it that Caesar was marching on Rome with his whole army, and quite clearly Pompey and the senatorial leaders could not get hold of any accurate information.[3]

On 14 January two messengers, L. Roscius and L. Caesar, were sent to Ariminum. The exact nature of their message from the Senate is not revealed. Perhaps they were to offer terms to Caesar, perhaps merely to delay him by offering negotiations. Pompey himself added a personal message:

> Caesar should not take as an insult to himself what Pompey had done in the interests of the Republic. He had always considered the good of the Republic more important than his private relationships, and Caesar should also lay aside his ambition and his anger for the sake of the Republic as his position demanded, and not allow his fury at the behaviour of his enemies to drive him to harm the Republic in the hopes of harming them.[4]

Caesar describes this message as an attempt by Pompey to excuse himself for his actions, implying that he felt guilty at this 'betrayal' of his former ally. In fact, as the repetition of the word 'Republic' shows, Pompey was emphasising his position as guardian of the constitution, and possibly countering the use as propaganda that Caesar was making of the Senate's violent treatment of his two tribunes.

Both commanders badly needed time, Caesar to allow his other legions to join him in Gaul, and to secure northern Italy before Pompey could get his troops into fighting order, and Pompey to collect his forces and plan the evacuation of Italy. Accordingly on 18 January Caesar sent Roscius and L. Caesar back with what appeared to be proposals for a peaceful settlement: Pompey should withdraw to Spain; both should disband their armies; there should be complete demobilisation in Italy; the 'reign of terror' should be brought to an end; there should be free elections and a return to constitutional government by Senate and people; he and Pompey should meet to discuss their differences and ratify these terms with an oath. To this list of proposals, which Caesar records, Cicero adds the agreement to hand over his provinces to successors, to give up his demand for candidature *in absentia*, and to come to Rome in person for elections.[5]

However, with the news of the fall of Ancona and Arretium Pompey had decided that the time had come to abandon Rome. The report of Caesar's crossing of the Rubicon had caused a wave of discontent in the Senate at Pompey's apparent slowness to take precautions. M. Favonius had challenged him to stamp his feet in order to raise an army, and although Cato proposed that Pompey be elected commander-in-chief of all Roman forces, Plutarch records that the reason he gave was not a military one but that those who created great crises should put an end to them. The proposal was not accepted.[6]

Replying to Favonius that the army could still be raised if the senators followed him and were prepared to abandon Rome and perhaps even Italy, Pompey took it upon himself to issue an edict declaring a *tumultus*, or state of civil war, and instructed all senators to leave Rome on pain of being considered partisans of Caesar. He himself left for Capua on the evening of 17 January and on 18 January he was followed by the consuls and the majority of senators. Quite clearly the evacuation took place in an atmosphere of panic and the consul Lentulus did not even have time to load the contents of the treasury on to carts before making his departure. For once Pompey's organisation had broken down.

If we are to generalise from Cicero's personal reaction to the abandonment of Rome it would seem to have been beyond the comprehension of many senators, and Dio, possibly using an eye-witness account as his source, gives a moving account of the agonising decisions the inhabitants of Rome had to take. But Cicero does add that it had a powerful effect on many of the townsfolk of southern

Italy. Caesar had marched on Rome, and no concessions could now be made to him.[7]

On 22 January Pompey, now joined by the consuls and many of the senators, was at Teanum Sidicinum, a few kilometres north-west of Capua. There he was overtaken by Titus Labienus, Caesar's senior legate in Gaul, who had abandoned his leader on the declaration of war and come over to the Pompeians. Opinions differ as to his motives. He had political connections with Pompey which went back at least as far as the sixties and he was also a Picene from Cingulum, and probably owed his early military career to Pompey's patronage. However, there is also reason to suppose that he had been increasingly dissatisfied with Caesar's treatment of him. Caesar seems to have dominated his legates in Gaul and given them little credit for their own successes, and had lately been showing greater favour to M. Antonius than to Labienus. The latter's cruelty and arrogance may have been partly responsible. Finally we know that in the previous December Caesar's enemies had been in touch with Labienus in Cisalpine Gaul, probably negotiating just such a move in the event of an invasion of Italy by Caesar.[8]

Pompey apparently had not been party to these overtures, and it has been suggested that some of the Catonians, in their desire to avoid the evacuation of Italy and to force Pompey to settle the issue as soon as possible, made use of Labienus to this end. Certainly he gave Pompey an encouraging account of Caesar's military strength, so much so that Pompey appears to have seriously considered the possibility of taking a stand against Caesar in Picenum. He sent one of his prefects of engineers, L. Vibullius Rufus, to that area to urge the garrison commanders there to greater efforts, to hasten the levying of troops, to stiffen the loyalty of the inhabitants, and to report accurately on the state of affairs. On 23 January Pompey, accompanied by Labienus, set out to join his two legions at Larinum in N. Apulia. He wrote to Cicero that within a few days he might be able to advance into Picenum and that Cicero might soon be returning to Rome.[9]

Shortly before Pompey left Teanum he received Caesar's reply to the messages which had been sent via Roscius and L. Caesar on 14 January. The terms appear at first sight to have offered the Catonians all that they wanted, although Pompey would not have readily agreed to withdraw to Spain. Cicero, however, who had met L. Caesar at Minturnae before he reached Teanum, and had been told the content of the message, thought that the terms were absurd and suggests that none of Caesar's legates took them seriously either. It has also been shown that in his account of these negotiations Caesar deliberately obscured the fact that he was seizing towns and building up his strength in north Italy while they were going on. It would appear that they were little more than a device to buy time.[10]

Pompey and the consuls had no doubts as to Caesar's intentions. Although they could not reject the terms without putting themselves morally in the wrong, they could call Caesar's bluff. Pompey entrusted the wording and the publication of their reply to his old ally P. Sestius, who had not yet left for Cilicia, and set out for Apulia. If Labienus was right about Caesar's military weakness there was no time to be lost.

Sestius' reply, carried back to Caesar at Ancona by the same two messengers, was that Pompey and the consuls accepted his proposals on the condition that he withdrew his troops from the towns he had already taken so that the Senate could return to Rome to discuss the situation. Until they received a guarantee that this was being done they would continue to levy troops. The reply was simultaneously published in order to achieve the maximum propaganda benefit from Caesar's expected rejection.

It is significant that Caesar in his account suggests that he had only taken Ariminum by this time, and justifies his rejection of the terms on the grounds that they were unfair. His annoyance is more likely to be due to the fact that he and not his enemies had been forced to turn down what could be claimed reasonable terms.[11]

In Campania and Apulia the levying of troops proceeded very slowly. The consuls had the job of mustering Pompey's old veterans, who had been settled at Capua under Caesar's law of 59, but Cicero reported to Atticus on 25 January that they were meeting with a poor response. Ten days later he revealed that the recruiting officers were not even daring to show their faces, and by 9 February any levying of troops was completely at a standstill. However, a potentially dangerous situation was averted when 5,000 trained gladiators from the school at Capua, who belonged to Caesar, were split up on Pompey's instructions and distributed among some 2,500 apparently loyal families for safe-keeping. Caesar suggests that the consul Lentulus actually contemplated using them, but was dissuaded by some of his saner advisers.[12]

Whatever Pompey's hopes had been of resisting Caesar's advance in Picenum, they must soon have been shattered by the first news he received from Vibullius. Hardly had Caesar read his last reply than Curio had taken the town of Iguvium. The praetor Thermus with his garrison of five cohorts had fled before Curio's arrival, and the cohorts had deserted shortly afterwards. The fall of Iguvium was probably the signal for the abandonment of Camerinum and so of all Umbria, and for the withdrawal of Scribonius Libo from Etruria. The northern approaches to Rome were now unguarded. Caesar himself moved rapidly down the east coast into Picenum. The townsfolk of Auximum threw out their garrison and its commander P. Attius Varus, and welcomed Caesar. Cingulum forgot its close associations with Labienus and offered Caesar troops; and Lentulus Spinther was forced to abandon Asculum. By 3 February Caesar was at Firmum, and three days later at Castrum Truentinum. Picenum had fallen to him without a blow being struck.

For all their supposed loyalty to Pompey the Picentines were not prepared to risk their farms and their homes to support him and the Optimates, who had done so little to help them in the past, in a private quarrel with Caesar. Whatever force the defence of the constitution had as a rallying cry among the members of the senatorial class it failed dismally among the hill farmers of north Italy. When personal livelihood was at stake the bonds of patronage and 'patriotism' were just too weak.

During his advance through Picenum Caesar was joined by his Twelfth Legion from Gaul, bringing his numbers in Italy up to two full legions supported by an increasing number of cohorts of new recruits and Pompeian deserters. By 4 February Pompey had clearly decided that he would have to put his original plan to evacuate Italy into operation, and had withdrawn to Luceria, where he had fourteen cohorts of the twenty which comprised his two legions. The rest were still on the road or had been sent ahead under Metellus Scipio to hold the embarkation port of Brundisium and the town of Canusium. Between Luceria and Capua there were some thirty cohorts of new recruits; he expected nineteen (discounting desertions) from Picenum and Umbria; and L. Domitius Ahenobarbus at Corfinium had a further twelve cohorts.

On about 5 February Pompey sent his legate Q. Fabius to Corfinium to urge Domitius to join him at once with all his forces or at least to send him the nineteen cohorts (five under Lucilius Hirrus which had escaped from Camerinum, and fourteen under Vibullius which included some of Lentulus Spinther's garrison from Asculum) which were on their way from Picenum. At about the same time he sent the tribune C. Cassius to the consuls at Capua with instructions to return with all speed to Rome and bring back the money from the inner treasury which had been left behind earlier. Lentulus, who does not seem to have known about the fall of Picenum, sent back a reply that Pompey should first advance into that district to cut off Caesar from Rome. The money remained in the treasury.

The critical events of the next fortnight can be followed in the series of despatches preserved in the eighth book of Cicero's letters to Atticus, supplemented by Caesar's own account and Cicero's personal comments.

On 8 February the cohorts from Picenum began to arrive at Domitius' camp at Corfinium, and Q. Fabius returned to Pompey at Luceria. Shortly after his arrival on 10 February Pompey wrote to Cicero:

> Q. Fabius reached me on 10 February. He announces that L. Domitius is on the march towards me with his own twelve cohorts and the fourteen cohorts which Vibullius has brought in; it was his intention to leave Corfinium on 9 February; C. Hirrus is following with five cohorts. I suggest that you come to me at Luceria. I think this will be the safest place for you.[13]

On 11 February Pompey received a despatch from Vibullius at Corfinium to the effect that Domitius had changed his plans. He promptly wrote again to Domitius:

> I am quite amazed that you send me no word and that I am kept informed on matters of public concern by others rather than yourself. With divided forces we can not match our enemy; if we combine our forces I hope that we can achieve something for the Republic and our common safety. Therefore, since you had decided, as Vibullius wrote to me, to leave Corfinium with your army on the 9 February and come to me, I wonder what reason there was for you to change your plan. For the reason Vibullius mentions in his letter is a trivial one, namely that you had been delayed by the news that Caesar had advanced from Firmum and reached Castrum Truentinum. For the nearer the enemy begins to approach, the faster you should have acted in order to join me before Caesar could hinder your march or cut you off from me.
>
> Therefore I ask you and urge you again and again, as I have consistently done in previous despatches, to come to me at Luceria on the first possible day, before the forces which Caesar has begun to collect can concentrate and cut you off from us. But if there are people holding you back in an attempt to protect their own country

houses, it is at least reasonable for me to demand that you should send me the cohorts which have come from Picenum and Camerinum, which have abandoned their own possessions.[14]

It should be noticed that Pompey does not issue orders to Domitius, nor does he explain his own strategy. He was technically only equal in rank to Domitius, and apparently felt that if the latter realised that he had now decided to abandon Italy altogether he would refuse to co-operate at all. What Domitius had in mind can only be guessed. If Rome was not to be left at Caesar's mercy the position at Corfinium was of great strategic importance. It controlled the roads from the east coast to Rome (*via Valeria*) and to Samnium and Campania, and if Caesar continued down the east coast into Apulia without taking it he would dangerously expose his rear. On the assumption that Caesar was to be fought in Italy there was everything to be said for holding him at Corfinium rather than Luceria. On 8 February, when Domitius agreed to withdraw, he thought that Caesar was at Firmum and probably likely to cross the Apennines by the road through Asculum well to his north; but the news that Caesar had advanced to Castrum Truentinum meant that he would have to consider the problem of Corfinium. Vibullius told Domitius that Caesar only had two legions, apparently unaware of the fact, which Pompey knew, that a third legion and several cohorts from Umbria and Etruria were expected shortly. On the information he had Domitius could expect to out-number Caesar by three to two, if he kept all his cohorts, and by more if Pompey came to his aid as he hoped.

To Pompey, of course, these considerations were now irrelevant. His sole object was to persuade Domitius to withdraw without revealing his plan to him until it was too late to adopt any other.

On 13 February he sent another legate D. Laelius with instructions to the consuls at Capua. With their approval one of them was to join him at Luceria, while the other took the Campanian levies, together with some troops recruited by Faustus Sulla, across to Sicily, there to be joined by Domitius with his twelve cohorts. The rest would congregate at Brundisium and cross from there to Dyrrachium in Greece. It would appear that Pompey had arranged for some of his transport ships to muster on the Campanian coast and others at Brundisium, and for troops to be evacuated from both sides of the peninsula. This was the first time that he had officially stated his policy of evacuation. Clearly he hoped that the consuls would be readier to accept the realities of the situation as he saw them than

Domitius. With their experience of levying reluctant recruits they would presumably be less willing to engage Caesar's veterans before it was absolutely necessary.[15]

Three days later (16 February) despatches began to arrive from Domitius. On receipt of the first Pompey replied:

Today, 16 February, M. Calenius has brought me a despatch from you, in which you write that you intend to keep watch on Caesar, and if he begins to march towards me along to coast, to come to join me in Samnium with all haste; but that if he should delay in your neighbourhood, you wish to offer resistance if he comes any nearer.

In my opinion that is an ambitious and courageous policy, but we have to be very careful in case by being divided we fail to match our enemy's numbers. He already has large forces and will shortly have larger ones. A commander of your skill should not only take into consideration how many cohorts Caesar has in the field, but the size of the cavalry and infantry forces he will shortly have collected. I have evidence for that in the message Bussenius sent me, in which he writes, as I am informed from other sources as well, that Curio is collecting the garrison forces which were in Umbria and Etruria, and marching towards Caesar. If these forces unite, although part of the army may be sent to Alba, and part may advance on you, although Caesar may not take the offensive but merely defend his own position, you will be in a sticky situation, and with the forces at your disposal you will be unable to keep Caesar's superior numbers far enough away to allow you to forage.

Therefore I urge you strongly to come here with all your forces as quickly as possible. The consuls have decided to do the same. I have given M. Tuscilius a message for you, that we must take precautions not to let the two legions come into sight of Caesar without the cohorts from Picenum. So do not be alarmed if you hear that I am withdrawing, if Caesar should happen to advance in my direction. I believe I must be careful not to get trapped. Because of the season of the year and the spirit of my soldiers I cannot build camp, nor is it desirable to collect my forces from all the towns in case I lose my line of retreat. So I have assembled no more than fourteen cohorts at Luceria. The consuls will either bring their forces here or go to Sicily. For we must either have a strong army with which we can be sure of being able to break through, or hold such areas as we can defend. Neither of those is true at the moment, because Caesar controls a large part of Italy, and we do not have an army as well equipped or as large as he does. So we must take care to put the interests of the Republic first. I urge you again and again to come to me as soon as possible with your whole force. Even now we can put the Republic back on its feet, if we adopt a common policy in this business. If we are divided we shall be weak. Of that I am certain.

After I had written the above, Sicca brought me a despatch and a message from you. As to your request that I come to join you, I feel that I can not do that, because I do not have much confidence in these legions.[16]

Still Pompey felt unable to reveal unambiguously his decision to evacuate Italy or to issue direct orders to Domitius. There is merely a hint that failure to comply with his request could lead to a further withdrawal. But, however persuasive Pompey's arguments may have been, they arrived too late. Already on 15 February Caesar had reached Corfinium and begun the blockade. On 17 February the news reached Luceria, and Pompey sent the following message to Domitius:

Your despatch was delivered to me on 17 February. You write that Caesar has pitched camp near Corfinium. What I thought and warned you would happen has happened. He does not want to join battle with you at present and he is bringing all his forces together and hemming you in to prevent your being able to march here directly and join your forces of loyal citizens with these legions of mine, about whose allegiance I still have doubts. So I am all the more disturbed by your despatch. I am not sufficiently confident of the allegiance of the men I have with me to risk a battle in which all the fortunes of the Republic are at stake, and the levies which have been raised for the consuls have not arrived here.

So do your best if you possibly can even now to extricate yourself and come here here as soon as possible before all the enemy's forces unite. The men from the levies can not get here quickly, and even if they could, you are fully aware how far one can trust men who do not even know each other against veteran legions.[17]

By the time this reply reached Corfinium the neighbouring town of Sulmo with a garrison of seven cohorts had already fallen; the Eighth Legion had arrived, and Curio had brought in a further twenty-two cohorts of recruits. With these forces Caesar was able to start building siege-works all round the city. Realising that escape for the whole army was impossible and that no relief was on the way, Domitius apparently decided to attempt to save his own skin and escape with a few friends. The troops, however, got wind of this plan, arrested Domitius, and offered to surrender themselves and their commander to Caesar. With deliberate clemency Caesar released Domitius and the other senators with him, and returned the 6,000,000 sesterces which Domitius had had to pay his troops. The thirty-one cohorts, however, were made to swear a new oath of allegiance to Caesar, and were eventually sent under the command of Asinius Pollio to seize Sicily from Cato. Caesar set out from Corfinium at noon on 21 February in hot pursuit of Pompey.

With the arrival of Domitius' last despatch Pompey had realised that the army at Corfinium was as good as lost. He promptly sent a further message to the consuls at Capua, informing them of the situation and of his reasons for not going to Domitius' aid. The message concluded:

> Therefore I have decided (and I see that M. Marcellus and the other members of the Senate who are here agree with me) to lead the force which I have with me to Brundisium. I urge you to collect as many troops as you can and come to Brundisium too as soon as possible. I suggest you equip the soldiers you have with you with the arms you were going to send to me. If you transport the remaining arms by mule to Brundisium you will have done the Republic a great service. Please pass this information on to our supporters. I am sending instructions to the praetors P. Lupus and C. Coponius to join you and bring you whatever troops they have.[18]

Pompey had now clearly abandoned his plan to garrison Sicily and decided to ship all his forces across to Greece. Leaving Luceria on 19 February ahead of his legions, he met the consuls at Canusium on the following day, and four days later was in Brundisium. Possibly because of his change of plan there were only enough transport ships collected for thirty out of his fifty cohorts. He decided that the consuls should cross first with their new recruits, and these were embarked and had left for Dyrrachium by 8 March. Pompey with his own two legions remained to await the return of the ships and to organise the defence of the port against Caesar.

He arrived on 9 March, after sixteen days of hard marching, and proceeded to set up camp outside the town walls. *En route* he had received the surrender of several more cohorts of Pompeians and captured Numerius Magius, another of Pompey's prefects of engineers, whom he sent on in advance with offers of a meeting between the two leaders to discuss peace. On Caesar's arrival Pompey seems to have sent Magius back, but we have no knowledge of the nature of his reply. Caesar's despatch to Oppius and Balbus, in which he mentions it, suggests that Pompey expressed interest. However, there was no reply to the second set of proposals which Caesar sent through Magius. Nevertheless Caesar seems to have remained hopeful, as he had been in January, that he could persuade Pompey to patch up their personal quarrel and withdraw his support from the Catonians. He continued to urge Cicero, and no doubt others, through the agency of Cornelius Balbus to use his influence with Pompey, and he sent Caninius Rebilus, a close friend of Scribonius Libo, into Brundisium to get Libo to talk with him as well.[19]

But Pompey was not to be drawn. He replied that in the absence of the consuls he had no power to negotiate. For him there was no thought of reconciliation, which could only mean subordination to Caesar. Indeed, if we can believe Cicero, it was possible to detect a growing bitterness and savagery in Pompey's character during the first months of 49. The country towns of Italy, which a year before had offered prayers for his safety, were now terrified of his anger and harshness. At Luceria he is said to have discussed the possibility of proscriptions after victory and to have uttered the ominous words, *Sulla potuit, ego non potero?*, 'Sulla could do it; shall I not be able to?' To Cicero there were signs that the Sullan terror was being resurrected.[20]

Once in Greece it was Pompey's plan to maintain a naval blockade on Italy, and trap Caesar between two great armies, the seven legions in Spain and the forces he knew he could muster in the East. As he waited at Brundisium for his transports to return he began to put the first phase of his plan into operation. Metellus Scipio and Pompey's elder son Gnaeus left for Scipio's province of Syria to collect troops and a fleet of warships. Vibullius Rufus, who had been released after the surrender of Corfinium, was sent out to the three legates of Spain, Varro, Petreius and Afranius, with instructions for organising the defence of the province. Two other commanders seem to have acted very much on their own initiative. L. Domitius had requisitioned seven ships from Igilium and Cosa on the coast of Etruria, manned them with clients from his own estates there, and sailed to Marseilles, the important port which controlled the land route from Italy to

Spain through his new province. P. Attius Varus, after his retreat from Auximum, had gone straight to Africa, a province he had previously governed, and assumed control in the absence of the official governor, Tubero, who had not yet arrived.

On the other hand Marcus Cato had abandoned Sicily to the Caesarian officer Asinius Pollio, and Marcus Cicero, in spite of two urgent requests by Pompey to join him, had discovered every possible excuse for not doing so and was still on the west coast watching events and trying to make up his mind which side to choose.[21]

Meanwhile, Caesar, in an attempt to trap Pompey in Brundisium, was busy blocking up the harbour mouth with earth moles from either side, joined across the deepest part by a string of rafts, each nine metres square, covered with a causeway of earth and protected with screens and towers. To counter this threat Pompey constructed towers for heavy artillery on a number of merchant ships and used these to destroy the rafts as they were floated into position.

In just over a week the fleet was back from Dyrrachium. Pompey embarked his two remaining legions, but before he could sail he had to cover the withdrawal of the troops who had been guarding the town walls by barricading and mining all but two of the streets leading to the harbour and leaving a picked force of archers and slingers to hold the fortifications till the last possible moment, and then race to board their ships. As one might expect, the operation ran smoothly with the loss of only two ships, in spite of the fact that Caesar was assisted by the townsfolk of Brundisium, who resented the treatment they had received from the soldiers and what Caesar called the insulting behaviour of Pompey himself.

On 17 March the evacuation was completed, and Caesar was left the master of Italy.

9 'DEAD MEN DON'T BITE': DYRRACHIUM AND PHARSALUS JANUARY TO SEPTEMBER 48

Once landed at Dyrrachium Pompey rapidly proceeded to build his new army. He had already sent instructions to all the client rulers of the East to provide troops, and in the provinces his governors and legates were hard at work. Before long the various units started to arrive at Beroea, a town in the lower Haliacmon valley of Macedonia sixty kilometres west of Thessalonica, which he had chosen as the training area for his army.

To the five legions of Roman infantry which had crossed from Italy were added four more. The veteran settlers in Crete and Macedonia provided one, as did the remains of two legions which had formed the permanent garrison of Cilicia; and in Asia the consul Lentulus was able to raise two legions by energetic recruitment. Furthermore Scipio in Syria was now in command of two legions which had survived Crassus' defeat against the Parthians in 53, but he had some difficulty in bringing them across the Amanus range into Cilicia, and did not get further than Pergamum before deciding to put his men into quarters for the winter.[1]

The list of cavalry units and light-armed auxiliaries reads like a gazetteer of the eastern world. Deiotarus and Castor of Galatia, Ariobarzanes of Cappadocia, and Taxiles of Lesser Armenia are reported as having led their troops in person, while other contingents came from all the eastern provinces as well as from the kingdoms of Lycia, Pisidia and Pamphylia, Paphlagonia, Pontus, Greater Armenia, Commagene and Egypt. The infantry were distributed among the legions; there were also 3,000 archers, 1,200 slingers, and, the pride of the army, 7,000 cavalry, mainly from the eastern kingdoms, but with some 800 herdsmen and slaves from Pompey's own estates.[2]

However, the real strength of the Pompeian cause lay in its fleet, estimated by Plutarch at 500 fighting ships with many other transports and light craft, but probably nearer 300 fighting ships in fact. They were under the supreme command of M. Bibulus, a man motivated more by hatred of Caesar, one would imagine, than by his love of Pompey, and divided into five flotillas commanded by Cn. Pompeius (sixty from Egypt), D. Laelius and C. Valerius Triarius (the Asiatic

Figure 7: Map of Northern Greece to illustrate the campaigns of 48.

fleet), C. Cassius Longinus (seventy from Syria), C. Marcellus and C. Coponius (twenty from Rhodes), and M. Octavius and Scribonius Libo (the fleets from Achaea and Liburnia). The task of the grand fleet was to maintain a patrol along the whole of the eastern coast of the Adriatic, to prevent corn ships from reaching Italian ports, and to safeguard the transport of corn and other essentials to the Pompeian forces and their supply bases. Sixteen ships were also sent to assist the Massiliots in their resistance to Caesar.[3]

Finally Pompey was particularly exercised by the problem of raising enough money to pay for the upkeep of this enormously expensive force. Thanks to the failure of the consuls to secure for him the contents of the Roman treasury he had lost 30,000,000 sesterces and a vast quantity of uncoined gold and silver to Caesar. This had to be made good by new taxes and other exactions from all the cities and kingdoms still under his control, and by forced payments of arrears and advances from the tax-collecting companies. Caesar describes in particular the extortionate methods of Scipio and his agents in Asia, where even the temple treasures of Diana at Ephesus were nearly seized. A mint was established at Apollonia, where coins were struck from the bullion collected.[4]

Pompey himself probably contributed the greater part of his own fortune. Caesar mentions that he paid a large reward to Antiochus of Commagene for his services, and one would imagine that he did not keep for himself the huge sums of interest which he was being paid by debtors such as Ariobarzanes. Certainly by the middle of June 48 we have Cicero's word for it that Pompey was in dire straits financially and borrowing a sum of 1,000,000 sesterces from Cicero.[5]

Plutarch describes the scene at the training grounds thus:

Pompey was exercising his infantry forces at Beroea. They were a mixed crowd and in need of training. He, however, did not sit idly on the side-lines, but took part in the training himself as if he were in the prime of his youth. It provided a great boost to the morale of the troops when they saw Pompey the Great, for all his fifty-eight years, fighting on foot in full armour, and then again on horseback effortlessly drawing his sword at full gallop and re-sheathing it with ease. Also at throwing the javelin he displayed strength as well as accuracy so that many of the young men could not better his distance. Kings of nations and rulers visited his camp and the number of leading Romans in his entourage was sufficient to form a full Senate.[6]

During the summer news began to arrive from other fronts of the war. At first all was encouragement. In July came an optimistic despatch from L. Afranius and M. Petreius in Spain. Unable to follow Pompey to Greece, Caesar had sent one of his legates in Gaul, C. Fabius, to seize the passes of the Pyrenees and make contact with the Pompeian forces in Spain, while he himself marched round from Italy with all speed. Afranius and Petreius had taken up their position at Ilerda, and with their superior knowledge of the countryside and some help from the weather they had succeeded in trapping the Caesarian legions in an area between the rivers Sicoris and Cinga and cutting off their supplies. The despatch was shortly followed by a new wave of supporters from Italy who thought that the war was nearly over and were anxious to join the winning side in time.

Then came news that the admirals Libo and Octavius had captured fifteen cohorts under C. Antonius, the brother of M. Antonius, whom Caesar had put in charge of the province of Illyricum to guard the eastern land approaches to Italy during his absence. They had trapped the Caesarians on the island of Curicta at the head of the Adriatic and defeated a naval force of forty ships under P. Cornelius Dolabella which had come to their aid. Having thus secured control of the northern Adriatic, Octavius tried to win over the Italian settlements along the coast, beginning with Salona, but he failed to shake their loyalty to Caesar and returned to Dyrrachium having added Antonius' cohorts to the Pompeian strength.[7]

Almost simultaneously (mid-August 49), the Pompeians won a great success in Africa. Here C. Curio, with two legions largely formed of the troops which had surrendered at Corfinium and been taken across to Sicily, had been decisively defeated by a Numidian army led by Saburra, one of the cavalry officers of King Juba. Juba, the son of Pompey's client King Hiempsal, had come to the aid of Attius Varus when Curio invaded Africa, and Saburra had lured the headstrong Curio into the desert south of Utica and cut the whole of his infantry to pieces. Juba was now in effective control of the province.

By then, however, the tide of fortune had turned in Spain. Displaying enormous energy in constructing a bridge and a ford across the Sicoris Caesar had reopened his supply lines, and used his superior cavalry to harass the Pompeian foraging parties to such good effect that Afranius and Petreius were forced to attempt a withdrawal to the Ebro. Having seized the initiative, Caesar pressed home his advantage with continuous attacks on the Pompeian column and finally forced the whole army (five legions) to surrender on 2 August.

Before long the two support legions under M. Varro in Further Spain had also surrendered at Corduba, and by mid-September Caesar's legate had finally besieged the obstinate Massiliots into capitulation.

Before the end of the year Caesar was back in Rome, where he had been elected dictator in his absence. Within eleven days he had held the consular elections for 48, and been himself chosen; taken steps to settle the current financial crisis; recalled all those exiled by the Pompeian 'purge' of 52; and moved on to Brundisium, where he had ordered an army of twelve legions plus cavalry to muster. Thanks to his phenomenal energy and speed he had wrested the initiative from Pompey. So far from allowing his rival to trap him in Italy between his Spanish and Asiatic armies, he was now in a position to bring the war to Pompey.

By the end of 49 Pompey felt ready to bring his army across from Macedonia to the Adriatic to put it in winter quarters near the stores depots which he had established at Dyrrachium, Apollonia and other towns along the coast of Epirus. He had by now been given supreme command of the war against Caesar by his 'Senate' (IIID).[8]

We have no means of knowing whether his strategy was to continue the naval blockade of Italy or to attempt an invasion. In view of his still superior naval strength and the loss of his Spanish legions the former is more likely, but the question is academic, for in his march along the Egnatian way towards Dyrrachium, Pompey was crossing the mountains of Candavia when he was met by his old prefect of engineers Vibullius Rufus bringing alarming news.

This was that on the night of 4 January Caesar had sailed from Brundisium with seven legions, and, catching Bibulus off his guard, managed to land unopposed at Palaeste on the mountainous coast between Oricum and Corcyra. Vibullius had been sent to Corcyra with a message for Pompey, and learning from Bibulus of his whereabouts had ridden at full speed day and night to catch him.

The gist of Caesar's message was that since both leaders had suffered serious losses in the past year now was the time to discuss peace while they were evenly matched. They should ask the Senate and People at Rome to frame terms, which they should accept, meanwhile having sworn publicly to dismiss their forces within three days.[9]

For Pompey to accept these terms would have been an admission of defeat. Caesar was now consul, and the Senate at Rome consisted of his supporters. He therefore sent no reply, but realising that his supply bases were in serious danger thanks to the timidity of Lucretius

Vespillo and Minucius Rufus, the commanders of the fleet at Oricum, and the unpreparedness of Bibulus, he ordered his army to head for Apollonia by forced marches.

Soon worse news arrived. L. Torquatus and L. Staberius, the garrison commanders of Oricum and Apollonia, had been forced by local support for Caesar to abandon their commands, and the whole of Epirus south of the river Apsus was lost. By redoubled efforts Pompey managed to reach the neighbourhood of Dyrrachium before Caesar, but the latter records that his numbers were reduced by the desertion of his Epirote recruits, and the rest turned into a panic-stricken rabble, which it took prompt action on the part of Labienus and the other officers to restore to some form of order.[10]

Thwarted in his bid for the great prize of Dyrrachium, Caesar withdrew south of the Apsus to consolidate his position and await the arrival of his remaining legions under the command of Fufius Calenus and M. Antonius. Pompey advanced and pitched camp opposite him, probably guarding the point where the southern extension of the Egnatian Way crossed the river, and waited. He was unwilling to risk a pitched battle. Even though his nine legions outnumbered Caesar's depleted seven, the latter were largely veteran, and Pompey wanted to increase his numerical superiority by the addition of Scipio's two legions, which he had sent for immediately on hearing the news of Caesar's crossing, while weakening Caesar by cutting off all supplies by sea.[11]

Appian mentions a number of cavalry skirmishes at this time, and records an attempt by Pompey to cross the river and join battle, perhaps at a time when Caesar himself was away from camp. Dio gives a slightly different version of the same story. Caesar was unwilling to risk battle until his reinforcements arrived, and it is unlikely that Pompey was prepared to attack a fortified camp. Appian's and Dio's sources may have mentioned some attempt to attack Caesar's supply lines.[12]

The success of Pompey's plan depended on Scipio's being able to reach Dyrrachium before Caesar's other legions could break the blockade. Bibulus had made some amends for his earlier blunder by capturing and burning thirty of Caesar's ships as they returned to Brundisium, and had set up permanent patrols from Sason island, just south of Apollonia, to Corcyra. However, conditions for the rowers were atrocious. It was now mid-winter and since Caesar had posted garrisons along the coast it was impossible to land to collect water or firewood, and all supplies had to be brought by sea from Corcyra.

These hardships drove Bibulus and Libo to open negotiations with Caesar in order to gain a temporary truce to allow the rowers to land for a while, but Caesar was not to be drawn, and shortly afterwards Bibulus died as a result of prolonged exposure and exhaustion. Pompey did not replace him in overall command of his navy, but repeatedly urged the individual flotilla commanders to increase their vigilance in maintaining the blockade. Libo, indeed, with a squadron of fifty ships, crossed to Brundisium to try to prevent Calenus and Antonius from even leaving harbour, so that the other admirals might have a breathing space in which to beach their ships for scraping and repair. But in spite of some initial success Libo was outwitted by Antonius in one engagement, lost one quadrireme, and was forced to withdraw from Brundisium.[13]

Meanwhile the troops and some officers in the two camps facing each other across the Apsus had begun to fraternise and even make their own arrangements for discussions. This was encouraged by Caesar, who remembered that such contact had helped to bring about the surrender of the Pompeians at Ilerda, but the danger was soon realised by Labienus and any contact between the two sides was forbidden. Pompey's own views about the possibility of an agreement had been made quite clear at a meeting with his advisers Vibullius, Libo, Lucceius and Theophanes, which Vibullius had called to discuss Caesar's earlier proposals: 'What good is life or citizenship to me if I am seen to enjoy it by Caesar's favour? It will be impossible to remove that impression when I am thought to have been brought back to the Italy which I left.'[14]

In late March the stalemate was finally broken when Antonius managed to cross with four more legions and land at the harbour of Nymphaeum, some fifty-seven kilometres north of Dyrrachium. This time Caesar's luck had been firmly on his side. The ships were carried up the coast past Apollonia by a south wind, and a fleet of warships under C. Coponius rowed out from Dyrrachium to intercept them. As the Caesarians reached the shelter of the harbour at Nymphaeum the wind suddenly veered to the south-west and drove the tiring Pompeian pursuers on to the unsheltered coast, wrecking the whole fleet. The blockade had been broken a second time.

It was now important that Pompey should prevent the two Caesarian armies from linking up. Breaking camp he marched north-east over a pass to a point a few kilometres south of the Egnatian Way and the Genusus river, which he knew Antonius must pass if he was to join Caesar. Yet again, however, he had to pay for his failure to win the loyalty of the local inhabitants. Not only had the Roman settlers at Lissus, just south of Nymphaeum, forced the Pompeian garrison commander there, M. Otacilius Crassus. to abandon the town, but the Greeks of the Genusus region revealed the position of Pompey's ambush to Antonius, and he was able to halt his march and stay in camp until he was joined by Caesar coming round by a detour to the east. To avoid being trapped himself, Pompey withdrew westwards along the Egnatian Way to Asparagium to protect the approaches to Dyrrachium.

The second failure of Pompey's blockade was followed by a valuable success. His elder son Gnaeus, who was in charge of the Egyptian fleet, received news that the garrison at Oricum had been reduced from one legion to three cohorts. Caesar had given up hope of bringing supplies in by sea, and once Antonius' trocps had arrived he decided to relieve the pressure on the Pompeian naval forces and his own commissariat and redeploy his troops by sending one-and-a-half legions to win support and gather supplies in Aetolia and Thessaly, and a further two legions under Domitius Calvinus to intercept Scipio in Macedonia. Gnaeus Pompey immediately took advantage of this new situation and in a clever and daring raid succeeded in attacking and burning Caesar's squadron of warships in the inner harbour at Oricum, and followed this up by destroying thirty transport ships which Antonius had left at Lissus.

Shortly after Pompey had encamped near Asparagium, the united Caesarian forces arrived on the southern bank opposite him, and on the following day Caesar drew up all his troops in battle-line to tempt Pompey into action. Pompey made no move, and the next day watched as Caesar withdrew eastwards along the river. He seems to have thought that Caesar was being forced to leave by supply difficulties. Scouts were sent out to observe this manoeuvre, and returned later with the news that a few kilometres away Caesar had crossed the river unopposed and headed north up a narrow and difficult mountain pass. Pompey must have realised that he had been outwitted once more. Caesar was aiming to cut him off from Dyrrachium.

Had he set out immediately on receipt of this news Pompey would have probably reached Dyrrachium first, but he under-estimated Caesar's speed and allowed his troops time to rest. When, after setting off before dawn the next day, he arrived in sight of his base, Caesar was already between them, having marched the fifty-five kilometres or so over the mountains with only the briefest of halts for rest.

At all costs Pompey now had to retain communications with

Dyrrachium by sea, and continue to keep Caesar starved of supplies. He established his new camp on the top of a rocky outcrop called Petra, overlooking the Egnatian Way and protecting a reasonable anchorage for his ships about seven kilometres south of his base, and sent out orders for part of his navy to assemble there and for the convoys from Asia and elsewhere to bring their cargoes of corn to his new camp. He knew that there was little food for Caesar in the immediate area, which he had recently ransacked himself, and he hoped that his cavalry would be able to harass Caesar's supply lines from the interior and any foraging parties. So long as his stronghold at Dyrrachium held out, he himself was safe.

But he can hardly have been prepared for Caesar's next move. His new camp was on some lower heights about two kilometres north of Petra across a valley. It was not long before Pompey noticed that enemy units were occupying a series of rugged hills which ran in a great arc east and then south-east of Caesar's camp, and constructing small forts on the summits. Where necessary the intervening gaps were being closed by a line of earthworks. Clearly Caesar was beginning to blockade the Pompeian position from the land. His motives, as he tells us himself, were three-fold: to prevent Pompey from getting fodder for his animals; to render his cavalry ineffective and thus protect his own foraging parties; and to reduce Pompey's standing in the eyes of the foreigners in his army by putting him on the defensive and making him openly refuse battle.[15]

To prevent this circumvallation being completed Pompey would have had to commit his troops to battle with Caesar's more experienced legions, and he was still unprepared to do this, at least until Scipio's reinforcements arrived. Having decided to continue with his policy of starving Caesar into submission, he was forced to start building an inner ring of fortifications, similar to Caesar's, enclosing as wide an area of grazing land as possible to stretch Caesar's lines to the limit. There were frequent skirmishes as both sides fought for the possession of certain points, but Pompey seems to have relied mainly on his slingers and archers and to have avoided fighting at close quarters.

Caesar records one battle in particular, fought about mid-June, for the control of the vital hill of Paliama, some five kilometres to the south of Pompey's camp. Had he held this position Caesar would have been able to draw his line very tightly round his enemy. Using archers and slingers and light armed infantry supported by catapults, Pompey dislodged the Caesarian Ninth Legion from its position, but he failed to take full advantage of the withdrawal and his pursuit was halted by an

Figure 8: Plan to illustrate the operations found around Dyrrachium.

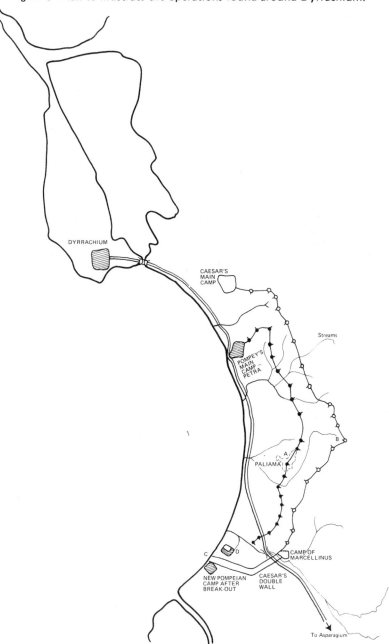

uphill counter-charge by the legionaries. The hill, however, was safe and Caesar was forced to continue building his fortifications on a wider arc. But in spite of the boast that Pompey was heard to make that he would not object to being called an incompetent commander if Caesar's legions escaped without serious losses, the number of casualties was very few (A in Figure 8).[16]

The suggestion that Pompey was being called incompetent in his own camp raises the question of morale among his men and especially among the leading senators in his entourage. Cicero, who was one of ten consulars there (before the death of Bibulus), later wrote about the many faults he found. 'Firstly, the forces, neither numerous nor warlike; secondly, apart from the commander, and a few others — I'm talking about the leaders — the rest had eyes only for plunder in the war itself, and their conversation was so bloodthirsty that I dreaded the thought of victory. Men of the highest rank were heavily in debt. The only good thing was the cause they were fighting for.'[17]

Cicero was among those who urged the acceptance of peace terms, but seeing that Pompey would have none of it, was in favour of the policy of attrition. More irritating still to Pompey than the advice of this most unmilitary supporter must have been his scathing criticisms of Pompey and his staff, which Plutarch records in his *Life of Cicero*, the squabbling and backbiting of the senators, and the friction between them and the more professional of his supporters, such as the Greek Theophanes. It was probably to protect his wife Cornelia from such unpleasantness as much as from the dangers of war that Pompey sent her to Mitylene on his arrival at Dyrrachium.[18]

By the end of June Caesar appears to have completed the circumvallation, and things were certainly not going as Pompey had expected. Admittedly Caesar was short of corn, but supplies were coming through and his men were feeding on barley, vegetables, meat and 'chara' bread, made by mixing the pounded roots of a local plant with milk. Within the blockade, however, fodder for the pack animals and horses was very scarce and the atmosphere was becoming foul with the stench of rotting carcasses. Caesar had also dammed the streams which flowed through the lines, effectively cutting off much of the fresh water supply, and hastily dug wells could not make good the loss.

If the army was not to be destroyed by disease during the summer and lose all its animals, Caesar's siege-works had to be breached. Pompey decided to lure Caesar himself away from the fortifications by means of a false message that some of the inhabitants of Dyrrachium were prepared to betray the town to him, and meanwhile launch a three-pronged attack against forts in the centre of the line. At two of these forts one cohort under L. Minucius Basilus and three under C. Volcatius Tullus put up heroic resistance against five of Pompey's legions until they were relieved by a force of two legions from the main camp under P. Sulla. The Pompeians were in fact cut off on a hill-top between the two lines for five days before Pompey could withdraw them, and Caesar reckoned the Pompeian losses at 2,000 (B in Figure 8).

At Dyrrachium Caesar himself had failed to take the town and only just escaped from ambush, but he soon hit back by building fortifications to cut off the two approaches to the town and prevent the cavalry horses which Pompey had shipped across from grazing in the countryside to the north.[19]

The return of these horses to the main camp only aggravated the situation and morale was further sapped by Caesar's now daily practice of offering battle between the two main camps, and forcing Pompey to draw up his battle-lines in order to keep up appearances, but so close to the camp walls that Caesar could not attack.

It was at this point that two Gallic cavalry officers from Caesar's army deserted in order to escape punishment for embezzlement of cavalry pay. Apart from their value as propaganda they also brought with them detailed information about the nature of the Caesarian siege-works and the system of patrols. As a result Pompey was able to plan a massive dawn offensive against the southern end of the line where it came close to the sea. Here Caesar had built a second wall 200 metres outside the main one to protect the defenders from sea-borne attacks from the rear, but this was unfinished and the area between the two walls undefended at the seaward end (C on Figure 8).

The attack came in three waves. Six legions launched a frontal assault on the fortifications, while units of light infantry and archers, with helmets protected by wicker masks against stones, landed behind the rear wall and between the two. The Caesarian Ninth Legion, which was positioned there, was routed, as was the small relief force which came to its aid from the nearest camp, that of P. Lentulus Marcellinus. The pursuit was only checked by large reinforcements brought up by Caesar and Antonius.

During the morning Pompey consolidated his newly-won position by building a camp south of the Caesarian walls for five of his legions, and sent the sixth back to reoccupy an old camp between those walls and his own previous defences (D in Figure 8). Hearing of this Caesar immediately sent a force of thirty-three cohorts to attack the single legion, and the left wing of this force succeeded in forcing its way into the camp. The cavalry and the rest of the right wing, however, were prevented from attacking the other side of the camp by a long earthwork which linked it to the nearby river, and by the time they had got across they were met by Pompey's cavalry coming to the rescue. Both they and the left wing were forced to retreat in haste as the five Pompeian legions moved up to the camp, and the encouraged Pompeians inside launched a counter-attack. But once again Pompey failed to press home his advantage. His advance relief force, which included the cavalry, was hindered by the same earthworks which had baffled the Caesarian right wing, and the main force was not allowed to pursue the defeated left wing in their absence. Caesar thought that Pompey was afraid of an ambush, so rapid was the Caesarian withdrawal, and wrote later that had Pompey kept up the pursuit he might have destroyed the whole of his army. Certainly it appears a weakness in Pompey that he was now reluctant to make a move that had not been planned in advance, but his men were not trained by experience to act with discipline in a sudden emergency, nor by all accounts were his centurions the loyal and battle-hardened officers that Caesar's were, capable of taking difficult decisions in the heat of battle on their own initiative. Caesar reckoned his own losses at about 1,000; Pompey's were presumably much less.[20]

However, not only did Pompey refrain from pursuing Caesar's routed forces and allow them to regroup in their camp; he also seems to have failed to notice his enemies' preparations for a total withdrawal. By dawn the next morning all Caesar's troops had left the area of Dyrrachium, and although Pompey sent his cavalry in pursuit as soon as the news reached him, Caesar had arrived at the Genusus near Asparagium and got most of his army across before they caught up. Moreover the cavalry which attacked Caesar's rear were driven off with considerable losses by a mixed force of cavalry and light-armed infantry.

Later the same day Pompey arrived with his infantry, and that night both armies stayed in their old camps on either side of the river, but the discipline in the Pompeian camp seems to have become very lax. When Caesar set out again at noon on the following day Pompey was apparently unable to pursue immediately because some of his men had gone back to their previous camp to retrieve the baggage they had left there. This delay gave Caesar thirteen kilometres and half a day's start over Pompey, which he was not able to make up in the next three days in spite of great effort. By this time Caesar had crossed the Apsus and reached Apollonia, and Pompey called off the chase. A great opportunity to capitalise on his success at Dyrrachium had been sadly missed.

But if Caesar later reflected that by thus letting him off the hook Pompey had lost the war, the Pompeians felt that by inflicting a nasty defeat on their enemy and breaking his siege they had won it. Messages proclaiming the virtual destruction of Caesar's army were sent to all their supporters and to all the towns of Greece, and Pompey was saluted as *Imperator*. He himself had the grace not to use the title in his victory despatches or to wreathe his *fasces* with laurel leaves, but he added to his party's unsavoury reputation for vindictiveness by allowing Labienus to insult and publicly execute his prisoners.

Although he was nominally commander-in-chief there is strong evidence that Pompey was beginning to crack under the strain of trying to control his subordinates. In previous campaigns he had of course chosen his own legates, but many of those now in his camp were men who felt that Pompey owed his position to them and were becoming increasingly dissatisfied with the way the war was being conducted.

After calling off his pursuit of Caesar, Pompey presumably paused to allow his baggage train and such troops as he had left behind to join him. One would imagine that he also took steps to replace some of the mules which had died during the siege. After a short while came the news that Caesar, with some six legions, had set out from Apollonia heading south. Four cohorts had been left to guard the sick and wounded at Apollonia.

Pompey conjectured that Caesar had taken one of two decisions, either to establish a camp near Oricum and wait for his remaining legions and cavalry from Brundisium, or take the southerly route over the mountains into Thessaly, link up with Domitius Calvinus, and attack Scipio. The second of these seemed to be more likely.

There was no lack of advice for Pompey from his fellow senators as to what move he should take. At a council of war L. Afranius, who had arrived from Spain during the siege of Dyrrachium with seven cohorts which he had salvaged from the disaster at Ilerda, argued that now was the time to retake Italy and recover the western provinces while Caesar was away. He was supported by many others whose chief concern seems to have been to return home and pick up the threads of their political careers. Pompey saw that militarily this course would have been disastrous. To leave Greece with Caesar undefeated would have involved the loss of his eastern allies and with them his control of the seas. It would not take Caesar long to march back to Italy through a friendly Illyricum, and he would be faced with a situation he had tried to avoid all along, a direct confrontation in Italy itself. In any case he would be losing face by turning his back on Caesar a second time, and be sacrificing Scipio to certain defeat.

Probably sending a message to Scipio to withdraw to Larissa in Thessaly and wait for him there, Pompey left a garrison of fifteen cohorts under M. Cato to guard the base at Dyrrachium, rejoined the Egnatian Way at Elbasan, and headed east through Candavia. Halting briefly at Heraclia he was met by an ambassador from the Dacian king, Burebistas, perhaps with instructions to negotiate an alliance with the Roman government, and the delay may have cost him the chance of catching Domitius Calvinus and his army by surprise. The latter had earlier made contact with Scipio and his legions in the upper Haliacmon valley, but Scipio had declined battle and Domitius was forced by shortage of supplies to withdraw towards Heraclia. When he was about four hours' march away, his scouts fell in with some of the Gallic cavalrymen who had deserted to Pompey at Dyrrachium. These recognised their old comrades, and with a blithe disregard for the importance of security gave them a full account of what had happened at Dyrrachium and the present position of the two main armies. The news was relayed to Domitius, who immediately wheeled round and headed south to meet Caesar.[21]

Pompey meanwhile pressed on south-east towards Larissa. As he was approaching the borders of Thessaly, at the very end of July, he received news from the leader of his supporters in the west of the state that Caesar was about to besiege the town of Gomphi. The inhabitants would not be able to hold out for long and appealed for help. This Pompey was too far away to provide, but at least he will have had the satisfaction of knowing that his deductions as to Caesar's movements had been correct. A few days later he joined Scipio at Larissa to learn that Caesar had stormed and plundered Gomphi and terrorised all Thessaly except Larissa into supporting him. He had now advanced to the plain of Pharsalus in the valley of the river Enipeus, some forty kilometres to the south of Larissa.

In a speech to his combined forces Pompey thanked his own army for their exertions and urged Scipio's men to share the rewards of the victory that had already been won. Then on 5 August with a force which now numbered some nine-and-a-half legions as well as 7,000 cavalry and numerous light-armed auxiliaries he also reached Pharsalus and encamped on the slopes of a hill to the north of the river, overlooking the camp of Caesar.

The details of the decisive battle which was fought on the Pharsalian plain four days later on 9 August 48 BC are still very much matters for debate. Caesar, our one surviving contemporary source, provides a very over-simplified account. He gives no precise information as to the site of the battle, probably exaggerates both the numbers and the casualties on the Pompeian side, treats the tactics virtually as an exercise in military theory, and differs on many points of detail and interpretation from later accounts. These in the main probably derive from the reports of Caesar's officer Asinius Pollio and some Pompeian survivors.[22]

The narrative which follows is based on the Caesarian framework, amended and supplemented where necessary from the other sources, and accepts the theory that in spite of Appian's siting of the battle south of the Enipeus, the course of the battle can best be explained by placing it on the north bank, probably between the modern villages of Bairakli and Lazar Bouga.

In pursuing Caesar from Epirus Pompey's strategy seems to have been one of continuing attrition. As Appian said:

> He thought it dangerous to risk everything on the outcome of one battle against trained and desperate men and Caesar's own brilliant luck. It would be easier and safer to wear them out by lack of supplies since they did not control any fertile territory, could make no use of the sea, and had no ships for a rapid escape. Using this powerful argument he decided to prolong the war and drive his opponents from famine to disease.[23]

In the Pompeian camp, however, relations between Pompey and his senior senators had gone from bad to worse. Accusations were being made that Pompey was deliberately prolonging the war in order to maintain his position of superiority. Domitius Ahenobarbus was openly referring to him as 'Agamemnon, King of Kings', and Favonius and Afranius are mentioned by Plutarch as jibers in a similar vein. Bitterness was also rife between Afranius and those who were demanding his trial for betrayal of the army in Spain, and between Domitius, Scipio and Spinther, who were arguing as to who should replace Caesar as *Pontifex Maximus* after his defeat. Consulships were being confidently apportioned for the next few years, and there was ominous discussion of proscriptions against those who had supported Caesar or remained neutral. A disturbing rumour was going the rounds of a plot among the cavalry to depose Pompey after defeating Caesar, and the linking of Cato's name with this was later alleged as one of Pompey's reasons for leaving him at Dyrrachium.[24]

The sources seem to be agreed that Pompey finally gave in to pressure from his advisers. The most weighty of them was probably Labienus, his cavalry commander, who was at pains to play down the quality of Caesar's troops and confidently predicted a victory. After his arrival in the plain of Pharsalus Pompey had a considerable strategic advantage. His camp, protected by a number of outpost forts, guarded the main route to his supply base at Larissa, along which reinforcements were probably arriving each day, and his superior cavalry was once more able to harass the Caesarian foraging parties, which were hampered by the fact that the corn growing in the plain was not yet ripe.

A day or so after his arrival Pompey revealed at a council of war that he had decided to join battle when a suitable opportunity presented itself, and he outlined his tactical plan. 'I have persuaded our cavalry, as soon as they get to close quarters, to attack Caesar's right wing from its unprotected flank, surround his line from the rear, and throw it into confusion and rout it before we have time to cast a single javelin at the enemy. They have assured me that they will do this. Thus, without danger to the legions and almost without bloodshed we shall bring the war to an end.' It was this assurance, probably given by Labienus, that was critical in making Pompey alter his plan. He was sincere in his reluctance to shed Italian blood in this war, as indeed was Caesar, and this attitude may partly explain his later behaviour in the battle. Labienus followed Pompey's speech with a disparaging account of Caesar's troops and an oath only to return to camp as victor, which was then taken by Pompey and the other commanders.[25]

For three days Pompey refused battle in spite of repeated invitations from Caesar, who drew his legions up in line on the plain each day. Pompey also took his men out of camp, but was careful to draw them up on the slopes, ready to fight only if Caesar would be rash enough to attack up the hill. Meanwhile his cavalry suffered one nasty setback in a skirmish with Caesar's cavalry which was strengthened by the inclusion of some specially trained infantry.

Finally, however, Pompey decided to offer battle on the morning of 9 August, the same morning that Caesar also decided to move camp and head up the valley to his north towards the town of Scotussa. The connection between these two decisions is by no means clear. Caesar claimed that his own plan was to secure easier supplies of corn and, while forcing Pompey to follow him and tire out his already exhausted troops, to seize an opportunity of attacking him on the march. He suggested that it was pure coincidence that Pompey decided to fight on the same day. The most convincing of Caesar's points is the first once, and it is probable that Pompey's strategy had worked in so far as it had forced Caesar to move his position. However, Caesar's intended line of march suggests that he hoped to be able to move round from Scotussa westwards to cut Pompey's communications with Larissa. If Pompey knew of this plan it would explain his decision to offer battle on the plain with an army which was preparing for marching rather than fighting on that day.[26]

Plutarch in his life of Brutus certainly suggests that on 8 August the Pompeians were expecting battle on the following morning. Then the night of 8 August brought a heavy thunderstorm after a day of sultry heat. As Pompey made a sacrifice, probably in the hope of good omens for the morrow, some of the intended victims escaped. This bad omen presumably contributed to a panic among the troops, which Pompey himself had to quieten, and their nerves will hardly have been steadied by the appearance of a fireball in the sky overhead. When Pompey himself finally got to sleep he was disturbed by a dream that he was decorating the temple to Venus Victrix at Rome with many spoils to the accompaniment of loud applause from the audience in his theatre. We have already seen that Pompey was a prey to superstition, and there may be reason to believe the accounts that he awoke in a thoroughly dejected and pessimistic frame of mind. Caesar claimed Venus as one of his ancestors, and this connection seems to have suggested to Pompey that he had been decking Caesar with spoils – viz. himself granting Caesar the victory.[27]

The night's storm was followed by a heavy mist in the early morning. By the time the sun finally broke through Pompey's scouts had probably confirmed that Caesar's preparations were well under way for striking camp. Pompey delivered a harangue to his troops (IIIE) and gave them the watchword 'Hercules is invincible'. Then leaving seven cohorts to guard his camp he led his army down on to the plain to deploy them across the space between the Enipeus and the lower slopes of the hills in three lines, each, so Frontinus tells us, about ten men deep. The front thus formed will have been about two kilometres long.[28]

If Pompey had hoped to catch Caesar at a disadvantage by this move, he under-estimated his opponent. In spite of the fact that the first animals of Caesar's baggage train were already moving up to the gates of the camp when the news of Pompey's advance was brought to him, Caesar was able to change his plan immediately and get his fighting troops out of the camp and into line of battle without any apparent confusion. If we may reinterpret an action recorded by Appian, he achieved this by having his engineers open gaps in the rampart and fill up the ditch with the material in order to avoid a serious 'log jam' at the gates.[29]

The distribution of forces on both sides can most easily be seen in Figure 9. Caesar gives his own numbers as 22,000 men in eighty cohorts (eight legions) and Pompey's as 47,000 men in 110 cohorts (eleven legions), but Professor Brunt has recently argued in favour of the lower estimate for the Pompeians of 38,000 men in eighty-eight cohorts which is found in Appian and Orosius, and probably derives from Pollio. It should be remembered that these numbers refer to legionaries, and do not include the light-armed troops provided by allied rulers. At all events Pompey had the advantage of numerical superiority, especially in cavalry, where his 7,000 heavily outnumbered Caesar's 1,000.[30]

Making sure that his right wing was well protected by the marsh on the banks of the Enipeus, perhaps over-flowing after the storm, Pompey concentrated the bulk of his cavalry on the left of his line. It was here, as we have seen, that he was confident that the battle would be won; and it was opposite this flank that Caesar made his most careful dispositions.

Pompey also gave instructions, apparently on the advice of one of his officers C. Triarus, that his infantry line should not charge at the outset of the battle, but should stand firm and allow the Caesarians to break their own ranks and exhaust themselves by charging twice the distance they would expect.

But he under-estimated the tactical skill and discipline of his opponents. When his cavalry did charge, accompanied by the slingers and archers on the left, the Caesarian cavalry steadily gave way. As the Pompeians began to wheel to the right to come round behind the Tenth Legion, they were suddenly met by a charge from eight cohorts of infantry which Caesar had withdrawn from his rear and kept hidden behind his cavalry in an oblique line. Using their javelins as stabbing spears, and apparently aiming at the faces of the Pompeians, they created panic in the massed ranks of horsemen and routed them completely. They massacred the now unprotected archers and slingers, and began to attack the rear of the Pompeian First and Third Legions. Rash and over-confident, Labienus had utterly failed his commander.[31]

Meanwhile, in spite of the disparaging remarks which Labienus had continued to make about the quality of Caesar's legions, and the drop

Figure 9: Diagram to illustrate the initial distribution of forces at the battle of Pharsalus. (Not to scale.)

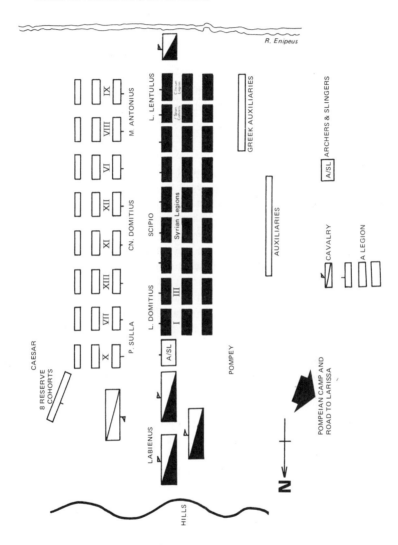

in morale they had suffered immediately after Dyrrachium, their discipline in the line had been faultless. Seeing the Pompeian infantry standing its ground, the front lines had of their own accord checked their charge half-way in order to recover breath before the assault. The Pompeians did in fact hold firm, hurled their javelins from a standing position, and drew swords to meet the attack. But the attack had only been made by the front two lines, and although the Pompeian legions fought well they were not prepared for the triple blow that fell on them. The rout of their cavalry was followed not only by the encirclement of their left flank, but by Pompey's own withdrawal from the battlefield and the entry of Caesar's third line, which he had kept fresh in reserve. At this point the allied auxiliaries might have been brought into action, but according to Appian these had fled for the camp as soon as the left wing began to give ground. Exhausted in the fierce mid-day heat and leaderless, the whole army turned in flight, and leaving the protection of the camp to the garrison and the auxiliaries, made for the hills behind.[32]

Caesar recalled that Pompey, who was directing his army on horse-back from a point probably just behind his own left wing, escaped from the battlefield on seeing the rout of the cavalry. Appian and Plutarch, on the other hand, suggest that it was not until he saw his infantry in retreat, and comment on his dazed and shattered appearance as he went slowly back to his camp and remained brooding in his tent until he heard that the Caesarians were breaking through the fortifica-tions. Only then did he strip himself of his general's cloak and insignia, seize a horse, and, acommpanied by Lentulus Crus, Lentulus Spinther, Favonius and one other, ride out through the back gate of the camp and up the road towards Larissa.[33]

This apparent desertion of the army by an experienced and popular commander needs some explanation. Caesar, who made little effort to spare the reputation if his defeated rival, talks of despair born of the collapse of all his hopes for a speedy victory. Dio believed that the totally unexpected defeat of the cavalry humbled his spirit, struck his reason with panic, and stripped him of all judgement. But perhaps Lucan, for all that he was at pains to portray Pompey as a tragic but heroic figure in his epic, also preserves an element of the truth. On his interpretation Pompey's departure was a calculated move to spare his army from total annihilation. 'He did not desire, as the wretched often do, to drag everything with him to destruction and make mankind share his own ruin . . . He did not lack the courage to face the swords, or to receive the death blow on his throat or chest; but he was afraid that, with Pompey's body strewn upon the field, his soldiers would refuse to flee and the whole world would fall prostrate upon the leader's corpse.' And we know from Appian and Florus (and thus probably from Livy) that at least in the later stages of the battle, after Pompey's departure, Caesar was urging his own men not to kill Roman citizens but to wreak their vengeance on the foreign auxiliaries.[34]

Although Caesar gives 15,000 as the number of Pompeians slain in the battle, Pollio's more moderate estimate of 6,000 may be nearer the truth. It would be wise to disregard rhetorical exaggerations of the carnage at Pharsalus and to see Pompey's action as that of a man who had seen his reluctant decision to try to end the war at one stroke rebound in his face, and come to the conclusion that to continue his own struggle with Caesar would now involve quite unjustifiable suffering and bloodshed for his fellow countrymen. His recent experiences with his aristocratic colleagues probably gave him little enthusiasm for the cause of a restored Republic on their terms. Military historians may fault Pompey for his lack of resolution (Napoleon's 'essential quality of a general') at Pharsalus. Probably he had already seen the destruction of his cause; in such circumstances resolution, perhaps, loses its value.[35]

Militarily Pompey's defeat should be attributed more to Caesar's tactical genius than to his own errors. It is generally agreed that Pompey's basic plan was simple and sound, and against any other commander would in all likelihood have succeeded. Against Caesar, however, it was not flexible enough, and too little provision was made for initial setbacks. Over-persuaded by his confident staff, Pompey had shown less than his usual care in planning, and his troops, in spite of protracted resistance by the centre of his line, were not of sufficient quality to make up for the deficiency. However, we should always remember, as the Roman historians did, that in civil war the emotional pressures on soldiers are not the same as in conventional war, and Caesar showed throughout that he knew just how to play on the emotions of his enemies. We may well wonder how many of them were certain what they were supposed to be fighting for.

We can not be sure whether in the month-and-a-half or so which followed Pharsalus Pompey ever seriously contemplated picking up the pieces of his shattered cause and continuing the struggle. After his escape from his camp he reached Larissa, where he was joined by thirty cavalrymen, and continued riding the same night through the vale of

Tempe towards the sea. Boarding a small river craft he and his companions sailed along the coast until they sighted a merchant ship whose captain, one Peticius, was willing to take them across to Amphipolis. There, according to Caesar, an edict was issued in Pompey's name that all the young men of military age in the province should muster to take the oath of allegiance to Pompey, but as he only stayed at Amphipolis for one night to borrow money from the town before sailing on to Mitylene, Caesar may be justified in concluding that the edict had been a ruse designed to put him off the scent.[36]

At Mitylene Pompey took on board his wife Cornelia and young Sextus. He had time, Plutarch records, for a brief discussion on Divine Providence with the philosopher Cratippus, but declined the citizens' offer of hospitality and advised them to surrender to Caesar. His next port of call was Attaleia (Antalya) in Pamphylia, and here there began to collect what might have become the nucleus of a new force − sixty senators and a number of triremes from the coastal cities of the eastern Mediterranean. Plutarch's account suggests that Pompey now indeed began to make a deliberate effort to raise more money and ships in Cilicia, picking up the threads of his old policy of a naval blockade.[37]

Be this as it may, he decided not to sail to Africa, where he learnt that Cato had taken the forces from Dyrrachium to join the arrogant Juba, or even to make contact with his elder son and the fleet at Corcyra. From Syedra in Cilicia he crossed to Cyprus to hear that Antioch, and thus the province of Syria, and the island of Rhodes had now declared against him. It was probably at this point that he made the fatal decision to collect as much money as he could from the citizens and tax-collectors on Cyprus and throw himself on the mercy of the new boy-king of Egypt, Ptolemy XIII. The advice was held by Plutarch to have come from Theophanes, and Pompey was thought to have contemplated even going to Parthia, to whose king he had earlier sent Lucilius Hirrus, and, on his arrival at Mitylene, King Deiotarus to negotiate terms for a possible alliance. It should be remembered that all this time Caesar was in pursuit and not more than a few days behind. Pompey's only hope was to find a ruler whose loyalty to him would outweigh the fear of reprisals from Caesar. The most loyal monarchs had already fought beside him and lost at Pharsalus. Ptolemy must have seemed the least dangerous of few possible choices.[38]

When the small flotilla arrived off the Egyptian coast it was learnt that Ptolemy was encamped with his army by Mount Casium, near Pelusium, engaged in a civil war of his own with his sister, Cleopatra. Pompey's request for aid was discussed by the king's council. This was controlled by three powerful courtiers who were virtually regents for the king, the eunuch Potheinus, Theodotus the king's tutor in rhetoric from Chios, and his army commander Achillas.

Anchored a short distance from the shore, Pompey saw a small boat put out towards his flagship. On board were a Roman tribune from the garrison which Gabinius had left for Ptolemy XII, and Achillas. Septimius, the soldier, whom Pompey recognised as a senior centurion from one of his earlier campaigns, greeted him as *Imperator*, and Achillas, in Greek, invited him to come on board, apologising for not having brought out a trireme more appropriate for his escort; the water between ship and shore was too shallow. Ignoring the warnings of his companions, who were alarmed by signs of activity by the king's ships anchored close inshore, and embracing Cornelia, Pompey took two of his centurions, a freedman by the name of Philip, and one slave, and climbed down into the boat. His departing words were a quotation from Sophocles:

Whoever goes to a tyrant's court becomes his slave, however free before.

As none of his companions appeared inclined to talk to him Pompey spent the short voyage perusing the speech in Greek he had written for delivery to Ptolemy. Then, as he rose to step ashore, he was stabbed from behind by Septimius. As he drew his toga over his face in order to die as decorum demanded, he was struck twice more by Achillas and one of his soldiers.

The treachery had not been that of Ptolemy, but of Theodotus, who had argued in council that this was the only safe course. Openly to reject or accept Pompey's request would have been to incur the enmity of either him or Caesar; but 'dead men do not bite'. It is easy to believe that Pompey was prepared for such a result and that he accepted it with the characteristic touch of fatalism which marked many of his actions and reported sayings towards the end of his life. The date was 28 September, one day before his fifty-ninth birthday, and the anniversary of his third and greatest triumph, that over Mithridates, in 61.

Pompey's head was cut off, taken to Ptolemy, and later presented, with his ring, to a horrified Caesar upon his arrival at Alexandria. His body was left on the shore and given a makeshift cremation by the loyal Philip, who was able to collect some of the ashes and give them to Cornelia. She eventually returned with them to Rome and interred them in the Alban palace.[39]

10 FACILE PRINCEPS?

About Pompey's distinctions there can be little dispute. Three times *triumphator*, conqueror of three continents and the sea between, it was he above all who created the Empire which Augustus and his successors were to increase and consolidate. At a time when Rome's internal and foreign foes might have dealt crippling damage to a state recovering from the disasters of the Sullan civil war, Pompey had dispersed all the threats (admittedly with considerable help) and left Rome undisputed mistress of the Mediterranean world. For the first time her foreign policy had injected into it a unity of thought and planning on a massive scale, and Pompey supplied the organising and administrative ability to put that planning into successful practice.

As a military tactician and strategist it is tempting to accept the admiring assessment of him by his contemporaries (other than Caesar) and allow the results to speak for themselves. It is unfortunate that we have no detailed accounts of most of his battles which would enable us to make for ourselves the sort of judgements which the *Gallic War* allows us to make about Caesar. The preceding narrative has attempted to present such evidence as there is as fully as possible. Without doubt Pompey made mistakes; in the civil war of 82; against Sertorius, especially at Lauro; and in the Civil War against Caesar. Except at Pharsalus these mistakes were not disastrous, and had little effect on the eventual outcome of the wars. Otherwise, his pertinacity and energy always saw him through.

It was in Pompey's nature to prefer cold, calculated planning to sudden inspired decisions in the heat of battle, and so he liked to win his battles by strategy, by so arranging things that he eventually came to grips with his opponent enjoying numerical superiority and the more advantageous position, and did not have to rely on tactical brilliance to win his victory. Often this led to prolonged campaigns and a policy of attrition, as against his three most brilliant adversaries, Sertorius, Mithridates and Caesar. But at other times he could move with lightning speed and decisiveness, as in Africa in 81 and against the pirates. In the end it must be remembered that only Caesar was ever able to take full advantage of the breathing space which Pompey's methods sometimes allowed a defeated enemy, and turn what might have been total disaster at Dyrrachium into victory at Pharsalus.

He was not, perhaps, an inspiring leader on the battlefield, but his men always knew that every care was being taken to maintain their supplies, to satisfy their physical needs, and to get them into the battle line with the greatest possible chance of success. With his troops Pompey was approachable, affable and reliable; after a campaign they were sure of generous rewards and a redoubtable champion for their own interests on discharge; his officers knew that he would help them in their future careers. All responded with confidence, loyalty, affection and remarkable displays of endurance.

There is probably most disagreement among historians when the discussion turns to Pompey's role as a politician. Certainly he followed in the footsteps of his father in not fitting neatly into any of the usual categories. He was not a member of a traditionally *nobilis* or Optimate family, but neither was he cast in the usual *popularis* mould. Nor is it particularly helpful to point to his long and close connection with the *equites*. Due partly to force of circumstance, partly, no doubt, to something in his own character, he came early to the conclusion that he was a man out of the ordinary, a Roman Alexander, who could earn by his services to his country a position of honour and prestige that was also quite out of the ordinary. This is well exemplified by his love of titles and outward display; his frequent references in his own speeches to his own achievements, and his reputation for personal pride and vanity.

In politics it would probably be correct to see him again as a strategist rather than a tactician, bringing to the Forum and the Senate the qualities which he displayed so clearly in his military campaigns. As he was reluctant to risk defeat in battle until he had taken every precaution to see that the odds were on his side, so in politics he refrained when possible from the open clashes with his rivals for power which might have brought rebuffs and damage to his pride. Rather he preferred to manipulate the situation, or in some cases just let it develop, until he was asked to step in and save his country or his friends. In this way he avoided being beholden to his supporters and ensured that it was he who was conferring the favours. It was part of this strategy to appear reluctant to accept commands, as can be seen most clearly in 67 and 66, or merely indifferent to the prospect (e.g. in the winter of 57-6 and in 54 and 53). Against Lepidus and Sertorius his youthful ambition was perhaps more apparent, but his commands against the pirates and Mithridates, the Corn Commission and his third consulship were all pressed upon him by popular or at least senatorial demand, and he was able to pose as the generous saviour of his people. Similarly he was able to win Cicero's support by securing his return from exile in 57 and regain Caesar's co-operation at Luca by making himself indispensible to him in early 56.

Sometimes the opposition — jealous *nobiles* or the equally ambitious Clodius (58-6), Crassus (56) or Caesar (51-48) — forced him into open political conflict, and here his showing was less impressive. Faced by the brick wall of the Catonians' stubbornness after his return from the East he proved a poor tactician in the Senate and at public meetings, and was driven to the coalition with Caesar in 60 and the use of violence in early 59. Similar opposition provoked the use of force at the magisterial elections for 55. In both cases the resort to violence was the result of desperation rather than a deliberate choice. As Clodius soon discovered, Pompey was himself highly susceptible to the threat of violence or assassination, an unexpected trait in one whose bravery on the battlefield was never called in question.

Unlike Caesar, but like Augustus, Pompey probably realised that open conflict with the Roman nobility was ultimately doomed to failure, and it is another mark of his pertinacity that the Catonians and other Optimates finally came to accept, albeit grudgingly, his leadership in the years 52-48. They may have come to believe that he would not use his power, as Sulla had, to crush all opposition; or perhaps they thought that they could make use of the growing rivalry between him and Caesar to break the latter and then reject Pompey again.

What use Pompey would have made of his victory had he won at Pharsalus we shall never know, in spite of Cicero's gloomy forebodings; but there are signs that it would have been closer to Augustus' use of his victory at Actium than to Caesar's solution. In all probability Pompey would have been content with a position of supremacy within the framework of the Roman constitution rather than above it. He seems to have viewed the constitution as an arrangement which could be adapted to meet the demands of a new empire and a united Italy without being overthrown. By 52 he had virtually reached a position where he was Rome's leader (*princeps*), pre-eminent in authority and honour, not interfering in the government of the ruling class except if he were called in to deal with an emergency. Behind this pre-eminence lay his vast wealth and *clientela*, and the army and the *imperium* which he held by reason of his proconsulship of Spain. This in its turn depended not on the annual allocation of provinces by the Senate but was granted by law for periods of five years. Contact with the assembly might have to be personal at times, but was more conveniently maintained through helpful tribunes. His tenure of a province did not demand his absence from Rome and Italy, for his legates could see to the day-to-day administration, and, especially now that his new theatre complex had provided a Senate House outside the city boundary, it did not prevent him from attending the Senate if he so chose.

In many ways the situation is similar to the position which Augustus created for himself after 23 BC. There were, however, some important differences. By then the ruling class had been forced by over eighteen years of civil war to accept the indispensability of a strong permanent *princeps*. Augustus had added the powers of a tribune to his own permanent proconsular *imperium*. And Augustus was able eventually to establish the dynastic principle. But it is not surprising that Pompey's image was carried in Augustus' funeral procession. It was his career rather than Caesar's that was the natural development between the dictatorship of Sulla and the Principate of Augustus.

There remains Pompey's character as a man. Shortly after his death Cicero wrote, 'I can not fail to grieve for his fate: for I knew him as a man of integrity and high moral character.' Such a judgement became standard in the years to come, as is shown by the brief sketch in Velleius (IIB) and the rather longer notices in Plutarch and Lucan, though we should not forget the criticisms of Cicero and Caelius and the comments of Sallust that he had 'an honest expression hiding a shameless heart', and was 'moderate in everything but his lust for power'. All such assessments must be comparative, but there can be little doubt that by the standards of his times Pompey was a leader who combined humanity with integrity and efficiency, capable of deep and lasting friendships, ready to forgive offences, less ruthless than many of his peers, and at least aware of the dangers and responsibilities of power. Add to this great personal vanity, pride bred of the consciousness of his own abilities, a reluctance to wear his heart on his sleeve, ambition and determination strong enough to drive him at times to deviate from some of his own standards of conduct, a tendency to superstition, occasional moodiness, a habit of blushing and appearing awkward on a public platform, and the picture begins to emerge of a highly complex character, hard to understand, sometimes infuriating, often admirable. Certainly he was a figure remarkable enough for his countrymen to call the thirty years from the dictatorship of Sulla to the dictatorship of Caesar the era of Pompey the Great.[1]

APPENDIX A
THE DOCUMENTARY SOURCES

The main continuous source for a study of Pompey must be PLUTARCH's (*c.* AD 46-120) *Lives*. Written in Greek, it relies on many no-longer extant earlier writers of varying quality, and only comparatively rarely are these quoted by name. Plutarch was enormously well-read, but as a biographer he was primarily interested in the character of his subject as illustrated by the events of his career and by numerous anecdotes and apophthegms, many of them clearly fictitious. The *Life of Pompey*, which can conveniently be found in Rex Warner's translation for Penguin Classics (*The Fall of the Roman Republic*), needs reading with care, but provides an invaluable framework for the historian. There is also much relevant information to be found in the *Lives* of Sulla, Caesar, Crassus and Cicero (same volume) and of Sertorius, Lucullus, the younger Cato and Brutus in the Loeb Classical Library (LCL).[1]

Of the works of contemporary writers those of CICERO (106-43 BC), CAESAR (100-44 BC) and SALLUST (86-*c*.34 BC) are the only ones which survive in any quantity. The *Letters* and *Speeches* of Cicero contain numerous references to Pompey, whom he knew well, dating from 70 to 47 BC. (There are several letters addressed to Pompey in person, and the collection contains a number actually written by him.) They are certainly our most important single source for this period. It would be misleading, though, to base an interpretation of Pompey's character and career solely on Cicero's assessment of him. Many of the speeches and letters were written in tones of fulsome flattery, others in moods of bitter disillusionment, and it is doubtful whether Cicero ever felt that he really understood his friend.[2]

Many relevant passages are quoted verbatim in the text; others can be found in Lacey and Wilson's selection entitled *Res Publica*, and in the two volumes in the Penguin Classics series (*Selected Works* and *Selected Political Speeches*), as well as in LCL, and Shackleton Bailey's translation of the *Letters to Atticus* (CUP). Some additional information, especially on the events of 52 is to be found in the commentary on five of Cicero's speeches by the apparently knowledgeable Q. ASCONIUS PEDIANUS (9 BC to AD 76).

Caesar's *The Civil War* (Penguin Classics) contains a full but biased account of the hostilities of 49 and 48. In its assessment of Pompey it needs to be balanced by reference to later writers who drew on a more favourable tradition.

Of the *Histories* of Sallust unfortunately only fragments survive. They include a number of speeches and letters from the seventies, and help to fill out the account of this poorly documented period. There are also some relevant passages in his *Conspiracy of Catiline* (translations in Lactor 6 and Penguin Classics). Sallust was a contemporary of Pompey, but opposed him politically as tribune in 52 and was a close adherent of Caesar in later years. He was not a great admirer of Pompey.[3]

Other contemporaries who wrote about Pompey and his campaigns were L. Voltacilius Pilutus, M. Terentius Varro, Posidonius of Apamea, and Theophanes of Mitylene, who all knew him and admired him. Their relevant works have not survived, but were probably used by the slightly later STRABO (*c.* 64 BC to AD 21) and Nicolaus of Damascus, who were in turn used by the Flavian historian JOSEPHUS* (*c.* AD 37 to after 94) in his work on *Jewish Antiquities*, and by other authors. Strabo's *Geography* contains much valuable information about the campaigns of 67-2, and Josephus is our best source for the Jewish campaign of 63 (translations in LCL).

The relevant books of LIVY's (59 BC to AD 17) *History of Rome* unfortunately survive only in very brief summaries (*The Periochae*), but were used by many later writers including CASSIUS DIO* (*c.* AD 163 to after 230), who wrote a long *History of Rome* in Greek, and provides us with the fullest continuous narrative of this period. Writing under the middle Empire (197–219) he was not the shrewdest interpreter of Republican history, but he is often the only source of much useful information. He claimed to have read nearly all the books on Roman history, but his method of selection seems to have been based on what he considered worth recording rather than on a critical assessment of the reliability of his sources.

Other writers in the so-called Livian tradition were: (i) LUCAN* (AD 39-65), the court poet of the age of Nero who wrote a long epic on the Civil War, often called the *Pharsalia*. The framework is historical, but the story is treated in a highly rhetorical fashion. It is valuable as showing how the memory of Pompey was treated a century or more after his death, and provides a generally favourable and credible picture of him. (ii) P. ANNIUS FLORUS* (*c.* second century AD), who wrote a series of compressed and rhetorical accounts of the wars he found in Livy and other writers, including those against Lepidus, Sertorius, Mithridates and the pirates. (iii) GRANIUS LICINIANUS (? second century AD), of whom little is known. The few surviving fragments of his *Handbook of Roman History* contain several references to the activities of Pompeius Strabo in the eighties. (iv) P. OROSIUS (5th century AD), a Christian writer whose *History against the Pagans* contains some helpful information about the eighties and the wars against Lepidus, Sertorius, Mithridates and the pirates.[4]

According to TACITUS (*c*. AD 55 to after 115), Livy was so full of praise for Pompey in his *History* that Augustus used to call him a Pompeian. How far this praise extended to the whole of Pompey's career rather than his stand against Caesar in 49-8 we have no way of telling. Tacitus himself saw Pompey not as a defender of the constitution, but as the natural though more devious successor to Marius and Sulla in the hunt for personal domination over Rome. His *Annals* and *Histories* contain several references to Pompey and many more to those of his descendants who played their parts in the history of the early Empire.[5]

The Greek historian APPIAN* (second century AD) contains much valuable detail in his books on the Mithridatic Wars and the Roman Civil Wars, but he can often be shown to be inaccurate, especially in his chronology. He seems to have used Posidonius, Livy and Sallust, as well as other, probably secondary, sources not used by Plutarch and Dio, in addition to the Caesarian officer Asinius Pollio, who began his work on Roman history in the year 60 BC.

Briefer, but also useful, is the work of C. VELLEIUS PATERCULUS* (*c*. 19 BC to after AD 31), a retired soldier writing under Tiberius. He uses some sources independent of Livy, but not very critically.

Other evidence is available from (i) the collection of *Memorable Deeds and Sayings* by VALERIUS MAXIMUS* (*e*. first century AD); (ii) the collection of *Military Stratagems* by Sex. JULIUS FRONTINUS* (*c*. AD 30-104), himself a general of considerable experience and ability; (iii) the vast *Natural History* of C. PLINIUS SECUNDUS* (AD 23/4-79); (iv) the *Life of Julius Caesar* and *The Lives of Famous Men* by C. SUETONIUS TRANQUILLUS (*c*. AD 69-140); and (v) the few quoted fragments in later authors of the Caesarian Greek writer DIODORUS SICULUS.

Translations of Livy's *Periochae*, Cassius Dio, Lucan, Florus, Tacitus, Appian, Velleius, Frontinus, Plinius, Suetonius and Diodorus can be found in LCL, and of Lucan, Tacitus and Suetonius in the

Penguin Classics series.

Convenient collections of source material for this period in translation are Lewis and Reinhold 1966, Sabben-Clare 1971, Lacey and Wilson 1970, and volumes 3, 6 and 7 in the Lactor series (produced by the London Association of Classical Teachers). These collections also contain further information about the authors.

Authors marked * are represented by quotations in Appendix B. These have been chosen mainly in order to illustrate (i) some of Pompey's qualities and achievements as a general (III A and B, V B and C, VII, VIII, IX); (ii) the surviving records of his triumphs (III C, VI); (iii) assessments of his career by later writers (II B, X, XI); (iv) speeches put into his mouth by Appian, probably to explain his interpretations of his actions at two critical points; it would be most unwise to assume that these have any basis in contemporary records (III D and E); (v) the sort of verbal criticism to which he was subject, especially during the period 59-2 (IV A and B).

This is by no means an exhaustive or even a representative selection. Many relevant passages have been translated or paraphrased in the text, and others which are easily available in published translations or source collections are referred to in the notes to the appropriate chapters. It should, however, give the reader some idea of the nature and style of the works from which the passages are taken and help towards the formation of some assessment of their value.

APPENDIX B
SELECTED PASSAGES IN TRANSLATION

I   The Asculum Inscription (ILS 8888; Degrassi ILLRP 515; Criniti 1970; Plate 1)

Cn. Pompeius Sex. f. imperator virtutis caussa equites Hispanos ceives Romanos fecit in castreis apud Asculum a.d. XIV K. Dec. ex lege Julia. In consilio fuerunt:

1.	L. Gellius L.f.Tro.	29.	C. Fornasidius C.f.Pol.
2.	Cn. Octavius Q.f.	30.	Cn. Pompeius Cn.f.Clu.
3.	M. Caecilius . . . f . . .	31.	Sex. Pompeius Sex.f.Clu.
4.	Ser. Sulpicius C.f.Ani.	32.	M. Hostilius M.f.Vel.
5.	L. Junius L.f.Gal.	33.	L. Aebutius L.f.Men.
6.	Q. Minucius M.f.Ter.	34.	Q. Hirtuleius L.f.Ser.
7.	P. Attius P.f.Ouf.	35.	L. Junius Q.f.Lem.
8.	M. Maloleius M.f.	36.	Q. Rosidius Q.f.Quir.
9.	(name lost)	37.	C. Tarquitius L.f.Fal.
10.	Aemilius Q.f.Pal.	38.	Q. Marcius L.f.Pap.
11.	Cn. Cornelius Cn.f.Pal.	39.	L. Opeimius Q.f.Hor.
12.	T. Annius T.f.Ouf.	40.	L. Insteius L.f.Fal.
13.	M. Aurelius M.f.Vol.	41.	T. Nonius T.f.Vel.
14.	L. Volumnius L.f.Ani.	42.	L. Nonius T.f.Vel.
15.	(name lost)	43.	C. Herius C.f.Clu.
16.	(name lost)	44.	L. Pontius T.f.Quir.
17.	T. Pompeius T.f.Cor.	45.	M. Lucanius M.f.Hor.
18.	C. Rabeirius C.f.Gal.	46.	L. Sergius L.f.Tro.
19.	D. Aebutius D.f.Cor.	47.	P. Pedanius P.f.Aim.
20.	M. Teiedius M.f.Pol.	48.	C. Laetorius C.f.Vel.
21.	C. Fundilius C.f.Quir.	49.	A. Fulvius A.f.Tro.
22.	M. Maianius M.f.	50.	Q. Ampidius Q.f.Aim.
23.	T. Acilius T.f.Vel.	51.	L. Minucius L.f.Vel.
24.	Cn. Oppius Cn.f.Vel.	52.	Ti. Veturius T.f.Vel.
25.	Q. Petillius L.f.Vel.	53.	Cn. Bussenius Cn.f.Ste.
26.	L. Terentius A.f.Vel.	54.	T. Petronius P.f.Fab.
27.	T. Terentius A.f.Vel.	55.	M'. Otacilius M'.f.Pol.
28.	L. Vettius L.f.Vel.	56.	L. Pullenius L.f.Men.

57.   M'. Aebutius M'.f.Pol.   59.   L. Otacilius L.f.Pup.
58.   P. Salvienus L.f.Mai.

Turma Salluitana. (Thirty names follow.)

Cn. Pompeius Sex. f. imperator virtutis caussa turmam Salluitanam donavit in castreis apud Asculum cornuculo et patella, torque, armilla, palereis; et frumentum duplex.

Translation:

[The following explanation of abbreviations should enable the reader to translate the names himself. In each name the first initial is the abbreviation of the *praenomen* (first name). Then comes the *nomen* (family name), followed by the abbreviation of the father's *praenomen* in the genitive case, and f. (*filius* = son of). Last comes the abbreviation of the tribe in which the family was enrolled for voting purposes. It will be noticed that different families of the same name can often be distinguished by their different tribes (e.g. see 17, 30 and 31), though it was possible to change tribes in certain circumstances. The eldest surviving son usually took his father's *praenomen*. Most families restricted themselves to very few *praenomina*. In inscriptions of this date the *cognomen* (third name), which usually either indicated a certain branch of the family or a physical or other peculiarity of the owner, was omitted. This often makes certain identification very difficult. The following can be identified with some probability: (for references in the text, see *index nominum*).]

Gnaeus Pompeius, son of Sextus, *imperator*, made (the following) Spanish cavalrymen Roman citizens as a reward for their valour in accordance with the Julian law. In the camp at Asculum. 17 November. In the council were:

1. L. Gellius Poplicola (Praetor 94, Consul 72, Censor 70); 2. Cn. Octavius Ruso (Praetor 91); 4. Ser. Sulpicus Galba; 5. L. Junius Brutus Damasippus (Praetor 82); 6. Q. Minucius Thermus (Quaestor 89); 10. M. Aemilius Lepidus (Consul 78); 11. Perhaps Cn. Cornelius Dolabella (Praetor 81); 13. Perhaps M. Aurelius Cotta (Consul 74); 18. C. Rabirius Postumus, defended by Cicero in 63; 28. L. Vettius Aninianus, the man who uncovered a plot against Pompey's life in 59; 30. Cn. Pompeius Magnus; 31. Probably Pompey's cousin, son of Strabo's brother Sextus Pompeius; 34, 37 and 40. Found later fighting in the army of Sertorius in Spain; 38. Perhaps the son of L. Marcius Philippus (Consul 91); 46. L. Sergius Catilina (Praetor 68, and leader

of the conspiracy of 63); 51. Perhaps L. Minucius Basilus of Cupra Maritima, later a notable Picene squire (Cic.de Off. 3.74); 55. Possibly M. Otacilius Crassus, father of the Pompeian commander at Lissus in 48.

[Abbreviations: *praenomina*: A. Aulus, C. Gaius, Cn. Gnaeus, D. Decimus, L. Lucius, M. Marcus, M'. Manius, P. Publius, Q. Quintus, Ser. Servius, Sex. Sextus, T. Titus, Ti. Tiberius. Tribes: Aim. Aemilia, Ani. Aniensis, Clu. Clustumina, Cor. Cornelia, Fab. Fabia, Fal. Falerna, Gal. Galeria, Hor. Horatia, Lem. Lemonia, Mai. Maecia, Men. Menenia, Ouf. Oufentina, Pal. Palatina, Pap. Papiria, Pol. Pollia, Pup. Pupinia, Quir. Quirina, Ser. Sergia, Ste. Stellatina, Ter. Teretina, Tro. Tromentina, Vel. Velina, Vol. Voltinia. N.B. This list only contains the abbreviations on the inscription and is not a complete list of *praenomina* or tribes.]

The cavalry unit from Saragossa. (Or led by Salluitus, or raised by S.) Gnaeus Pompeius, son of Sextus, *imperator*, as a reward for valour presented the Salluitan cavalry unit in the camp at Asculum with the following decorations and a double ration of corn: the small silver spear and paten; torc, armlet and badges of honour.

II   Velleius Paterculus *History of Rome*, Book 2.

(A)   Ch. 21. I have already mentioned how the State had employed the distinguished services of Gnaeus Pompeius, the father of Pompey the Great, in the Marsic War, and especially in Picenum, and how he had taken the city of Asculum, around which, although the armies had been scattered in many other regions, 75,000 Roman citizens and more than 60,000 Italians had fought on one day. While Cinna was making war on his own country, Pompeius, thwarted in his hope of prolonging his consulship, behaved in such an ambiguous and uncommitted fashion that everything he did was to his own advantage and he seemed to be merely watching for the right opportunity as he moved himself and his army this way and that according to where the hope of power shone brightest. But finally he came to grips with Cinna in a fierce and mighty battle; it was joined and fought beneath the very walls and eyes of the city of Rome, and words can scarcely express how disastrous the outcome of it was to participants and onlookers alike. Afterwards, when a plague was wreaking havoc in both armies, exhausted as they were by the war, Gnaeus Pompeius died. The pleasure felt at his death was almost matched by the loss of those citizens who had died by the sword or the plague, and the Roman People vented on his dead body the anger which it had felt for him during his lifetime.

Whether there were two or three families called Pompeius, the first of that name to hold the consulship was Quintus Pompeius with Gnaeus Servilius about 167 years ago (141 BC).

(B)   Ch. 29. 113 years ago, shortly before L. Sulla's arrival in Italy, Gnaeus Pompey, the son of that Gnaeus Pompeius whose splendid exploits in the Marsic War during his consulship I have mentioned above, being 23 years old took a great risk at his own expense and on his own initiative and, splendidly succeeding in his attempt, raised a strong army from Picenum, which was crammed full of *clientes* whom he had inherited from his father, in order to liberate and restore the grandeur of his country. It would take many volumes to do justice to the greatness of this man, but the scale of my work demands that he be described in a few words.

His mother was Lucilia, a woman of senatorial stock. He himself was outstandingly handsome, not with the sort of beauty which merely graces youth, but with an air of grandeur and firmness which suited his rank and fortune and accompanied him to the end of his life. A man of exceptional integrity and uprightness, he was also a fair orator; he had a fierce passion for power, provided that it was offered to him out of honour and did not have to be seized by force; in war he was a highly experienced commander, in peacetime a most restrained citizen, except when he was afraid that he might have some rival; he was firm in his friendships, yet forgiving when offended; if he made up a quarrel you could trust him perfectly, and he was always ready to accept an apology; he rarely, if ever, used his power violently; he was free from almost every vice, unless it should be counted among the worst sins in a free state which was also mistress of the world to object to seeing anyone his rival in greatness when he ought to have held all citizens his equals. Brought up to a life of soldiering from the time he came of age on the staff of that shrewdest of generals, his own father, he had trained his character, which was noble and capable of learning what was right, with such remarkable shrewdness in the art of war that, while Metellus won greater praise from Sertorius, Pompey was more greatly feared.

III   Appian *Roman History*

(A)   *The Civil Wars.* [After mention of a battle at Clusium between Sulla and Carbo.] In the plain of Spoletium Pompeius and Crassus, both legates of Sulla, killed about three thousand of the Carbonians and besieged their opposing commander Carrinas. Eventually Carbo sent another force to help Carrinas, but Sulla heard of this, laid an ambush for them on their march, and killed about two thousand. Carrinas got away one dark night during a heavy rainstorm, and although some of the besiegers heard a noise they took no notice of it because of the rain. Carbo sent eight legions under Marcius to relieve his colleague Marius at Praeneste, at the news that he was being hard pressed by hunger. Pompey attacked them from ambush at a narrow pass, and after routing them and causing a large number of casualties he trapped the rest on a hill-top. Marcius managed to escape from this predicament by not extinguishing his fires one night, but his army blamed him for the ambush and there was a serious mutiny. One complete legion marched back to Ariminum under its standards without orders, and the rest dispersed piecemeal to their homes, with the result that only seven cohorts remained with Carbo.

(B)   Ibid. Ch. 96. And this was the state of affairs in Italy. Pompey sent some troops to capture Carbo, who had fled from Africa to Sicily with many distinguished followers and from there to the island of Cossyra. He ordered his officers to put the others to death without even bringing them into his presence, but he had Carbo brought with his feet in chains before him, and although he had been three times consul he delivered a harangue to him in public before executing him and sending his head to Sulla.

(C)   *The Mithridatic Wars* Chs. 116-17. At the end of the winter Pompey distributed rewards to the army; 1,500 Attic drachmas (6,000 sesterces) to each soldier and in like proportion to the officers, the whole, it is said, amounting to 16,000 talents (384,000,000 sesterces). Then he marched to Ephesus, embarked for Italy, and hastened to Rome, having dismissed his soldiers at Brundisium to their homes, a democratic action which greatly surprised the Romans. As he approached the city he was met by successive processions, first of youths, farthest from the city, then bands of men of different ages came out as far as they severally could walk; last of all came the Senate, which was lost in wonder at his exploits, for no one had ever before vanquished so powerful an enemy, and at the same time brought so many great nations under subjection and extended the Roman rule to the Euphrates. He was awarded a triumph exceeding in brilliancy any that had gone before, being now only thirty-five years of age [in fact forty-five]. It occupied two successive days, and many nations were represented in the procession from Pontus, Armenia, Cappadocia, Cilicia and all Syria, besides Albanians, Heniochi, Achaeans of Scythia, and Eastern Iberians. Seven hundred undamaged ships were brought into the harbours. In the triumphal procession were two-horse-carriages and litters laden with gold or with other ornaments of various kinds, also the couch of Darius, the son of Hystaspes, the throne and sceptre of Mithridates Eupator himself, and his image, eight cubits high, made of solid gold, and 75,100,000 drachmas of silver coin; also an infinite number of wagons carrying arms and beaks of ships, and a multitude of captives and pirates, none of them bound, but all arrayed in their native costumes.

(117) Before Pompey himself, at the head of procession, went the satraps, sons, and generals of the kings against whom he had fought, who were present (some having been captured and others given as hostages) to the number of 324. Among them were Tigranes, the son of Tigranes, and five sons of Mithridates, namely, Artaphernes, Cyrus, Oxathres, Darius and Xerxes, also his daughters, Orsabaris and Eupatra. Olthaces, chief of the Colchians, was also led in the procession, and Aristobulus, king of the Jews, the tyrants of the Cilicians, and the female rulers of the Scythians, three chiefs of the Iberians, two of the Albanians, and Menander the Laodicean, who had been chief of cavalry to Mithridates. There were carried in the procession images of those who were not present, of Tigranes and of Mithridates, representing them as fighting, as vanquished, and as fleeing. Even the besieging of Mithridates and his silent flight by night were represented. Finally it was shown how he died, and the daughters who chose to perish with him were pictured also, and there were figures of the sons and daughters who died before him, and images of the barbarian gods decked out in the fashion of their countries. Moreover, a tablet was carried along with this inscription: 'Ships with brazen beaks captured, 800; cities founded in Cappadocia, 8; in Cilicia and Coele-Syria, 20; in Palestine the one which is now Seleucis. Kings conquered: Tigranes the Armenian, Artoces the Iberian, Oroezes the Albanian, Darius the Mede, Aretas the Nabataean, Antiochus of Commagene.' These were the facts recorded on the inscription. Pompey himself was borne in a chariot studded with gems, wearing, it is said, a cloak of Alexander the Great, if anyone can believe that. It seems to have been found among the possessions of Mithridates that the inhabitants of Cos had received from Cleopatra. His chariot was followed by the officers who had shared the campaigns with him,

some on horseback and others on foot. When he arrived at the Capitol he did not put any of the prisoners to death, as had been the custom of other triumphs, but sent them all home at the public expense, except the kings. Of these Aristobulus alone was at once put to death, and Tigranes somewhat later. Such was the character of Pompey's triumph.[1]

(D)   *Civil Wars* Bk. 2, Chs. 50-51. [Speech attributed to Pompey at Beroea in late 49.] When all was in readiness Pompey called the senators, the knights, and the whole army to an assembly and addressed them as follows: 'Fellow-soldiers, the Athenians, too, abandoned their city for the sake of liberty when they were fighting against invasion, because they believed that it was not houses that made a city, but men; and after they had done so they presently recovered it and made it more renowned than ever before. So, too, our own ancestors abandoned the city when the Gauls invaded it, and Camillus hastened from Ardea and recovered it. All men of sound mind think that their country is wherever they can preserve their liberty. Because we are thus minded we sailed hither, not as deserters of our native land, but in order to prepare ourselves to defend it gloriously against one who has long conspired against it, and, by means of bribe-takers, has at last seized Italy by a sudden invasion. You have decreed him a public enemy, yet he now sends governors to take charge of your provinces. He appoints others over the city and still others throughout Italy. With such audacity has he deprived the people of their own government. If he does these things while the war is still raging and while he is apprehensive of the result and when we intend, with heaven's help, to bring him to punishment, what cruelty, what violence is he likely to abstain from if he wins the victory? And while he is doing these things against the fatherland certain men, who have been bought with money that he obtained from our provinces of Gaul, co-operate with him, choosing to be his slaves instead of his equals.

(51) 'I have not failed and I never will fail to fight with you and for you. I give you my services both as soldier and as general. If I have any experience in war, if it has been my good fortune to remain unvanquished to this day, I pray the gods to continue all these blessings in our present need, and that I may become a man of happy destiny for my country in her perils as I was in extending her dominion. Surely we may trust in the gods and in the righteousness of the war, which has for its noble and just object the defence of our country's constitution. In addition to this we may rely upon the magnitude of

the preparations which we behold on land and sea, which are all the time growing and will be augmented still more as we come into action. We may say that all the nations of the East and around the Euxine Sea, both Greek and barbarian, stand with us; and kings, who are friends of the Roman people or of myself, are supplying us soldiers, arms, provisions, and other implements of war. Come to your task then with a spirit worthy of your country, of yourselves, and of me, mindful of the wrongs you have received from Caesar, and ready to obey my orders promptly.'

(E) Ibid. Ch. 72. [Speech attributed to Pompey before Pharsalus.] 'You, my fellow soldiers, are the leaders in this task rather than the led, for you urged on this engagement while I was still desirous of wearing Caesar out by hunger. Since, therefore, you are the marshalls of the lists of battle, conduct yourselves like those who are greatly superior in numbers. Despise the enemy as victors do the vanquished, as young men do the old, as fresh troops do those who are wearied with many toils. Fight like those who have the power and the means, and the consciousness of a good cause. We are contending for liberty and country. On our side are the laws and honourable fame, and this great number of senators and knights, against one man who is piratically seizing supreme power. Go forward then, as you have desired to do, with good hope, keeping in your mind's eye the flight of the enemy at Dyrrachium, and the great number of their standards that we captured in one day when we defeated them there.' [C, D and E transl. Horace White. Loeb.]

IV. **Valerius Maximus** *Memorable Deeds and Sayings*

(A) Bk. 6, Ch. 2, Sec. 8. Helvius Mancia of Formiae, a freedman's son and a very old man indeed, was prosecuting L. Libo before the censors (possibly in 55). In the trial Pompey the Great reproached him with his humble birth and old age, remarking that he had been sent back from the underworld to accuse the defendant. 'You are right, Pompey,' he replied 'I do indeed come from the underworld, and I come to accuse Libo. But while I was tarrying there I saw the bloody Gnaeus Domitius Ahenobarbus weeping because, though a man of the highest nobility and the sternest integrity and the staunchest of patriots, he had been killed in the very prime of his youth on your orders. I saw Marcus Brutus, a man of no less distinction, hacked by the sword and complaining that his fate was due first to your treachery and then to your cruelty. I saw Gnaeus Carbo, who was the fiercest protector of your boyhood and your father's property in his third consulship, bound in the chains which you had ordered to be clamped on him, and protesting that contrary to all laws of right and wrong he had been slaughtered by you, a mere Roman knight, when he held the highest office in the State. I saw the practorian Perpenna in the same plight and uttering the same plaintive cry cursing your brutality, and all of them with one voice complaining that they had died uncondemned at your hands – the teenage butcher.'[2]

This provincial, still stinking of his father's slavery, a man of unbridled rashness and intolerable spirit, was allowed with impunity to reopen the deep wounds of the civil wars now long covered with scars. It was indeed very brave to curse Gnaeus Pompey, but at the same time it was perfectly safe.

(B)   Ibid. Sec. 7. Once when Pompey was wearing a white bandage on his leg Favonius remarked to him, 'It does not matter on what part of your body you wear your crown.' By scoffing at a scrap of rag he was reproaching him with having royal power. But Pompey's expression did not change one whit. He was careful to avoid either of two possibilities – smiling and seeming gladly to acknowledge his power, or frowning and seeming to admit it. It was this tolerance of men of lower nature and fortune which made him so approachable to people.[3]

V   Sextus Julius Frontinus *Stratagems*

(A)   Bk. IV, v. 1. When Gnaeus Pompey's soldiers threatened to plunder the money which was being carried for his triumph, Servilius urged him to divide it among them in order to avoid a mutiny. Pompey declared that he would not hold his triumph, and would even die rather than submit to the insubordination of his soldiers. He then reproved them severely and threw his laurel-wreathed *fasces* in their faces, telling them to start by plundering those, and by the suggestion of so hateful an action he restored their discipline.[4]

(B)   Ibid. II, v. 31. Then there was the occasion in Spain when Sertorius had his camp near that of Pompey outside the town of Lauro. There were only two areas where foraging was possible, one close by, the other further away, and Sertorius gave orders that the nearer one should be frequently raided by light-armed troops, but that no soldier should go anywhere near the more distant one. Eventually he persuaded the enemy that the remoter area was the safer. One day, when the Pompeians had set out for this area, Sertorius ordered Octavius Graecinus with ten cohorts armed in Roman fashion, and ten cohorts of Spanish light-armed troops, and Tarquitius Priscus with two thousand cavalry to go and set an ambush for the foragers. These men energetically carried out their orders. They reconnoitred the ground and hid the above-mentioned troops by night in a neighbouring wood. In front they posted the light-armed Spaniards, who were best suited to guerrilla warfare; the troops who were equipped in Roman fashion they placed further into the wood, and positioned the cavalry furthest away from the enemy so that their plan should not be given away by the noise of the horses. They then ordered everyone to rest in strict silence until three hours after sunrise. When the Pompeians, who suspected nothing, were fully laden with forage they began to think of returning, and those who had been on guard, deceived by the quietness of the ambushers, were also slipping away to collect fodder. First the Spaniards were let loose, and with characteristic Spanish *élan* they poured down on the stragglers, who were expecting nothing of the sort, and routed them with a considerable number of casualties.

Then, before resistance to this attack could be organised, the heavier-armed troops burst forth from the wood and overwhelmed the Romans who were regrouping, putting them to flight, while the cavalry charged those who were already fleeing and followed them all the way back to camp, cutting them to pieces. Care was also taken that no one should escape, for 250 cavalrymen who had been kept in reserve were sent on ahead at the gallop, and by using short cuts they were easily able to overtake those who had fled first, turn and attack them before they could reach Pompey's camp. On hearing of this Pompey sent out a legion under D. Laelius to protect his foragers. The cavalry immediately withdrew to the right, as if they were retreating, and then moved round the legion and attacked it too from the rear, while those who had pursued the foragers were already charging it from the front. Thus the legion was sandwiched between two lines of enemy and crushed, with the loss of its commanding officer. Pompey was leading out the whole of his army to help the legion when Sertorius also displayed his own troops drawn up on the hills and thwarted Pompey's plan. Thus in addition to the double loss which had been caused by the same cunning stroke, Sertorius forced Pompey to be a helpless onlooker as his own men were mown down. This was the first battle between the two commanders. Livy recounts that out of Pompey's army 10,000 men and all the transport were lost.

(C)   Ibid. II, v. 33. When Pompey was fighting Mithridates in Armenia, and the latter had the advantage over him in the number and quality of his cavalry, he positioned three thousand light-armed troops and five hundred cavalry by night hidden by the brushwood which grew between the two camps. Then at first light he sent out his cavalry against the enemy position drawn up in such a way that, when the whole of the enemy cavalry and infantry joined battle, they could withdraw gradually without breaking ranks until they gave the ambushers room to play their part and rise to attack the enemy from the rear. When this move had gone according to plan, those who appeared to be running away turned about, and Pompey was able to cut to pieces the panic-stricken enemy thus trapped in the middle, and by bringing up his infantry to close quarters put even the horses themselves to the sword. In that battle Pompey destroyed the confidence which the king had had in his cavalry.

VI   Pliny the Elder *Natural History*

Bk. VII, Ch. 26, Secs. 95 and 97-9. But it is relevant to the fame not just of one man but of the Empire of Rome to detail at this point all the records of Pompey the Great's victories and his triumphs, which matched in splendour the exploits not only of Alexander the Great but almost of Hercules and father Bacchus.

(97) Afterwards he was sent out with command over every sea and then to the East, and brought back countless titles for his country, like the victors at the sacred games who win their crowns not for themselves but for their countries. He bestowed these honours on the city in the shrine of Minerva which he dedicated from the proceeds of the sale of booty as follows:

'Gnaeus Pompey the Great, Commander-in-Chief, has brought to an end thirty years of war; 12,183,000 men he routed, scattered, slew or received into surrender; 846 ships he sunk or captured; he accepted the capitulation of 1,538 towns and forts, and subdued the lands from the Maeotians to the Red Sea; here he duly fulfils his vow to Minerva.'

(98) This is his summary of his achievements in the East. But the announcement of the triumph which he held on the 28 September in the consulship of M. Piso and M. Messalla ran as follows: 'When he had liberated the sea-coast from the pirates and restored the command of the sea to the Roman People, he celebrated his triumph over Asia, Pontus, Armenia, Paphlagonia, Cappadocia, Cilicia, Syria, the Scythians, the Jews, the Albanians, Iberia, the island of Crete and the

Bastarnae, and in addition to these over King Mithridates and King Tigranes.'

(99) The topmost peak of that glorious achievement (as he himself said at a public meeting when he delivered a speech about his campaigns) was that although he had received Asia as the furthest province of the Empire he had returned it to the People as the heart of their fatherland.

VII Cassius Dio *History of Rome*

Bk. XXXVI, Chs. 20-23. I will now relate the progress of Pompey's career. Pirates always used to harass those who sailed the sea. even as brigands did those who dwelt on land. There was never a time when these practices were unknown, nor will they ever cease probably so long as human nature remains the same. But formerly freebooting was limited to certain localities and small bands operating only during the summer on sea and on land; whereas at this time, ever since war had been carried on continuously in many different places at once, and many cities had been overthrown, while sentences hung over the heads of the fugitives, and there was no freedom from fear for anyone anywhere, large numbers had turned to plundering. Now the operations of the bandits on land, being in better view of the towns, which could thus perceive the injury close at hand and capture the perpetrators with no great difficulty, would be broken up with a fair degree of ease; but those on the sea had grown to the greatest proportions. For while the Romans were busy with their antagonists, the pirates had gained great headway, sailing about to many quarters, and adding to their band all of like condition, to such an extent that some of them, after the manner of allies, assisted many others. (21) When these wars had been ended, the pirates, instead of desisting, did much serious injury alone by themselves both to the Romans and to their allies. They no longer sailed in small force, but in great fleets; and they had generals, so that they had acquired a great reputation. First and foremost they robbed and pillaged those sailing on the sea, no longer permitting them any safety even during the winter season, since as a result of their daring, practice, and success they made voyages in security even then; and next they despoiled even those in the harbours. For if anyone ventured to put out against them, he would usually be defeated and perish; but even if he conquered, he would be unable to capture any of the enemy by reason of the speed of their ships. Accordingly they would return after a little, as if victors, and would ravage and set in flames not only farms and fields, but also whole cities; some places, however, they conciliated, so as to gain naval stations and winter quarters in a friendly land as it were.

(22) As these operations of theirs met with success it became customary for them to go into the interior, and they inflicted many injuries on those even who had nothing to do with the sea. This is the way they treated not only the distant allies of Rome, but even Italy itself. For, believing that they would obtain greater gains in that quarter and also that they would terrify all the others still more if they did not keep their hands off that country, they sailed into the very harbour of Ostia as well as other cities in Italy, burning the ships and pillaging everything. Finally, as no attention was paid to them, they took up their abode on the land, disposing fearlessly of whatever men they did not kill, and of whatever spoils they took, just as if they were in their own land. And though some plundered here and some there, since of course it was not possible for the same persons to do harm throughout the whole length of the sea at once, they nevertheless showed such friendship one for another as to send money and assistance even to those entirely unknown, as if to their nearest of kin. In fact, this was one of the chief sources of their strength, that those who paid court to any of them were honoured by all, and those who came into collision with any of them were despoiled by all.

(23) To such an extent did the power of the pirates grow that their hostility became a grave and constant menace, admitting of no precaution and knowing no truce. The Romans, of course, heard of these deeds from time to time, and even saw a little of what was going on, in as much as imports in general ceased coming in and the corn supply was shut off entirely; but they paid no serious attention to it at the proper time. Instead they would send out fleets and generals only as they were stirred by individual reports, but accomplished nothing; on the contrary, they caused their allies all the greater distress by these very means, until they were finally reduced to the last extremity. Then at length they came together and deliberated for many days as to what really should be done. Wearied by the continued dangers and perceiving that the war against the pirates would be a great and extensive one, and believing, too, that it was impossible to assail them all at once or yet individually, in as much as they helped one another and there was no way of driving them back everywhere at once, the people fell into great perplexity and despair of making any successful move. In the end, however, one Aulus Gabinius, a tribune, set forth his plan. He had either been prompted by Pompey or wished in any case

to do him a favour; certainly he was not prompted by any love of the common welfare, for he was a most base fellow. His plan, then, was that they should choose from among the ex-consuls one general with full power against all the pirates, who should command for three years and have the use of a huge force, with many lieutenants. He did not directly utter Pompey's name, but it was easy to see that if once the populace should hear of any such proposition, they would choose him. [Trans. E. Cary Loeb]

VIII P. Annius Florus *Short History of Rome*

Bk. III, Ch. 6, Secs. 7-14. Thus Pompey, who had also been successful previously, now seemed to deserve the victory [*sc.* over the pirates], and he was also given control of the war against Mithridates. Wishing to put an end once and for all to this plague which was scattered over the whole sea, he attacked with almost super-human armament. For he had a very large number of fleets of his own and provided by his Rhodian allies, and with many legates and captains he encompassed the whole shoreline from the Atlantic to the Black Sea. Gellius was put in charge of the Etruscan Sea; Plotius of the Sicilian; Atilius blockaded the gulf of Liguria; Pomponius the coast of Gaul; Torquatus the sea of the Balearics; Tiberius Nero the straits of Cadiz, the entrance to the Mediterranean; Lentulus the coast of Libya; Marcellinus the coast of Egypt; Pompey's sons the Adriatic; Terentius Varro the Aegaean and Ionian Seas; Metellus the Pamphylian coast; Caepio the coast of Asia; Porcius Cato placed his ships across the very jaws of the Propontis and locked them like a door. Thus, throughout every harbour, bay, hiding place, retreat, promontory, strait and peninsula of the sea all the pirates were shut in and harassed, as it were by hunters with their nets. Pompey himself made for Cilicia, the source and fountain-head of the war. The enemy did not refuse to fight, but their daring appeared to spring from desperation at being overwhelmed rather than from confidence; it amounted to no more than rowing into battle for the first onslaught. When they saw that their ships were surrounded on all sides, they immediately threw away their weapons and oars and pleaded for their lives by rhythmical clapping on every side – the usual signal of those begging for mercy. Never have we won such a bloodless victory; but no people has ever proved more loyal in later years. This was due to the remarkable foresight and planning of the general, who removed that race of seafarers far from the sight of the sea, and virtually tied them to inland farms. At the same time he recovered the use of the sea for our ships and restored his own men to the land. What should strike you first about this victory? Its speed? It was won within forty days. Its good fortune? Not even a single ship was lost. Its permanence? The pirates were no more.

IX   Flavius Josephus *Jewish Antiquities*

Book XIV, Secs. 57-73. Pompey was enraged at this treachery, and, putting Aristobulus under guard, he went to the city in person. Jerusalem was strongly defended on all sides except the north, where there was a weakness. For it is surrounded by a broad, deep ravine, taking in the temple, which is itself strongly fortified by a stone wall all round. (58) Amongst the citizens there was virtual civil war, for they could not come to any agreement about the present dangerous situation. Some were for surrendering the city to Pompey, while the adherents of Aristobulus urged that they should close the gates against him and also declare war on him for holding their leader under arrest. Before the others could make a move they seized the temple and cut down the bridge which connected it with the city, making ready for a siege. (59) The other party let the Roman army in, and handed the city and the palace over to Pompey. He sent his legate Piso with a force to garrison both of these, and fortified the houses opposite the temple and those which surrounded it outside the city. (60) He then offered to come to terms with the defenders, but when they refused to listen to his proposals he began to build a second wall round the temple. In all these moves he was enthusiastically helped by Hyrcanus. He himself pitched camp outside the city to the north of the temple, where it was vulnerable. (61) Even there great towers had been constructed, and a ditch had been dig, and the temple was surrounded by a deep ravine. For where the bridge had been destroyed there was a sheer side facing the city. Here Pompey had begun to raise a mound, working every day with great difficulty, and sending his troops to cut down all the timber in the neighbourhood. (62) When the mound was high enough (and it had been a hard task to fill the ditch because of its enormous depth) he moved up the siege engines and artillery, which had to be brought from Tyre, and began to knock down the temple walls with rock-hurling catapults. (63) The only reason why the defenders did not prevent the mound being completed was the Jewish custom of resting on the seventh day. For our law allows us to defend ourselves against aggressors who are actually attacking, but does not allow us to take action against an enemy who is doing anything else.

(64) The Romans knew this perfectly well, and on those days which we call the Sabbath they refrained from shooting at the Jews or coming to grips with them, but built up their mound and siege towers, and brought up the artillery ready to go into action the next day. (65) The following fact will give some idea of the extreme devotion we show to God and our rigid observance of the laws. Never during the whole siege were the priests prevented by fear from performing their tasks. Twice a day, early in the morning and at the ninth hour [*c.* 3 o'clock p.m.] they performed their ceremonies at the altar, and not even the difficulties caused by the attacks made them omit any of the sacrifices. (66) Indeed, when the city was captured in the third month, on the day of Fasting during the 179th Olympiad in the consulship of Gaius Antonius and Marcus Tullius Cicero, the enemy rushed in and were slaughtering those in the temple, (67) but the priests who were sacrificing continued with their service all the same; they were not driven to run away either by fear for their lives or by the numbers of those who were already dead; they thought it better to meet the fate that was coming to them right there by the altars than to neglect any of their appointed duties. (68) This is not merely a legend to glorify their fictitious devotion; it is a true story, attested by all those who wrote the history of Pompey's campaigns, including Strabo and Nicolaus and Titus Livius, the author of The History of Rome.[5]

(69) The siege-engine, then, was brought up, and the largest of the towers was shaken and collapsed, creating a breach through which the enemy rushed. First over the wall was Cornelius Faustus Sulla, son of the dictator, with his contingent. After him on the other side of the breach was the centurion Furius with his men, and in the middle, yet another centurion, Fabius, with a strong party. (70) There was slaughter everywhere. Some Jews were killed by Romans, others by their own countrymen; others actually threw themselves down the ravines or set fire to the houses and died in the flames, unable to bear their fate. (71) The death toll of Jews was about 12,000; the Romans lost very few. Absalom, Aristobulus' uncle and father-in-law was among the prisoners. Grave sacrilege was committed against the sanctuary of the temple, which had previously neither been entered or seen. (72) For Pompey and a considerable retinue went inside and saw those things which only the high priests are allowed to see. There was a golden table and a sacred candelabrum and libation vessels and a store of spices, as well as the sacred money in the treasury amounting to 2,000 talents (48,000,000 sesterces). Out of respect for our religion Pompey touched none of these, but in this also fully justified his

reputation for integrity. (73) The following day he instructed the temple servants to purify the temple and to make the customary offering to God. He restored the High Priesthood to Hyrcanus, partly in return for his valuable services, but mainly because he had prevented the Jews throughout the country from fighting on the side of Aristobulus. He executed the ringleaders of the resistance. He then distributed suitable rewards for bravery to Faustus and the others who had led the attack over the wall.

X   *The Latin Anthology* No. 402

Pompeius totum victor lustraverat orbem,
    At rursus toto victus in orbe iacet:
Membra pater Libyco posuit male tecta sepulchro;
    Filius Hispana est vix adopertus humo.
Sexte, Asiam sortite tenes. divisa ruina est:
    Uno non potuit tanta iacere solo.

O'er all the world once Pompey cast his wide-victorious eyes;
    Through all the world in latter days a vanquished Pompey lies:
The father's limbs ill-covered rest beneath a Libyan mound;
    Far off the elder son lies dead, scarce hid by Spanish ground.
In Asia Sextus' lot to fall; thus they their ruin share;
    One soil alone could not suffice so great a loss to bear.

XI   **M. Annaeus Lucanus** *Pharsalia*

(A) Bk. 1, lines 98-157. For a brief space the jarring harmony was maintained, and there was peace despite the will of the chiefs; for Crassus, who stood between, was the only check on imminent war. So the Isthmus of Corinth divides the main and parts two seas with its slender line, forbidding them to mingle their waters; but if its soil were withdrawn, it would dash the Ionian sea against the Aegaean. Thus Crassus kept apart the eager combatants; but when he met his pitiable end and stained Syrian Carrhae with Roman blood, the loss inflicted by Parthia let loose the madness of Rome. By that battle the Parthians did more than they realise: they visited the vanquished with civil war. The tyrants' power was divided by the sword; and the wealth of the imperial people, that possessed sea and land the whole world over, was not enough for two. (111) For, when Julia was cut off by the cruel hand of Fate, she bore with her to the world below the bond of affinity and the marriage which the dread omen turned to mourning. She alone, had Fate granted her longer life, might have restrained the rage of her husband on one side and her father on the other; she might have struck down their swords and joined their armed hands as the Sabine women stood between and reconciled their fathers to their husbands. But loyalty was shattered by the death of Julia, and leave was given to the chiefs to begin the conflict. (120) Rivalry in worth spurred them on; for Magnus feared that fresher exploits might dim his past triumphs, and that his victory over the pirates might give place to the conquest of Gaul, while Caesar was urged on by continuous effort and familiarity with warfare, and by fortune that brooked no second place. Caesar could no longer endure a superior, nor Pompey an equal. Which had the fairer pretext for warfare, we may not know: each has high authority to support him; for, if the victor had the gods on his side, the vanquished had Cato. The two rivals were ill-matched. The one was somewhat tamed by declining years; for long he had worn the toga and forgotten in peace the leader's part; courting reputation and lavish to the common people, he was swayed entirely by the breath of popularity and delighted in the applause that hailed him in the theatre he built; and trusting fondly to his former greatness, he did nothing to support it by fresh power. (135) The mere shadow of a mighty name he stood. Thus an oak-tree, laden with the ancient trophies of a nation and the consecrated gifts of conquerors, towers in a fruitful field; but the roots it clings by have lost their toughness, and it stands by its weight alone, throwing out bare boughs into the sky and making a shade not with leaves but with its trunk; though it totters doomed to fall at the first gale, while many trees with sound timber rise beside it, yet it alone is worshipped. But Caesar had more than a mere name and military reputation: his energy could never rest, (145) and his one disgrace was to conquer without war. He was alert and headstrong; his arms answered every summons of ambition or resentment; he never shrank from using the sword lightly; he followed up each success and snatched at the favour of Fortune, overthrowing every obstacle on his path to supreme power, and rejoicing to clear the way before him by destruction. Even so the lightning is driven forth by wind through the clouds: with noise of the smitten heaven and crashing of the firmament it flashes out and cracks the daylight sky, striking fear and terror into mankind and dazzling the eye with slanting flame. It rushes to its appointed quarter of the sky; nor can any solid matter forbid its free course, but both falling and returning it spreads destruction far and wide and gathers again its scattered fires.

(B) Bk. 9, lines 186-214. Though all alike dared to revile Heaven, and blamed the gods for Pompey's death, yet a tribute as welcome to the shades of Magnus came in the words of Cato: few as they were, but they came from a heart fraught with truth. He said: 'The citizen who has fallen, though far inferior to our ancestors in recognising the limits of what is lawful, was yet valuable in our generation, which has shown no respect for justice. He was powerful without destroying freedom; he alone, when the people were willing to be his slaves, remained in private station; he ruled the Senate, but it was a Senate of kings. (195) He based no claims upon the right of armed force; what he wished to receive, he wished that others should have the power to refuse him. He acquired enormous wealth; but he paid into the treasury more than he kept back. He snatched the sword; but he knew how to lay it down. He preferred war to peace; but he was a lover of peace even when he wielded the weapons of war. It pleased him to accept office, and it pleased him also to resign it. His household was pure and free from extravagance, and never spoilt by the greatness of its master. His name is illustrious and revered among all nations, and did much service to our own State. Sincere belief in Rome's freedom died long ago, when Sulla and Marius were admitted within the walls; (205) but now, when Pompey has been removed from the world, even the sham belief is dead. No tyrant need blush in future: there will be no pretence of military command, and the Senate will never again be used as a screen. Fortunate was he, because his last day followed close on defeat, and because the Egyptian butchers forced upon him the death he should have courted. He might perhaps have stooped to go on living under the tyranny of his kinsman. Happiest of all men are those who know when to die; and next come those upon whom death is forced. For myself, if destiny bring us into the power of others, I pray that Fortune will make Juba play the part of Ptolemy: I am willing enough that he should keep me for Caesar, on condition that he keeps me with my head cut off.' [Lucan translations by J.D. Duff, Loeb.]

NOTES

Chapter 1

1. *Asculum inscription:* Taylor 1960, p. 177; Criniti 1970.
2. *Politics:* esp. Gelzer 1969; Badian 1958; Taylor 1949.
3. *Toga virilis:* 17 March was the date of the festival of *Liberalia*, at which this ceremony usually took place. cf. Fowler 1899, p. 56.
4. *Tribes:* Taylor 1960; *Citizenship:* Sherwin-White 1939; *Pompeius:* Duchesne 1934.
5. *Lucilius:* West 1928; Porphyrio on Hor. Serm. II. 1.29; Pompey's mother may have been from a different branch of the same family. *Other families:* Varro, Minucius.
6. *Siege:* Vell. Pat. II. 21; *Training:* Cic. Imp. Cn. Pomp. 10.
7. Or. V. 18.
8. *The 90s:* Badian 1958, ch. IX; 1957; *Equites:* Brunt 1965 (2).
9. Brunt 1971, pp. 224-7.
10. App. BC I.63; Sall. H. II. 21. M; I follow Badian (1955) in ascribing the Sallust fragment to the year 88 rather than 80, and to Strabo rather than his son.
11. Or. V. 19. 10.
12. Gr. Lic. XXXV. p. 18. *Candidature:* One of the consuls of each year had the task of holding the elections for the following year, and of receiving and accepting or rejecting nominations. He could thus have some influence over the election of his successors. cf. Taylor 1949. *Death of Strabo:* Most authorities relate that he was killed by a thunderbolt, but this probably stems from a misunderstanding of an original phrase meaning 'struck by disease' (cf. CAH IX p. 264, n. 1). Plutarch (Pomp. 1) retains the story of an assassination attempt by Cinna on Strabo which was foiled by Pompey. This is rejected as unlikely by Badian (1958, p. 239, n. 6) on fairly subjective grounds. Plutarch and others attest the unpopularity of Strabo, and this is borne out by the description of his disturbed funeral (Gr. Lic. XXXV. p. 23. Tuebner 1904, ed. Flemisch; and App. B. II. A). His main faults apparently were treachery (probably his ambivalent attitude in 87 as seen from Octavius' point of view) and greed (his retaining of the Asculum booty). For the theory that he was not the man '*dis ac nobilitati perinvisus*' mentioned by Cicero (pro Corn., Asc. p. 79 Cl.) and thus not one of the men accused under the *lex Varia*, see Badian 1969. It is likely that much of the tradition hostile to Strabo is the result of propaganda disseminated by his enemies at a later date.
13. *The period 87-3:* Bulst 1964; Badian 1962.
14. Plut. Pomp. 4; Cic. Br. 230; Val. Max. VI. 2. 8.
15. *Cinna's expedition:* Wilkes 1969 p. 34; Plut. Pomp. 5.
16. *Cinna's death:* Badian 1962 p. 59; *Posidonius:* Strasburger 1965.
17. Plut. Pomp. 8.
18. Plut. Pomp. 8. 4.
19. Cic. Imp. Cn. Pomp. 11; Diod. XXXIX. 20; Plut. Pomp. 10. Also Val. Max. 9. 13. 2.
20. The chronology of the African campaign and the date of Pompey's first triumph are notoriously difficult to establish. The reconstruction followed

238 *Notes*

here is that of Badian (1955), who argues for a swift campaign and a triumph at the earliest date possible on the present evidence. If we accept Plutarch's assertion that the African campaign only lasted forty days (Pomp. 12) and suppose that an intercalary month was inserted before March 81, it seems just possible to squeeze the necessary events into the time available.

21. *The meeting*: Plut. Pomp. 14; Venus was also the patron goddess of Sulla, who will not have been overjoyed at the implication that she was favouring Pompey as generously as himself.
22. Badian 1955.
23. Plut. Pomp. 2. Alexander was also Pompey's hero. Examples of conscious imitation of him are frequent, and were noticed by contemporaries. cf. Weinstock 1971, p. 37.

Chapter 2

1. Plut. Pomp. 14. 5.
2. *Mucia and the Metelli*: Wiseman 1971.
3. *Optimates* and *Populares*: 'Optimates' is a term frequently used both by the ancient authors and by modern historians, and it may be helpful to offer a definition here. Cicero explained the term in his *Republic* as follows: 'When certain men control the State by virtue of their wealth, their distinction, or any form of power, this is a faction, but they call themselves "Optimates" (the best people).' (Rep. 3. 23.) In fact the title was applied to the clique of more reactionary *nobiles* and their supporters who were concerned to reserve for themselves the right to control the decisions of the Senate and the electoral and legislative assemblies by the traditional means of *amicitiae* and *clientela*. To an Optimate the theoretical sovereignty of the Roman people should always be subordinate in practice to the authority of the Senate; the Senate should be controlled by those whose family, traditions and wealth fitted them to provide the senior magistrates of Rome and to guide their decisions.

Any politician who did not enjoy the support of the Optimates, or who wanted to propose reforms or programmes contrary to their interests, had to find ways of countering their formidable power. Many of the most successful methods had been demonstrated by the Gracchi brothers, Tiberius and Gaius, during their tribunates of 133 and 123 and 122, and by C. Marius and the tribune L. Appuleius Saturninus in 103 and 100. Tribunes had the right of proposing legislation in the Council of the Plebs (*concilium plebis*), which was in fact the Assembly of the People excluding the members of the very few Patrician families. They could also veto the proposals of other megistrates. As ten tribunes were elected each year, and they did not require the qualifications of age and previous office which consuls required, it was not difficult for ambitious and active men to secure election. If they were brave enough to stand up to the various forms of moral and physical obstruction which their opponents would use against them, they could, without the consent of the Senate, get far-reaching legislation passed in the Plebeian council which, on their interpretation of the constitution, was perfectly legitimate.

Agrarian reforms in the interests of the landless; grants of free or cheap corn to poor citizens; legislation to take control of the law courts out of the hands of the Senate; decisions concerning Rome's relations with foreign kings; and the allocation of land to discharged soldiers; all these and more had been passed in the last half-century by tribunes who adopted what was known as the *popularis* or popular line. This word, which is often used as the opposite of Optimate, describes rather the methods used by politicians than their policies, which might be designed to further the selfish interests of a few individuals just as much as to put right glaring social injustices. The *populares* were by no means a political party, even in the sense that the Optimates were, and, although it is possible to trace a certain continuity of thought and even ideals in the actions of men whom their contemporaries called *popularis*, the factions which opposed the Optimates from time to time nearly always centred round one leading personality, whose motives should not necessarily be construed as democratic or idealistic (cf. Lactor 7, Ch. IV).

4.   Pompey was, however, a believer in the value of law and order. If the Sullan regime could guarantee that, it would appear to him worth supporting.

5.   Plut. Pomp. 15. 1-2. cf. App. B. I.

6.   Syme, 1964 pp. 183 ff.

7.   Plut. Pomp. 15. 3.

8.   *Lepidus' speech*: Sall. H. I. 55. M; Lactor 6, p. 4 (Transl.).

9.   *Philippus' speech*: Sall. H. I. 77. M; Lactor 6, p. 7 (Transl.).
      Consultum ultimum: The Ultimate Decree; passed in an emergency by the Senate giving consuls and magistrates a guarantee of senatorial support for such measures as they saw fit to take to restore normality. It claimed to be able to suspend some of the constitutional checks on the magistrates, but its legality was challenged by some *populares*. cf. Lactor 7, p. viii.
      Interrex: a magistrate appointed, in the absence or illness of both consuls, usually to hold elections; could only hold office for five days, after which, if he had not fulfilled his purpose, another would be appointed.

10.   Oros. V. 21. 16-18.

11.   Plut. Pomp. 16. To this campaign may belong the episode recorded by Frontinus (Str. I. ix. 3), when some of Pompey's soldiers got out of hand and massacred the Senate of Mediolanum (Milan). In order to punish the culprits Pompey had recourse to a piece of trickery to avoid a possible mutiny.

12.   Plut. Sert. 15. 2.

13.   App. BC. I. xiii. 108; Plut. Pomp. 17. 3-4. *Military inexperience*: However, Mamercus Lepidus does seem to have won something of a reputation as a legate in the Social War. cf. Broughton 1952, p. 43.

14.   *The size of the army and the Sertorian War in general*: Oros. V. 23. 1-15. Galba: Peter, HRF. p. 237. Note also how many other foreign commitments required the attention of Rome's generals in 77. Thus Ap. Claudius Pulcher and Cn. Cornelius Dolabella (Macedonia), L. Licinius Lucullus (Africa), P. Servilius Vatia (Cilicia) and possibly A. Terentius Varro (Asia), in spite of their qualifications, were just not available for Spain. cf. Ch. 2, p. 48, and the speech of Cotta, Sall. H. II. 47. M; Lactor 6, p. 13 (Transl.).

15.   *Pompey's description*: Sall. H. II. 98. 4. M; Lactor 6, p. 17. *Saluvii*: Caes. BC. I. 35. 4.

16.   Cic. Imp. Cn. Pomp. 10-11; Luc. viii. 808.

17.   Plut. Pomp. 18. 3; Sert. 18.

18.   Plut. Pomp. 18. 3.

19.   Oros. loc. cit. n. 14.

20.   App. BC. I. xiii. 110; Plut. Pomp. 19; Sert. 19.

21.   App. loc. cit.

22.   *Pompey's letter*: Sall. H. II. 98. M; Lactor 6, p. 17 (Transl.).
23.   App. BC. I. xiii. 112-15; Front. Str. 2. xi. 2.
24.   App. BC. I. xiii. 113; Liv. Per. XCVI; App. Mith. 72. 308; Bennett 1961.
       The consuls of 72: Gellius and Lentulus Clodianus acted in Pompey's
       interests in 72, were censors in his first consulship in 70, and legates of
       his in 67. Gellius had probably been the senior member of Strabo's
       consilium in 89 (I). cf. p. 53.
25.   Sall. H. III. 43. M.
26.   Cic. Verr. 2. V. 153.
27.   Caes. BC. I. 61. 3.
28.   *Calagurris*: Oros. loc. cit.
29.   *Triumphal monument*: cf. Weinstock 1971, p. 37, for another, perhaps
       conscious, reminiscence of Alexander. Pliny N.H. VI. 26. 96.

Chapter 3

1.   *Speech of Macer*: Sall. H. III. 48. M; Lactor 6, p. 20 (Transl.).
2.   For the theories that Pompey attempted to meddle with the affections
       of Cotta's troops at the siege of Heraclea, and that Verres in Sicily led a
       virtual counter attack on Pompey's clients there: Ward 1968, 1970;
       Badian 1958, pp. 282 ff. Against this: Gruen 1971.
3.   Plut. Crass. 11. 2; App. BC. I. xiv. 119.
4.   Plut. Crass. 12. 1.
5.   Sherwin-White 1956. It may be that Crassus also needed special dispensa-
       tion if, as can be argued, he had been praetor in 72, not 73. In that case he
       would have been all the more willing to co-operate with Pompey. cf.
       Broughton 1952, pp. 110, 118 and 120.
6.   Cic. Verr. I. 15. 44-5.
7.   Plut. Crass. 12.2; Stockton 1973.
8.   Plut. Pomp. 22.
9.   *Timing of the lex Aurelia and the possibility of an earlier bill*: Stockton
       1973, postscript.
10.   Plut. Pomp. 23. 1-2.
11.   *Lex Plotia*: Smith 1957.
12.   Plut. Pomp. 23. 3.
13.   Plut. Luc. 34.
14.   *Piracy*: Ormerod 1924. Lewis and Reinhold 1966, pp. 327-30. Lacey and
       Wilson 1970, No. 15.
15.   Plut. Pomp. 25. 4.
16.   Plut. Pomp. 25, 26; Dio XXXVI. 23-37, esp. 24.5 and 6.
17.   Dio XXXVI. 25 and 26.
18.   Dio XXXVI. 31-6.
19.   Ormerod 1923; Groebe 1910.
20.   Cic. Imp. Cn. Pomp. 12. 34.
21.   Plut. Pomp. 27.
22.   Flor. III. 6. 7-14 (I. 41).
23.   App. Mith. XIV 95 and 96; Flor. loc. cit.
24.   Plut. Pomp. 28.
25.   Reynolds 1962; Virgil G. IV. 125 ff.
26.   Cic. Imp. Cn. Pomp; Dio XXXVI. 43. 2; Lacey and Wilson 1970, Nos.
       16 and 17.
27.   Plut. Pomp. 30.

Chapter 4

1. Pliny NH. vi. 51 f. (qualities of water of the Caspian; trade routes to India); xii. 20 (ivory); xii. 111 (balsam); xxv. 5 (Lenaeus and Mithridates' medical books). *Theophanes*: see n. 8.
2. *Freedmen*: e.g. Demetrius, Plut. Pomp. 40.
3. Plut. Pomp. 30-42; App. Mith. XV. 97 to XVII. 119; Dio XXXVI. 45-54; XXXVII. 1-23. See also esp. Magie 1950; Anderson 1922; Jones 1937; Van Ooteghem 1954.
4. Plut. Pomp. 32.
5. Dio XXXVI. 48 and 49; Plut. Pomp. 32. 5-7; App. Mith. XV. 99-100; Front. Str. 2. i. 12; Flor. III. 5. 21 ff (I. 40. 21 ff).
6. Plut. Pomp. 35. 2 and 3; Strabo XI. 4. 5; Dio XXXVII. 4; Front. Str. 2. iii. 14.
7. Vell. Pat. II. 40. 1.
8. Strabo XI. 2. 2; XI. 4. 2; XI. 5. 1; XI. 14. 4; XI. 14. 11; Pliny – see n. 1. Plut. Pomp. 35 and 36.
9. Dobias 1931; Downey 1951.
10. Strabo XII. 3. 31. Aulus Gellius Noct. Att. XVII. 16. 2. (The blood of poison-eating ducks.)
11. Chap. IV, pp. 98 ff.
12. Cic. Att. VI. 1. 3 ff.
13. *The Jewish campaign*: Plut. Pomp. 41; App. Mith. XVI. 106; Dio XXXVII. 15. 2-19; and esp. Josephus Ant. Jud. XIV. 1-81.
14. App. Mith. XVI. 107.
15. See n. 13.
16. Alexander the Great had used similar methods.
17. Plut. Pomp. 42.
18. Cic. De Div. II. 53; Grenade 1950.
19. *Pompey's settlement*: Jones 1937; Fletcher 1939; Magie 1950; Van Ooteghem 1954, pp. 244 ff; Marshall 1968; Wellesly 1953; Adcock 1937.
20. *Lex Pompeia*: Marshall 1968.
21. Strabo XII. 3. 1; Fletcher 1939.
22. See pp. 186 ff.
23. App. Mith. XVII. 114.
24. *Legislation of 52*: Chap. VII, pp. 157 ff.
25. *The victory despatch*: claiming that all wars both on land and sea had been brought to an end. It was welcomed with a grant of a further *supplicatio*, this time of twelve days. cf. Cic. de prov. cons. 27; Weinstock 1971, p. 38. *Theophanes*: Strabo XIII. 2. 3; Plut. Pomp. 42. 4; For another wealthy and powerful Asiatic client, Pythodorus: Strabo XIV. 1. 42.

Chapter 5

1. *Quintus' advice: Commentariolum Petitionis* 5; Lactor 3 (Transl.). Cic. Att. I. 1.
2. Cic. Q. F. III. 8. 4.
3. cf. Ch. 3, pp. 74 and 77.
4. Stockton 1971, pp. 57 ff.
5. *Tribunate of Cornelius and Gabinius*: Ch. III, pp. 66 ff; Davison 1930. *Prosecution of Manilius*: Phillips 1970. Lactor 7, pp. 11 ff.
6. Sall. Cat. 18; Suet. Jul. 9; Stockton 1971, pp. 73 ff; Stevens 1963;

Seager 1964. Note that Catilina's nomination may have been rejected because it was submitted too late.

7.   *Reform programme*: Stockton 1971, pp. 82 ff. This view is not universally accepted. cf. Seager, JRS 1971, p. 273.

8.   Asconius ed. Clark, pp. 82 ff. (*In orationem in toga candida*.)

9.   *Rullus' agrarian bill*: Cic. Contra Rullum; Hardy 1913; Sumner 1966; Lacey and Wilson 1970, No. 22.

10.   Stockton 1971, p. 88.

11.   This interpretation does, however, suggest a remarkable ignorance of Pompey's interest or stupidity in not anticipating Pompey's coolness on the part of Cicero.

12.   Plutarch (Cic. 18) records that the conspirators planned to seize Pompey's children and hold them as hostages to secure a peaceful settlement with him on his return.

13.   *Cato and Metellus*: Plut. Cato min. 20. 2; 26-9.

14.   Cic. Fam. V. 7.

15.   Cic. Att. I. 12. 3.

16.   Plut. Pomp. 43. 2 and 3; App. Mith. 116.

17.   Cic. Att. I. 14. 1.

18.   Cic. Att. I. 14.

19.   Ibid.

20.   Cic. Att. I. 13. 4.

21.   *L. Afranius*: Allen 1951.

22.   Lugli 1946; Van Ooteghem 1954, pp. 317 ff; Blake 1947, p. 244.

23.   Cato did, however, oppose the granting of two extraordinary additional privileges, those of wearing triumphal dress and a golden crown at the races, and a *toga praetexta* and laurel wreath at the theatre. Weinstock 1971, p. 38.

24.   Cic. Att. I. 18. 5; Dio XXXVII. 49. 3; Sabben-Clare 1971, Nos. 3 and 6.

25.   One may well wonder why Pompey did not decide to stand for a second consulship in 59 himself, as he was now legally entitled to do. Possibly he had no desire to face as consul a largely hostile Senate in its present mood. For the election of Caesar and the formation of the coalition: Sabben-Clare 1971, Nos. 9-17; Stanton 1975.

26.   Caesar no doubt also reminded Pompey that he had given his support to the *Lex Manilia* in 66.

Chapter 6

1.   For the sources on Caesar's consulship: Sabben-Clare 1971, Nos. 18-50. For the dating of the legislation: Taylor 1967.

2.   Dio XXXVIII. 4 and 5; Sabben-Clare, No. 18.

3.   *The Egyptian question*: Shatzman 1971.

4.   *Augur*: The college of sixteen augurs was responsible for divining before every important public action whether it would enjoy the support of the Gods. Membership of the college was an honour and brought with it some political advantages. It is not known when Pompey was elected to the college.

5.   Cic. Att. II. 16. 2; Sabben-Clare, No. 27. *Proud kings*: Cic. Att. II. 8. 1; and cf. Sabben-Clare, Nos. 39-43.

6.   For the view that this Caepio was in fact M. Brutus, Cato's nephew: Syme 1939, p. 34. According to Plutarch (Pomp. 47. 6) Pompeia herself

was also engaged to Sulla's son Faustus.

7.   *The Vettius affair*: McDermott 1949; Allen 1950; Taylor 1950; Rowland 1966 (also on Crassus' relations with Caesar and Pompey at this time); Sabben-Clare, No. 32.

8.   *Death of Brutus*: Ch. II, p. 42; M. Brutus the younger was mentioned by Vettius at the first enquiry (Att. II. 24); Aemilius Paullus was the son of Lepidus (cos. 78); Stockton 1971, p. 185.

9.   Cic. Att. II. 19; Sabben-Clare, No. 41; Lactor 7, pp. 53 ff.

10.   *Tyranny*: Dunkle 1967.

11.   Cic. Att. II. 21. 3 ff.

12.   Cic. Att. II. 23. 2. *Sam(p) siceramus*: Ch. 4, p. 11. This was obviously a well-used nickname for Pompey at this time.

13.   Cic. Q. F. I. 2.

14.   *Consular elections*: Lindersky 1965. *Unofficial dictator*: Cic. Q. F. I. 2. 15.

15.   *Clodius*: Lintott 1967 and 1968 passim; Seager 1965; Gruen 1966 (2); Rowland 1966.

16.   Plut. Cic. 31. 3.

17.   Dio XXXVIII. 30; Asconius ed. Clark, p. 47; Sabben-Clare, Nos. 141-5.

18.   Asc. pp. 46 and 47.

19.   The vote was, unusually, taken in the Centuriate assembly, where the wealthier voters had greater influence. Stockton 1971, p. 193. *Cicero's recall*: Sabben-Clare, Nos. 146-54.

20.   Anderson 1963.

21.   Pliny NH. VII. 34; XXXV. 59 (Polygnotus); 114 (Antiphilus); 126 (Pausias); 132 (Nicias of Athens); XXXVI. 41 (Coponius). Van Essen 1934; Havelock 1971, pp. 117, 150-51, 268 (Pasiteles).

22.   Brown 1951. The style, according to Brown, 'betrays the hand of a sculptor of the mid-1st century BC, a sculptor of the first rank, Greek trained or well versed in the classicising hellenism of contemporary eclecticism'.

23.   Syme 1961.

24.   *Corn Commission*: Sabben-Clare, Nos. 155-7; Lactor 7, pp. 65 ff.

25.   *Maius imperium*: Balsdon 1957. Metellus: Ch. III, p. 74.

26.   Plut. Pomp. 49. 4. 'Harbours, markets, distribution of crops, in short all the operations of farmers and shippers.'

27.   *Relations with other nobiles*: Gruen 1969.

28.   Plut. Pomp. 50. Note his terse reply to hesitant captains during a period of stormy weather: 'To sail is necessary, to live is not.'

29.   *The attack on the Lex Campana*: Stockton 1962; Cic. Q. F. II. 1.

30.   *The Egyptian question*: Shatzman 1971; Sabben-Clare, Nos. 164-8; Dio XXXIX. 12-16.

31.   *The oracle*: Dio XXXIX. 15. 2.

32.   Cic. Q. F. II. 3. 2 ff.

33.   cf. Ch. VI, p. 127 f.

34.   *The trial of Sestius*: Pocock 1926.

35.   *The trial of Caelius*: Austin 1960.

36.   For the suggestion that Pompey let Cicero think he (Cicero) had persuaded him to support Domitius' proposal: cf. Pocock 1926, p. 27; Cic. Phil. II. 24.

37.   *Conference of Luca*: Sabben-Clare, Nos. 172-91.

38.   cf. esp. Cic. Fam. I. 9; Sabben-Clare, No. 177.

39.   Dio XXXIX. 25. 1 and 2.

40.   Dio XXXIX. 27. 2. The election and second consulship of Pompey and Crassus: Sabben-Clare, Nos. 192-208.

41. The sources suggest that in fact the *Lex Trebonia* left the allocation of Spain and Syria to lot, perhaps to make it seem closer to usual constitutional practice. Even so, the lot must have been a pure formality. cf. Plut. Cato min. 43; Crass. 16; Dio XXXIX. 33. 2; Sabben-Clare, Nos. 195-7.
42. Cic. Att. IV. 9; Sabben-Clare, No. 198.
43. Dio XXXIX. 33. 3.
44. *The theatre*: Platner and Ashby 1929, p. 146; p. 428; pp. 515 ff; Nash 1968, vol. II, plates 1216-23. The incorporation of the temple was apparently designed to avoid censure for building a permanent theatre, a Greek institution which might corrupt Roman youth. According to the extant remains (in the Piazza di Grottapinta) the facade of the *cavea* consisted of three superimposed arcades (Doric, Ionic and Corinthian) built of peperino and fronted by red granite columns. The diameter of the theatre was about 155 m, and the length of the *scaena* or stage about 95 m. The truth of Pliny's statement (NH. XXXVI. 115) that it held 40,000 spectators is now doubted. Also Van Ooteghem 1954, pp. 402 ff; Robathan 1950, p. 166; Blake 1947, pp. 149, 254. *The house*: Plut. Pomp. 40. 5.
45. Cic. Fam. VII. 1.
46. *Deaths of Carbo, etc.*: Val. Max. 6. 2. 8; Cic. Fam. I. 8. 2.
47. Dio XXXIX. 55. 3.
48. Jos. Ant. Jud. XIV. 82-104.
49. Cic. Red. Quir. 16; Red. Sen. 5; Dom. 66. For other such references see Gelzer 1969, p. 45.

Chapter 7

1. *Violence*: Lintott 1968.
2. *The scandal*: Sabben-Clare 1971, Nos. 236-40. The vote of the century which voted first (*centuria praerogativa*) was considered to affect the votes of all the other centuries.
3. *Obnuntiatio*: the announcement by a magistrate that he had observed bad omens which would necessitate the postponement of an assembly.
4. Cic. Q. F. II. 13. 5; Att. IV. 18. 3; Q. F. III. 8.
5. Plut. Pomp. 53. Sabben-Clare, Nos. 251-3.
6. Dio XXXIX. 62. 2; Cic. Att. IV. 18. Sabben-Clare, Nos. 244-50.
7. App. BC. II. 3. 20; Plut. Pomp. 54. 2 and 3.
8. Cic. Att. IV. 19. 2.
9. Plut. Pomp. 54. 3; Dio XL. 46. 1; App. BC. II. 3. 20. cf. Sabben-Clare, Nos. 271-9.
10. Plut. Pomp. 55; Syme 1939, pp. 40 and 45; Anderson 1963, Ch. 2; (Pompey's marriage alliances in general).
11. Asc. ed. Clark, pp. 30 ff (*In Milonianam*). On this and the rest of 52: Sabben-Clare, Nos. 290-324. Lactor 7, pp. 73 ff.
12. Dio XL. 48 ff.
13. Asc. p. 36.
14. Asc. pp. 33 ff.
15. cf. Cic. *pro Milone*.
16. Plut. Pomp. 55. 4 f; App. BC. II. 4. 25.
17. For a full discussion of this whole thorny problem: Cuff 1958; Stockton 1971, pp. 247 ff and 1975; Jameson 1970. Sources: Sabben-Clare, Nos. 326-44 (51 BC).

18. Suet. Jul. 28. 3; Sabben-Clare, No. 320.
19. Cic. Att. V. 11. 3; Fam. III. 8. 10; Sabben-Clare, Nos. 338 and 339.
20. Cic. Att. V. 7; Fam. II. 8. 2; VIII. 1. 3.
21. (Cic.) Fam. VIII. 8. 9; Sabben-Clare, No. 343. Lactor 7, pp. 79 ff.
22. App. BC. II. 4. 26. The money used to build the *Basilica Aemilia*. The bribe 36,000,000 sesterces, though Velleius (II. 48. 3.) gives the figure as 100,000 sesterces. Sources: Sabben-Clare, Nos. 350-54.
23. *Curio*: Lacey 1961; Sabben-Clare, Nos. 355-60. Caelius (Cic.) Fam. VIII. 6. 5.
24. Dio XL. 61 and 62; Caelius loc. cit.
25. *The debate on the provinces*: Sabben-Clare, Nos. 361-6.
26. App. BC. II. 4. 28; Sabben-Clare, No. 368; also Nos. 367-73.
27. Plut. Pomp. 57. 1-3. cf. Daly 1950.
28. Plut. Pomp. 57. 4 and 5; App. BC. II. 4. 29 and 30.
29. App. BC. II. 4. 28.
30. Caelius (Cic.) Fam. VIII. 14; Sabben-Clare, No. 378. Cic. Att. VI. 8. 1.
31. Cic. Att. VII. 7. 5.
32. Cic. Att. VII. 2. 5.
33. App. BC. II. 4. 30; Sabben-Clare, No. 381.
34. Ibid.
35. Von Fritz 1942.
36. Cic. Att. VII. 4; Sabben-Clare, No. 385.
37. Cic. Att. VII. 8; Sabben-Clare, No. 388.
38. App. BC. II. 4. 32; Plut. Pomp. 59. 3; Suet. Jul. 29. 2; Sabben-Clare, Nos. 383, 397, 391.
39. cf. Ch. VII, p. 170 and previous note.
40. Livy Ep. CIX; App. BC. II. 4. 33. Sabben-Clare, No. 401. It should be noted that the dates given in this account are those of the Roman calendar before it was reformed by Caesar. They do not correspond to the dates of the lunar calendar. At the beginning of 49 the Roman calendar was about forty-six days ahead of the moon, and by the battle of Pharsalus about sixty days ahead. This was because no intercalary month had been inserted for several years.

Chapter 8

1. *Faustus Sulla*: cf. Ch. VI, p. 126 and note 6. Faustus had eventually married Pompeia.
2. *Scribonius Libo*: now more closely connected with Pompey since his daughter Scribonia had married Pompey's younger son Sextus.
3. (Cic.) Att. VII. 8. 4; App. BC. II. v. 36; Plut. Pomp. 60; Dio XLI. 4-9.
4. Caes. B.C. I. 8. 3; On this mission and the early exchanges of messages between Caesar and Pompey: Von Fritz 1941.
5. Caes. B.C. I. 9. 3; Cic. Fam. XVI. 12.
6. *Favonius' challenge*: cf. Ch. VII, p. 166. Plut. Pomp. 61. 1.
7. Dio loc. cit; Cic. Att. VII. 11.
8. Syme 1938; Tyrrell 1972.
9. *Prefect of engineers*: the title given to an ADC of the general in the Roman army at this period.
10. Cic. Att. VII. 13A; Von Fritz 1941.
11. Caes. B.C. I. 11.
12. Cic. Att. VII. 14; 21; 23. Caes. B.C. I. 14. 4.

13.   Cic. Att. VIII. 11A. *The siege of Corfinium*: Shackleton Bailey 1956;
      Burns 1966.
14.   (Cic.) Att. VIII. 12B.
15.   (Cic.) Att. VIII. 12A. 3.
16.   (Cic.) Att. VIII. 12C.
17.   (Cic.) Att. VIII. 12D.
18.   (Cic.) Att. VIII. 12A.
19.   (Cic.) Att. IX. 7C
20.   (Cic.) Att. VIII. 11; 16; IX. 7; 10.
21.   (Cic.) Att. VIII. 11A-D.

Chapter 9

1.   *Lentulus*: Josephus Ant. Jud. XIV. 228 ff. *Scipio*: ibid. 123-6. Caesar sent
      the Jewish prince Aristobulus, whom he released from prison in Rome,
      to win support in Syria, but he was poisoned by Pompeian partisans there.
      Scipio also executed Aristobulus' son Alexander on Pompey's instructions.
      cf. Dio XLI. 18. 1. Lucilius Hirrus seems to have been sent on an embassy
      to Parthia at this time, perhaps to secure the co-operation of the king in
      not attacking the eastern provinces while they were thus denuded of
      troops. Caes. B.C. III. 82. 4.
2.   App. BC. II. viii. 49; Caes. B.C. III. 3 ff; Also Lucan Phars. IV. 169-297.
3.   Plut. Pomp. 64; App. and Caes. loc. cit; *numbers of ships*: Van Ooteghem
      1954, p. 590.
4.   Caes. B.C. III. 31-3.
5.   Caes. B.C. III. 4. 5; (Cic.) Att. XI. 3.
6.   Plut. Pomp. 64. 1-3.
7.   Wilkes 1969, pp. 40-41.
8.   For the speech which Appian at this point attributes to Pompey: App.
      BC. II. viii. 50 and 51 (Ap. III. E).
9.   Caes. B.C. III. 10.
10.   Caes. B.C. III. 13. 2-3.
11.   For the topography of this campaign: Veith 1920; Rice Holmes 1923;
      Van Ooteghem 1954 ad loc.
12.   App. BC. II. viii. 56; Dio XLI. 47.
13.   For an alternative interpretation of Libo's raid: Fuller 1965, pp. 214-15.
14.   Caes. B.C. III. 18.
15.   Caes. B.C. III. 43. 3.
16.   Caes. B.C. III. 45. 2-6.
17.   Cic. Fam. VII. 3. 2.
18.   Plut. Cic. 38.
19.   *The attack on Dyrrachium*: Dio XLI. 50. 3-4.
20.   Caes. B.C. III. 70; also Plut. Pomp. 65. 5.
21.   *Burebistas*: Mihailov 1956, No. 13 (IGBR).
22.   *The battle of Pharsalus*: Rice Holmes 1923; Van Ooteghem 1954; Rambaud
      1955; Gwatkin 1956; Gelzer 1960; Fuller 1965; Pelling 1973. The sources
      differ over the distribution of forces, as over most other details.
23.   App. BC. II. x. 66.
24.   Plut. Pomp. 67; Caes. B.C. III. 83.
25.   Caes. B.C. III. 86. 3 and 4; 87.
26.   Caes. B.C. III. 85; Plut. Pomp. 68.
27.   Plut. Brut. 4; Pomp. 68; App. BC. II. x. 69. For the suggestion that his

dejection was due to the recurrence of aestivan malaria: cf. Van Ooteghem 1954, p. 627; *Dreams*: Brenk 1975.

28.   Front. Strat. II. iii. 22.
29.   App. BC. II. xi. 75.
30.   Brunt 1971, pp. 691 ff.
31.   Pompey had himself used similar tactics in Albania in 65. Ch. IV, p. 85.
32.   Appian (BC. II. xi. 79) and Plutarch (Pomp. 69. 4) say that the Pompeians did not throw their javelins but used them as thrusting spears to break the enemy charge. *Escape of the allies*: App. BC. II. xi. 80.
33.   App. BC. II. xi. 81; Plut. Pomp. 72. 1 and 2; Caes. B.C. III. 94. 5.
34.   Caes. B.C. III. 94. 5; Dio XLII. 1; Luc. Phars. VII. 654-5; 669-72; App. BC. II. xi. 80; Flor. IV. 2. 50. See also Luc. Phars. VI. 319-29.
35.   *Pollio's estimate*: App. BC. II. xi. 82; *Lack of resolution*: Fuller 1965 p. 239.
36.   Caes. B.C. III. 102. 3.
37.   Plut. Pomp. 74-6.
38.   Plut. Pomp. 76. 5.
39.   According to Pliny (NH V. 68) there was a mound known as the tomb of Pompey not far from Pelusium, by Mt. Casius. This is not inconsistent with Plutarch's narrative, as a mound raised over the ashes of the pyre could well claim to be a tomb. Tradition held that Pompey lay buried in Egypt. cf. Ap. X.

Chapter 10

1.   (Cic.) Att. XI. 6; Sall. H. II. 16. M; II. 17. M. Luc. Phars. 1. 98-157 and 9. 186-214.

Appendix A

1.   *Plutarch*: Russell, D.A. *Plutarch*.
2.   *Cicero*: Stockton 1971; Holliday 1969.
3.   *Sallust*: Syme 1964.
4.   *Lucan*: Holliday 1969; Lintott 1971.
5.   Tacitus on Livy: Ann. IV. 34; on Pompey: esp. Hist. II. 38; Ann. III. 28.

Appendix B

1.   NB: The cities founded in Bithynia are omitted in this document. It is also difficult to justify the claim to have conquered Darius the Mede. Aristobulus was not immediately put to death. cf. Ch. IX, n. 1. On this triumph and its novelties: Weinstock 1971, pp. 38 ff.
2.   Pompey's reproach is presumably an example of his rather heavy sense of humour, involving a pun on the word *inferi* = lower beings or underworld.
3.   The date of this incident is probably 60 (Cic. Att. II. 3. 1). The bandage was to cover an ulcer. The point of the jibe is a rather recherché reference to an action of Alexander the Great. He had once used his own diadem as a bandage to staunch the bleeding of a head wound he had

accidentally inflicted on his bodyguard Lysimachus. Lysimachus later became one of the kings who succeeded Alexander, and this action was regarded as having been an omen of his future kingship. cf. Weinstock 1971, p. 335.

4.   The reading, and thus the dating, of this passage is that of Badian 1955.
5.   The date given here seems to be impossible, for the Day of Fasting, which is presumably the Day of Atonement, of the 179th Olympiad would have fallen in October 64. The expression 'Day of Fasting' may be due to confusion in one of Josephus' sources between Fast Day and Sabbath and the temple may have fallen on one sabbath in July of 63 before the end of the 179th Olympiad in that month. Alternatively the number of the Olympiad may be wrong and the temple have fallen on 10 October 63. This would certainly allow more time for the activities in Syria earlier in the year.

SELECT BIBLIOGRAPHY OF MODERN WORKS

Adcock, F.E., 'Lesser Armenia and Galatia after Pompey's settlement of the East', *JRS*, 1937, pp. 12 ff

Ahl, F.M., 'The pivot of the Pharsalia', *Hermes*, 1974, pp. 305 ff

Allen, W., 'The Vettius affair once more', *TAPA*, 1950, pp. 153 ff

_____ 'The Lucii Afranii of Cicero Att. I. 16. 13', *TAPA*, 1951 pp. 127 ff

Anderson, J.G.C., 'Pompey's Campaign against Mithridates', *JRS*, 1922, pp. 99 ff

Anderson, W.S., 'Pompey, his friends and the literature of the first century BC', *Univ. of Calif. Publ. in Class. Phil.*, vol. 19, 1963, no. 1, pp. 1-88

Austin, R.G., *Cicero pro Caelio* (ed.), 3rd edn., 1960 (Oxford)

Badian, E., 'The date of Pompey's first triumph', *Hermes*, 1955, pp. 107 ff

_____ 'Caepio and Norbanus', *Historia*, 1957, pp. 318 ff

_____ *Foreign Clientelae* (Oxford, 1958)

_____ 'The early career of A. Gabinius', *Philologus*, 1959, pp. 99 ff

_____ 'Waiting for Sulla', *JRS*, 1962, pp. 47 ff

_____ *Roman Imperialism in the late Republic* (Oxford, 1968)

_____ 'Quaestiones Variae', *Historia*, 1969, pp. 447 ff

Balsdon, J.P.V.D., 'Long-term commands at the end of the Republic', *Class. Rev.*, 1949, pp. 14 ff

_____ Review of Gelzer: *Pompeius*, in *Historia*, 1950, pp. 296 ff

_____ 'The proposal to give Pompey *Maius Imperium* in Sept. 57', *JRS*, 1957, pp. 16 ff

Bennett, W., 'The death of Sertorius and the coin', *Historia*, 1961, pp. 459 ff

Blake, M.E., *Ancient Roman Construction in Italy from the Prehistoric Period to Augustus* (Washington, 1947)

Brenk, F.E., 'The dreams of Plutarch's Lives', *Latomus*, 1975, pp. 336 ff

Broughton, T.R.S., *The Magistrates of the Roman Republic* (New York, 1952)

Brown, F.E., 'Magni Nominis Umbrae', *D.M. Robinson Studies*, 1951, vol. 1, pp. 761 ff

Brunt, P.A., '*Amicitia* in the late Roman Republic', *Proc. Camb. Phil.*

Soc., 1965, pp. 1-20

_____ 'The *Equites* in the Late Republic', *Sec. Int. Conf. of Ec. Hist.*, 1 (The Hague, 1965)

_____ 'Italian aims at the time of the Social War', *JRS*, 1965, pp. 90 ff

_____ *Italian Manpower 225 BC – AD 14* (Oxford, 1971)

Bulst, C.M., 'Cinnanum Tempus', *Historia*, 1964, pp. 307 ff

Burns, A., 'Pompey's Strategy and Domitius' stand at Corfinium', *Historia*, 1966, pp. 74 ff

Caldwell, W.E., 'An Estimate of Pompey', *D.M. Robinson Studies*, 1951, vol. II, pp. 954 ff

Collins, H.P., 'The decline and fall of Pompey the Great', *Greece and Rome*, 1953, pp. 98 ff

Criniti, N., *L'Epigrafe di Asculum di Gn. Pompeo Strabone* (Milan, 1970)

Cuff, J.P., 'The Terminal Date of Caesar's Gallic Command', *Historia*, 1958, pp. 445 ff

Daly, L.W., 'Vota publica pro salute alicuius', *TAPA*, 1950, pp. 164 ff

Davison, J.A., 'Cicero and the *lex Gabinia*', *Class. Rev.*, 1930, pp. 224 f

Dobias, J., 'Les premiers rapports des Romains avec les Parthes et l'occupation de la Syrie', *Journal of the Czechoslovak Oriental Institute*, Prague, 1931, pp. 215 ff

Downey, G., 'The occupation of Syria by the Romans', *TAPA*, 1951, pp. 149 ff

Duchesne, J., 'Note sur le nom de Pompée', *Ant. Class.*, 1934, pp. 81 f

Dunkle, J.R., 'The Greek tyrant and Roman political invective of the Late Republic', *TAPA*, 1967, pp. 151 ff

Fletcher, W.G., 'The Pontic cities of Pompey the Great', *TAPA*, 1939, pp. 17 ff

Fuller, J.F.C., *Julius Caesar: Man, soldier and tyrant* (London, 1965)

Gelzer, M., *Pompeius* (Munich, 1949)

Grenade, P., 'Le mythe de Pompée et les Pompéiens sous les Césars', *Rev. des Etudes Anciennes*, 1950, pp. 28 ff

Groebe, P., 'Zum Seerauberkriege des Pompeius Magnus', *Klio*, 1910, pp. 374 ff

Gruen, E.S., 'The Dolabellae and Sulla', *AJP*, 1966, pp. 385 ff

_____ 'P. Clodius, instrument or independent agent', *Phoenix*, 1966, pp. 120 ff

_____ 'Pompey, the Roman aristocracy and the conference of Luca', *Historia*, 1969, pp. 71 ff

_____ 'Pompey, Metellus Pius and the trials of 70-69 BC: the perils

of schematism', *AJP*, 1971, pp. 1 ff
_____ *The Last Generation of the Roman Republic* (London, 1974)
Gwatkin, W.E., 'The father of Pompey the Great', *TAPA*, 1940,
  p. xxxvii
_____ 'Some reflections on the battle of Pharsalus', *TAPA*, 1956,
  pp. 109 ff
Hardy, E.G., 'Consular provinces between 67 and 52 BC', *Class. Rev.*,
  1917, pp. 11 ff
_____ 'The policy of the Rullan proposal in 63 BC', *Journal of
  Philology*, 1913, pp. 228 ff
Havelock, C.M., *Hellenistic Art* (London, 1971)
Holliday, V.L., *Pompey in Cicero's Correspondence and Lucan's Civil
  War* (The Hague, 1969)
Jameson, S., 'The intended date of Caesar's return from Gaul', *Latomus*,
  1970, pp. 638 ff
Jones, A.H.M., *The Cities of the Eastern Roman Provinces* (Oxford,
  1937)
Knight, D.W., 'Pompey's concern with pre-eminence after 60 BC',
  Latomus, 1968, pp. 878 ff
Lacey, W.K., 'The tribunate of Curio', *Historia*, 1961, pp. 318 ff
Lacey, W.K. and Wilson, B.W.J.G., *Res Publica. Roman Politics and
  Society according to Cicero* (Oxford, 1970)
Langlois, V., 'Soli et Pompeiopolis', *Rev. Arch.*, 1853, pp. 358 ff
Lewis, N. and Reinhold, M., *Roman Civilisation. Sourcebook I:
  The Republic* (New York, 1966)
Lindersky, J., 'Constitutional aspects of the consular elections in 59
  BC', *Historia*, 1965, pp. 421 ff
Lintott, A.W., 'P. Clodius Pulcher – Felix Catilina?', *Greece and Rome*,
  1967
_____ *Violence in Republican Rome* (Oxford, 1968)
_____ 'Lucan and the History of the Civil War', *Class. Quart.*, 1971,
  pp. 488 ff
_____ 'Cicero and Milo', *JRS*, 1974, pp. 62 ff
Lugli, G., 'Albano Laziale – scavo dell' "Albanum Pompeii" ', *Atti
  della Accademia Nazionale dei Lincei*, 1946, vol. VII, pp. 60 ff
McDermott, W.C., 'Vettius ille, ille noster index', *TAPA*, 1949, pp.
  351 ff
Magie, D., *Roman Rule in Asia Minor* (Princeton University, 1950)
Marshall, A.J., 'Pompey's organisation of Bithynia-Pontus: two
  neglected texts', *JRS*, 1968, pp. 103 ff
Mihailov, G., *Inscriptiones Graecae in Bulgaria repertae* (Sophia, 1956)

Nash, E., *Pictorial Dictionary of Ancient Rome* (London, 1968)

Ormerod, H.A., 'The distribution of Pompey's forces in the campaign of 67 BC', *Liverpool Annals of Arch. & Anth.*, 1923, pp. 46 ff

———   *Piracy in the Ancient World* (Liverpool and London, 1924)

Parker, H.M.D., *The Roman Legions* (Oxford, 1928)

Pelling, C.B.R., 'Pharsalus', *Historia*, 1973, pp. 249 ff

Phillips, E.J., 'Cicero and the prosecution of C. Manilius', *Latomus*, 1970, pp. 595 ff

Platner, S.B. and Ashby, T., *A Topographical Dictionary of Ancient Rome* (Oxford, 1929)

Pocock, L.G. (ed.), *Cicero in Vatinium* (London, 1926; Amsterdam, 1967)

———   'Pompeiusve parem', *Class. Phil.*, 1927, pp. 301 ff

Poulsen, Fr., 'Les portraits de Pompeius Magnus', *Rev. Arch.*, 1936, pp. 16 ff

Rambaud, M., 'Le soleil de Pharsale', *Historia*, 1955

Reynolds, J., 'Cyrenaica, Pompey and Cn. Cornelius Lentulus Marcellinus', *JRS*, 1962, pp. 95 ff

Rice Holmes, T., *The Roman Republic and the Founder of the Empire* (Oxford, 1923)

Robathan, D.M., *The Monuments of Ancient Rome* (Rome, 1950)

Rowland, R.J., 'Crassus, Clodius and Curio in the year 59 BC', *Historia*, 1966, pp. 217 ff

Sabben-Clare, J., *Caesar and Roman Politics 60-50 BC* (Oxford, 1971)

Sanford, E.M., 'The career of Aulus Gabinius', *TAPA*, 1939, pp. 64 ff

Scullard, H.H., *From the Gracchi to Nero* (London, 1963)

Seager, R., 'The first Catilinarian Conspiracy', *Historia*, 1964, pp. 338 ff

———   'Clodius, Pompeius and the exile of Cicero', *Latomus*, 1965, pp. 519 ff

Shackleton Bailey, D.R., 'Expectatio Corfiniensis', *JRS*, 1956, pp. 57 ff

———   (ed.), *Cicero – Epistulae ad Atticum* (6 vols, Cambridge, 1965-70)

Shatzman, I., 'The Egyptian question in Roman politics 59-54 BC', *Latomus*, 1971, pp. 363 ff

———   *Senatorial Wealth and Roman Politics* (Brussels, 1975)

Sherwin-White, A.N., *The Roman Citizenship* (Oxford, 1939)

———   'Violence in Roman Politics', *JRS*, 1956, pp. 1 ff

Smith, R.E., 'The Lex Plotia Agraria and Pompey's Spanish veterans', *Class. Quart.*, 1957, pp. 82 ff

Stanton, G.R. and Marshall, B.A., 'The coalition between Pompeius and Crassus', *Historia*, 1975, pp. 205 ff

Stevens, C.E., 'The "Plotting" of 66/65 BC', *Latomus*, 1963, pp. 397 ff

Stockton, D.L., 'Cicero and the Ager Campanus', *TAPA*, 1962, pp. 471 ff

_____ *Cicero – A Political Biography* (Oxford, 1971)

_____ 'The First Consulship of Pompey', *Historia*, 1973, pp. 205 ff

_____ 'Quis iustius induit arma?', *Historia*, 1975, pp. 232 ff

Strasburger, H., 'Poseidonius on problems of the Roman Empire', *JRS*, 1965, pp. 40 ff

Sumner, G.V., 'Cicero, Pompeius and Rullus', *TAPA*, 1966, pp. 569 ff

Syme, R., 'The Allegiance of Labienus', *JRS*, 1938, pp. 113 ff

_____ *The Roman Revolution* (Oxford, 1939)

_____ 'Who was Vedius Pollio?', *JRS*, 1961, pp. 23 ff

_____ *Sallust* (Cambridge, 1964)

Taylor, L.R., *Party Politics in the Age of Caesar* (Berkeley, 1949)

_____ 'The date and meaning of the Vettius affair', *Historia*, 1950, pp. 45 ff

_____ 'The voting Districts of the Roman Republic', *Papers and Monographs of the American Academy in Rome*, vol. XX, 1960

_____ 'The dating of major legislation and elections in Caesar's first consulship', *Historia*, 1967, pp. 173 ff

Tyrrell, W.B., 'Labienus' departure from Caesar in January 49 BC', *Historia*, 1972, pp. 424 ff

Van Essen, C.C., 'Literary evidence for the beginnings of Roman Art', *JRS*, 1934, pp. 154 ff

Van Ooteghem, J., *Pompée le Grand. Batisseur d'Empire* (Louvain/ Paris, 1954)

Veith, G., *Der Feldzug von Dyrrhachium zwischen Caesar und Pompejus* (Wien, 1920)

von Fritz, K., 'The Mission of L. Caesar and L. Roscius in January 49 BC', *TAPA*, 1941, pp. 125 ff

_____ 'Pompey's Policy before and after the Outbreak of the Civil War of 49 BC', *TAPA*, 1942, pp. 145 ff

Ward, A.M., 'Caesar's support of Pompey in the trials of M. Fonteius and P. Oppius', *Latomus*, 1968, pp. 802 ff

_____ 'Cicero and Pompey in 75 and 70 BC', *Latomus*, 1970, pp. 58 ff

Weinstock, S., *Divus Julius* (Oxford, 1971)

Wellesly, K., 'The extent of the territory added to Bithynia by Pompey', *Rh. M.*, 1953, pp. 293 ff

West, A.B., 'Lucilian Genealogy', *AJP*, 1928, pp. 240 ff
Wilkes, J.J., *Dalmatia* (London, 1969)
Wiseman, T.P., 'Celer and Nepos', *Class. Quart.*, 1971, pp. 180 ff

INDEX NOMINUM

GENERAL INDEX